Spenser's Forms of History

Spenser's Forms
of History

B<small>ART VAN</small> E<small>S</small>

OXFORD
UNIVERSITY PRESS

OXFORD
UNIVERSITY PRESS

Great Clarendon Street, Oxford OX2 6DP

Oxford University Press is a department of the University of Oxford.
It furthers the University's objective of excellence in research, scholarship,
and education by publishing worldwide in

Oxford New York

Auckland Bangkok Buenos Aires Cape Town Chennai
Dar es Salaam Delhi Hong Kong Istanbul Karachi Kolkata
Kuala Lumpur Madrid Melbourne Mexico City Mumbai Nairobi
São Paulo Shanghai Singapore Taipei Tokyo Toronto

Oxford is a registered trade mark of Oxford University Press
in the UK and in certain other countries

Published in the United States
by Oxford University Press Inc., New York

© Bart van Es 2002

The moral rights of the author have been asserted
Database right Oxford University Press (maker)

First published 2002

British Library Cataloguing in Publication Data

Data available

Library of Congress Cataloging in Publication Data

Data applied for

ISBN 0–19–924970–9

1 3 5 7 9 10 8 6 4 2

Typeset in Garamond
by Regent Typesetting, London
Printed in Great Britain
on acid-free paper by
Biddles Ltd,
Guildford and King's Lynn

For my parents, Henk and Dieuwke

Preface

IT WAS EDMUND SPENSER himself who, in a letter accompanying the 1590 *Faerie Queene*, first coined and applied to himself the term 'Poet historical'. Ever since that time readers have attempted to delineate the unquestionably central relationship between Spenser and 'history'. Traditionally, academic studies have concentrated on *The Faerie Queene* and its exposition of providential patterns in history—whether those of Protestant teleology or dynastic epic. This work has done much to reveal Spenser's complex relationship with the grand narrative of his church and nation's past. The resulting picture of a visionary poet confronting the harsh realities of time is important and true, but nevertheless incomplete.

This book attempts to broaden the historical canvas. It starts from the proposition that, rather than simply presenting a single unified view of his nation's place in history, Spenser utilized a range of 'forms of history'. Six of these 'forms'—chronicle, chorography, antiquarianism, euhemerism, analogy, and prophecy—constitute the building blocks of this study. Across a series of discursive essays the work demonstrates the ways in which Spenser explored and manipulated available means of approaching the past. As well as illustrating the facility with which Spenser adopts these modes of writing it draws attention to the conflicts within and between them. The poet to some extent worked to resolve such tensions, but he also exploited them.

The book forwards a more multifaceted 'Poet historical' than has hitherto been recognized. Spenser, it argues, was genuinely engaged with the complexities of contemporary history writing. He was at once serious, playful, and politically astute about the ways in which his nation's past was being interpreted. Repeatedly he can be seen to complicate elements within his own work which, at first sight, appear conventional and conservative. In particular, the poet demonstrates a profound awareness of historical forms—allowing them in many ways to permeate the literary forms of his own writing. He looked in detail at the style and substance of his sources (from regional descriptions to mythological compendia). Reading Spenser's work alongside a wide range of historical and quasi-historical texts, this study attempts to draw out the wealth of interconnections between them. In doing so it also draws attention to interpretative histories, tracing changes over time to the ways individual narratives could be read. The study thus provides the sketch of a changing cultural landscape—of significance not just for Spenser, but for many of his contemporaries Renaissance England, it is argued, governed its approach to the past by means of historical form. Although not always fully self-conscious, the choice of a particular mode, at a particular time, involved intellectual judgement and political tact. In the light of this contention Early Modern historical narratives need to be read with a new kind of critical awareness.

This work grew out of a doctoral dissertation passed by the University of Cambridge, and I would like to express my thanks to the teachers, colleagues, friends, and family whose help has contributed to its completion. In the first place my gratitude is due to Colin Burrow who has supervised this project throughout. I am also very grateful to Richard McCabe, Andrew Hadfield, Patrick Cheney, and Claire Preston who each read and commented upon portions of the work whilst in progress. The advice and support of Anne Barton, John Kerrigan, Marie and Richard Axton, Anne Lake Prescott, John Carey, Eric Griffiths, Catherine Bates, and the late Jeremy Maule have been invaluable. The help of Chris Tilmouth, Bruno Currie, Peter McDonald, Peter Conrad, Christopher Butler, Richard Hamer, Christopher Haigh, Colin McAdam, Jason Yiannikkou, Peregrine Rand, Tore Rem, and many other friends at the Universities of Oxford and Cambridge is also deeply appreciated. I am grateful to the British Academy for the award of a scholarship, as well as to Queens' College, Cambridge, where I began my thesis, and to the Dean and Students of Christ Church, Oxford, whose award of a Junior Research Fellowship enabled me to complete this book. Thanks are due to the staff of the Cambridge University Library (in particular those of the Rare Books Room) as well as to those of the Cambridge and Oxford English Faculty Libraries, the British Library, the Bodleian, and the college libraries of Queens' and Trinity, Cambridge, and Christ Church, Oxford. I would like to express my appreciation of the friendly assistance of Professor Arthur Kinney, Professor Kirby Farrell, and the editorial board of *ELR*. The chapters on prophecy and antiquarianism first appeared in their journal in a slightly different form, the former under the title '"Priuie to his Counsell and Secret Meaning": Spenser and Political Prophecy', *ELR* 30 (2000), 3–31; the latter as 'Discourses of Conquest: *The Faerie Queene*, the Society of Antiquaries, and *A View of the Present State of Ireland*', *ELR* 32 (2002), 127–59. In addition, an article containing material from the chapter on chorography is set to appear in a forthcoming issue of *Spenser Studies*. I am grateful for the dedication of Sophie Goldsworthy, Sarah Hyland, Frances Whistler, and Sylvia Jaffrey at Oxford University Press, as well as to the Press's two anonymous readers. They have helped to make this a stronger book. I wish to thank my mother, father, and brother for their constant support in many ways. Finally, I thank my wife Anne Marie, and children Josie, Beatrice, and Edgar for their love, help, and patience.

B.v.E.

Contents

Abbreviations

DNB	Dictionary of National Biography
ELH	English Literary History
ELR	English Literary Renaissance
N&Q	Notes and Queries
OED	Oxford English Dictionary, 2nd edition
PMLA	Publications of the Modern Language Association of America
SP	Studies in Philology

Introduction

Reading Spenser Historically

In 1612—more than a decade after Spenser's death—Michael Drayton published the first part of *Poly-Olbion*. It is a survey of the nation: as it is now, as it was in the past, and as it exists in the past/present of mythology. In spite of its proclaimed novelty the work is, in more than one sense, a backward-looking composition. Its rearward glance catches the land's history and poetry alike, and regarding both it displays a sense of temporal disjunction. *Poly-Olbion* feels out of joint with its time. This is most graphically apparent in its conflicting prefaces.[1] For here, alongside a zealous defence of the integrity of received stories about 'the ancient people of this Ile', it also forwards a very progressive and sceptical assessment of that ancient British history. These two versions of the nation's past continue to sit directly alongside each other throughout the volume. Thus, as Drayton vaunts the glories of Merlin and King Arthur, John Selden (the poem's antiquarian annotator) systematically points the reader towards manuscripts and architectural remains that offer damning evidence against the poet's 'fiction'. Both men stick doggedly to their side of the story, each makes strident claims for the 'truth' of what he writes.[2] Most remarkably of all, as they do so, poet and antiquarian

---

[1] See *Poly-Olbion*, in J. William Hebel (ed.), *The Works of Michael Drayton*, 5 vols. (Oxford: Shakespeare Head Press, 1933; repr. Oxford: Basil Blackwell, 1961), IV. iii*, and *passim*. Drayton's general preface aggressively condemns what it assumes to be an unappreciative age. His pessimism proved well founded: ten years on a considerable portion of the original print run would still remain unsold, allowing the 1622 additions to be appended to the remaining stock.

[2] T. D. Kendrick, *British Antiquity* (London: Menthuen, 1950; repr. 1970), 103, did not doubt that Drayton believed passionately in the old history first related by Geoffrey of Monmouth, and Jean R. Brink, *Michael Drayton Revisited*, Twayne's English Authors Series, 476 (Boston: Twayne, 1990), 87, agrees with his verdict. Joseph M. Levine, *Humanism and History: Origins of Modern Historiography* (Ithaca: Cornell University Press, 1987) argues that the inclusion of the notes makes it 'perfectly plain' that Drayton 'knew and appreciated the difference' between the respective fact and fiction (p. 52). Anne Lake Prescott, 'Drayton's Muse and Selden's "Story": The Interfacing of Poetry and History in *Poly-Olbion*', *SP* 87 (1990), 128–35, argues for a more playful interchange between the two voices; for developments on this view see also D. I. Galbraith, *Architectonics of Imitation in Spenser, Daniel, and Drayton* (Toronto: University of Toronto Press), 121–9, and John E. Curran, Jr. 'The History Never Written: Bards, Druids, and the Problem of Antiquarianism in *Poly-Olbion*', *Renaissance Quarterly*, 51 (1998), 498–525. Andrew

alike lay claim to the figure of England's 'Poet historical', Edmund Spenser.

The conflict of historical visions in *Poly-Olbion* provides the snapshot of a changing situation that is of vital importance for understanding Edmund Spenser. By the time that the first part of Michael Drayton's poem was published, the intellectual climate surrounding ancient history had already changed significantly from that which impressed itself upon *The Faerie Queene*. The mythical tale of the Britons and their kings had, as Ferguson puts it, been 'driven from center-stage' by new historical interests.[3] Little by little, antiquarians such as Selden had shifted the status of it and other pseudo-histories towards the purely poetic. Classical myth, too, had begun to be regarded differently by historians.[4] Even in 1612, however, that process was far from complete. In spite of the nonchalance with which Drayton refers to 'the Illustration of this learned Gentleman', and for all Selden's confidence about the intention of the poet, the stories that they deliver about the past rub uncomfortably against one another. Drayton speaks with passion of his 'friends, the Cambro-Britans' (p. vii*) and spiritedly offers his backing for the tales of '*Britaine*-founding *Brute* . . . which now the envious world doth slander for a dreame' (p. 9). Selden, on the other hand, feels deeply uneasy about these old narratives. Glossing Drayton's reference to the mythical King Arthur, he tells us that 'the *Bards* songs have, with this kind of unlimited attribut so loaden him, that you can hardly guesse what is true' (p. 87). What Selden had begun by calling 'Personating Fictions' (p. viii*) soon become '*false tales*' (p. 88). Far from illustrating their 'clothed Truth' (p. viii*) as he had promised, the antiquarian shuns them altogether, telling us 'from such I abstaine, as I may' (p. 89).

Hadfield, 'Spenser, Drayton, and the Question of Britain', *Review of English Studies*, 51 (2000), 582–99, argues for the existence of anxieties about the stability of English identity in a British context.

    [3] Arthur B. Ferguson, *Clio Unbound: Perception of the Social and Cultural Past in Renaissance England*, Duke Monographs in Medieval and Renaissance Studies, 2 (Durham, NC: Duke University Press, 1979), 111. For an accessible translation of the Briton history see Geoffrey of Monmouth, *The History of the Kings of Britain*, trans. Lewis Thorpe (London: Penguin, 1966). An authoritative survey of its impact is offered by J. S. Tatlock, *The Legendary History of Britain: Geoffrey of Monmouth's Historia Regum Britanniae and its Early Vernacular Versions* (Berkeley: University of California Press, 1950). On its historicity see David N. Dumville, *Histories and Pseudo-histories of the Middle Ages* (Aldershot: Variorum, 1990).

    [4] For one survey see Arthur B. Ferguson, *Utter Antiquity: Perceptions of Prehistory in Renaissance England* (Durham, NC: Duke University Press, 1993). The quasi-historical status of Classical myth is still in evidence in the prefatory verse of *Poly-Olbion* where the gloss sets out Julius Caesar's ancestral links to Aeneas and his mother Venus.

Although it is fought out only in prefaces and endnotes, there is in *Poly-Olbion* a conflict between different readings of the past. This is true not just of ancient texts but also of more recent arrivals. Spenser, even at this early date, had become the subject of historical controversy: both Drayton and Selden attempted to recruit him to their cause. Drayton's position as a Spenserian is well known. As time went on he and the rest of the 'shepherd nation' drew increasingly on the nostalgia and discontent summed up by Queen Elizabeth's 'arch poet'.[5] For Drayton Spenser's historical poetry had profound emotional and moral resonance; by insisting on the truth of Arthurian legend he confirmed connections with the older poet. Yet for Selden too the kind of history that Spenser wrote was important. While Drayton drew the poet back in time by investing him with quasi-Medieval authority, Selden pulled in the opposite direction, making Spenser a conduit for progressive historical values. On more than one occasion he called upon the poet as witness. Taking Spenser as a precedent, Selden stressed the exclusive 'poetical' domain of legendary histories. The story of St George, for example, lacked 'true antiquity' and was therefore 'symbolicall' rather than 'truely proper' (p. 85). It was with great satisfaction that Selden observed that 'our admired *Spencer* hath made him an embleme of Religion' (p. 85).

The divergent readings of *Poly-Olbion* testify at once to a complex national debate about the past, and to uncertainty surrounding the figure of Edmund Spenser. To some the poet might appear as the voice of a more faithful age: a time that placed moral as well as aesthetic value on old histories. Yet there were also elements in his work that allowed for other readings: there were expressions of scepticism and even signs of progressive historical thought. Drayton and Selden were not alone in disputing the historical status of Spenser's output. While Spenser lived a patriotic yeoman of Kent had already provided manuscript annotations confirming the accuracy of *The Faerie Queene*'s chronicle history.[6] For the

---

[5] On the Spenserian quality of Drayton's project see Joan Grundy, *The Spenserian Poets: A Study in Elizabethan and Jacobean Poetry* (London: Edward Arnold, 1969), 128–42, and W. B. Hunter (ed.), *The English Spenserians: The Poetry of Giles Fletcher, George Wither, Michael Drayton, Phineas Fletcher and Henry More* (Salt Lake City: University of Utah, 1977). A more recent study of the poet's imitators is provided by Michelle O'Callaghan, *The 'Shepheards Nation': Jacobean Spenserians and Early Stuart Political Culture, 1612–1625* (Oxford: Oxford University Press, 2000). Drayton's backward vision was still more evident in the 1622 edition which, through a new preface and a dedicatory poem by William Browne, mourned the passing of Elizabeth, Sidney, and Spenser (p. 393).

[6] For these annotations by John Dixon, which checked the chronicles of *Faerie Queene* II.x and III.iii against those of Fabyan, see Graham Hough (ed.), *The First Commentary on 'The Faerie*

antiquarian Sir James Ware, on the other hand, the poet was to become the representative of an advanced historical movement.[7] Whereas in *Poly-Olbion* the rival voices of history and legend are unmistakable, in Spenser's works the line between the two seems to have shifted considerably in response to the demands of readers.

The years since Spenser's death—like those of his life—saw changes in the perceived place of history, both in the work of poets and within a wider national culture. Although, as D. R. Woolf says, 'few scholars would now agree that there was anything terribly revolutionary about developments in English historical writing', he, along with many other scholars, nevertheless depicts a hesitant movement towards a more accurate, analytical perspective on the past.[8] As the term 'history' gradually shifted its significance towards that of an academic discipline, so its place in the works of Spenser changed under the influence of literary schools and fashions. This is true not only of sixteenth- and seventeenth-century readers. In the academic writing of the twentieth century, too, the place of history in the works of Spenser has altered. Where Romantic critics such as Coleridge had admired the absence of history in *The Faerie Queene*, the editors of the early twentieth-century Variorum edition greatly increased its presence by means of a sustained search for historical allegory.[9]

Each age develops its own readings of the past. The current one, it is widely recognized, has a fondness of plurals. Recent scholarship, especially on English nationhood, has enabled new thinking about the significance of history in the works of Spenser. Richard Helgerson's *Forms of Nationhood*—a work implicitly acknowledged in this study's title—performed a seminal role in the discovery of such exchanges.[10] Cartographic, religious, or legal texts are now routinely recognized as

Queene' (privately published, 1964), 12–15. For details of Dixon's life see Bart van Es, 'The Life of John Dixon, *The Faerie Queene*'s First Annotator', *N&Q* 246, NS 48: 259–61.

[7] For details see Ch. 3, especially in its discussion of Sir James Ware's *The Historie of Ireland, Collected by Three Learned Authors* (Dublin, 1633).

[8] D. R. Woolf, *The Idea of History in Early Stuart England: Erudition, Ideology, and 'The Light of Truth' from the Accession of James I to the Civil War* (Toronto: University of Toronto Press, 1990), p. xi. See also Woolf, *Reading History in Early Modern England* (Cambridge: Cambridge University Press, 2000).

[9] See *Coleridge's Miscellaneous Criticism*, ed. T. M. Raysor (London: Constable, 1936), 36, and *The Works of Edmund Spenser: A Variorum Edition*, ed. Edwin Greenlaw *et al.*, 11 vols. (Baltimore: Johns Hopkins University Press, 1932–49). The latter also drew on earlier commentaries, notably Upton's.

[10] *Forms of Nationhood: The Elizabethan Writing of England* (Chicago: University of Chicago Press, 1992).

useful entry-points for the exploration of Early Modern literature. The ways in which authors appropriate and transform historical narrative has likewise been the subject of productive enquiry.[11] To a degree such work is indebted to the New Historicism, but it also owes much to an increased sensitivity to multifaceted cultural and political identities. Writers such as David Baker, Colin Kidd, and Claire McEachern have facilitated a greater understanding of the politics of national history.[12] As a result, the ways in which stories about the past go to shape the present have come more openly into view.

In the case of Edmund Spenser too, the scholarship of the last twenty years has greatly expanded available ways of reading. It is equally difficult here to give an adequate account of developments. A lasting impression was certainly made by Harry Berger, whose awareness of Spenser's changeful 'state of present time' has been hugely instructive, especially when combined with subsequent political readings.[13] More recent Spenser scholarship—even where not directly dealing with historical thinking—has also greatly complicated our understanding of Spenser's place within history. Montrose has written brilliantly on the instability of the Spenserian subject.[14] Helgerson, Rambuss, Cheney, amongst others,

[11] Annabel Patterson's 'Sir John Oldcastle as a Symbol of Reformation Historiography', in *Religion, Literature, and Politics in Post Reformation England: 1540–1688*, ed. Donna B. Hamilton and Richard Strier (Cambridge: Cambridge University Press, 1996), 6–21, and Lisa Jardine, 'Encountering Ireland: Gabriel Harvey, Edmund Spenser, and English Colonial Ventures', in Brendan Bradshaw, Andrew Hadfield, and Willy Maley (eds.), *Representing Ireland: Literature and the Origins of Conflict, 1534–1660* (Cambridge: Cambridge University Press, 1993), 60–75, are but two examples of this far-reaching development.

[12] David J. Baker, *Between Nations: Shakespeare, Spenser, Marvell, and the Question of Britain* (Stanford: Stanford University Press, 1997), Colin Kidd, *British Identities before Nationalism: Ethnicity and Nationhood in the Atlantic World, 1600–1800* (Cambridge: Cambridge University Press, 1999) and Claire McEachern, *The Poetics of Nationhood, 1590–1612*, Cambridge Studies in Renaissance Literature and Culture, 13 (Cambridge: Cambridge University Press, 1996). Such work is also related to what is sometimes called 'eco-criticism', with its interest in regional identities and cultural geography.

[13] 'Archaism, Immortality, and the Muse in Spenser's Poetry', *The Yale Review*, 58 (1968), 214–31, is a typical example. Berger's *Revisionary Play: Studies in the Spenserian Dynamics* (Berkeley: Univerisity of California Press, 1988) collects the bulk of these earlier essays. Its introduction, by Louis Montrose, provides a productive political counterpoint. For a more critical perspective, see Richard A. McCabe, 'Self-consuming Discourse: Spenserian Poetics and the "New" New Criticism', *Review*, 13 (1991), 185–99.

[14] Louis Adrian Montrose, 'The Elizabethan Subject and the Spenserian Text', in Patricia Parker and David Quint (eds.), *Literary Theory/Renaissance Texts* (Baltimore: Johns Hopkins University Press, 1986), 303–40, sits alongside a number of other articles that examine the interrelationship between genre, politics, and history in Spenser's work. Also influential, for example, is David Norbrook, *Poetry and Politics in the English Renaissance* (London: Routledge & Kegan Paul, 1984).

have transformed conceptions of the poet's career.[15] On top of this an accumulation of studies have effected a ground-shift in the perceived significance of Ireland for the work of Spenser. Amongst this last grouping a number of scholars—notably Andrew Hadfield and Christopher Highley—have already productively combined innovative thinking on historical works with wider developments in Spenser Studies.[16] Using a broader canvas, David Galbraith's recent work on 'imitation' has again sought out the connections between the poet and historical writing.[17] In combination with earlier scholarship on providence and dynastic epic, such criticism is working to reveal an increasingly multifaceted 'Poet historical'.[18]

The present book builds upon a very long tradition of 'reading Spenser historically'. It begins with the premise—amply confirmed by centuries of commentary—that the poet thought deeply about the significance of the past. It differs from earlier studies in three principal ways. In the first place it widens the domain of 'history' by including

[15] Richard Helgerson, *Self-Crowned Laureates: Spenser, Jonson, Milton and the Literary System* (Berkley: University of California Press, 1983), Richard Rambuss, *Spenser's Secret Career*, Cambridge Studies in Renaissance Literature and Culture, 3 (Cambridge: Cambridge University Press, 1993), and Patrick Cheney, *Spenser's Famous Flight: A Renaissance Idea of a Literary Career* (Toronto: University of Toronto Press, 1993). See also the essays collected in Judith H. Anderson, Donald Cheney, and David A. Richardson (eds.), *Spenser's Life and the Subject of Biography* (Amherst, Mass.: University of Massachusetts Press, 1996).

[16] Andrew Hadfield, *Edmund Spenser's Irish Experience: Wilde Fruit and Salvage Soyl* (Oxford: Clarendon Press, 1997) and Christopher Highley, *Shakespeare, Spenser, and the Crisis in Ireland*, Cambridge Studies in Renaissance Literature and Culture, 23 (Cambridge: Cambridge University Press, 1997).

[17] Galbraith, *Architectonics*.

[18] The place of providential history was proclaimed in unequivocal terms in E. M. W. Tillyard's *The Elizabethan World Picture* (London: Chatto & Windus, 1943, repr. 1958), e.g. pp. 12–15. Since then numerous critics have provided subtle readings on the tone and structure of Spenser's historical vision. One influential account is to be found in Angus Fletcher, *The Prophetic Moment: An Essay on Spenser* (Chicago: University of Chicago Press, 1971), which uses the archetypes of 'temple' and 'labyrinth' to model the exploratory perspective on time in *The Faerie Queene*. Certainly his thinking influenced Michael O'Connell's *Mirror and Veil: The Historical Dimension of Spenser's 'The Faerie Queene'* (Chapel Hill: University of Carolina Press, 1977) which sets up a similar opposition between revelation and quest in describing the poet's mindset. That opposition was placed in a wider European context by Andrew Fichter, *Poets Historical: Dynastic Epic in the Renaissance* (Yale: Yale University Press, 1982), while the complexity of Spenser's art in relation to providence was more fully explored in McCabe's exceptionally learned study *The Pillars of Eternity: Time and Providence in 'The Faerie Queene'* (Dublin: Irish Academic Press, 1989). Other studies include Catherine Rodgers, *Time in the Narrative of 'The Faerie Queene'* (Salzburg: Institut für Englische Sprache und Literatur, 1973), Nancy Pope, *National History in the Heroic Poem: A Comparison of the Aeneid and* The Faerie Queene (New York: Garland, 1990), Claus Uhlig, *Klio und Natio: Studien zu Spenser und der Englischen Renaissance* (Heidelberg: Universitätsverlag, 1995), and Thomas F. Bulger, *The Historical Changes and Exchanges as Depicted by Spenser in 'The Faerie Queene'* (Lewiston, NY: Edwin Mellen Press, 1993).

within it material (including prophecies, political tracts, and regional descriptions) not routinely contained within that category. While such material has been discussed before it has rarely been in relation to a wider historiographical context. Antiquarianism and chorography, for example, are not often brought together with universal chronicles. Their shared status as 'histories' has been too little recognized. Secondly, because this study is unusually wide in its definition of 'history', it is uncommon too in the range of texts in which it finds a historical influence. Work on Spenser and history has traditionally focused on *The Faerie Queene*, but here less prominent pieces including the *Complaints, Colin Clouts Come Home Againe*, and *The Shepheardes Calender* also receive sustained attention. Thirdly, this study distinguishes itself through a focus on 'form'. As with the word 'historical', the word 'form' as used here defines neither a modern nor an Elizabethan concept.[19] Rather it is something that falls between the two. The work thus marks a new departure by setting out a nebulous but influential genre-system governing Early Modern English approaches to the past.[20]

Through the concept 'forms of history' this book explores Spenser's engagement with an important Elizabethan discourse. It looks, for example, at the intersection of panegyric and apocalyptic history, or at the respective capabilities of chorography and chronicle. It attempts to reveal the intellectual and political energies released in such exchanges and to demonstrate the way in which Spenser harnesses them. Spenser could think about 'chronicle' in terms of a defined set of moral values. When writing from an antiquarian perspective, those values could be radically different. In poetry, however, these and other forms could meld

---

[19] As noted in J. G. A. Pocock's *The Ancient Constitution and the Feudal Law: A Study of English Historical Thought in the Seventeenth Century, a Reissue with a Retrospect* (Cambridge: Cambridge University Press, 1987), 255, it is difficult to find the right vocabulary to define 'the historical' in the Early Modern period. The word 'history' attached to an antiquarian tract would have appalled many Renaissance historians, yet at the same time the word was used very casually in relation to fictional accounts. To a degree the concept 'forms of history' is indebted to Hayden White, *Metahistory: The Historical Imagination in Nineteenth-Century Europe* (Baltimore: Johns Hopkins University Press, 1973), 1–42. The 'forms' set out here, however, are more likely than those of White to have been a conscious presence in the minds of writers and readers.

[20] The word 'system' should be employed cautiously—it is not intended here to imply any formal Renaissance hierarchy of 'kinds'. Rather, it gestures towards the loose categories described by David Duff (ed.), *Modern Genre Theory* (London: Longman, 2000), pp. x–24. It should also be noted that generic boundaries in Renaissance historiography have been explored in detail by Woolf, *The Idea*, and Ferguson, *Clio*. On more formal Renaissance concepts of genre, see Rosalie Colie, *The Resources of Kind: Genre-Theory in the Renaissance*, ed. Barbara K. Lewalski (Berkeley: University of California Press, 1973), or Lewalski (ed.), *Renaissance Genres: Essays on Theory, History, and Interpretation* (Cambridge, Mass.: Harvard University Press, 1986).

together. As a strongly political and moralistic writer, Spenser could deploy them to a wide variety of ends. This study attempts to trace in Spenser's output the interacting strands of that historical vision. In a sense it tries to recover the particulated perspectives of *Poly-Olbion*. For in its depictions of the past and in its readings of Edmund Spenser, that work has much to tell about the significance of 'forms of history'.

Early Modern Histories

Any account of Spenser's sense of history juggles conflicting demands. On the one hand it must be located on a (not always consistent) line of development towards a more modern historiography. The long-established argument for the Renaissance recovery of such concepts as 'anachronism', 'awareness of evidence', and 'interest in causation' holds within it an important element of truth: irrefutably, late sixteenth-century England was gradually moving towards a new understanding of its distant past.[21] On the other hand, what such accounts of progressive struggle find more difficult to convey is the simultaneous highly diverse picture presented by a synchronic approach. If, in retrospect, it is possible to trace such developments as the decline of the chronicle, or the abandonment of myths about the country's Briton heritage, these conclusions were inevitably beyond the reach of late sixteenth-century observers.[22] Edmund Spenser's poetic vision was the product of competing historiographic perspectives: as well as a developing enthusiasm for the new knowledge about Britain's past, he also displays an understanding of other older and equally complex histories.[23] His vision was neither fully theorized nor fully consistent, but nevertheless one that expressed and played brilliantly upon the cross-currents of the Elizabethan dialogue with the past.

[21] See e.g. Peter Burke, *The Renaissance Sense of the Past* (London: Edward Arnold, 1969), 1 and *passim*. Burke's formulation is confirmed by the research of Levine, *Humanism and History*, 11.

[22] Kendrick, *British Antiquity*, concludes that the antiquarian thought of the 16th cent. is 'complex, almost to the point of becoming entirely contradictory and confusing' (p. 104). See also Stuart Piggott, *Ancient Britons and the Antiquarian Imagination: Ideas from the Renaissance to the Regency* (London: Thames & Hudson, 1989), 8.

[23] On Spenser's use of the medieval quasi-historical tradition of romance, see Andrew King, *'The Faerie Queene' and Middle English Romance: The Matter of Just Memory* (Oxford: Oxford University Press, 2000). King's study illustrates the generic shading of romance into historical writings and hagiography (p. 69) and the ways in which Spenser 'can create from a highly complex literary-historical tradition with strong political associations a dynastic, national, and Protestant epic with its own coherences' (p. 180). See also Robert A. Albano, *Middle English Historiography* (New York: Peter Lang, 1993).

In analysing the background of that dialogue, it is important to stress that doubts about ancient records had always existed. Higden's *Universal Chronicle*, almost certainly written in the 1320s, set a pattern adopted by many subsequent compilers by transposing a mass of available material while expressing uncertainty about a number of specific elements.[24] The demonstration of what Ferguson calls 'ambivalence' had for a very long time been an available response for compilers who nevertheless tended to reproduce accepted narratives.[25] It is there in a masterful way, for example, in Hardyng's *Chronicle* of 1436 which repeatedly advances and then recoils as it presents questionable accounts, such as the legends concerning the name by which the island of Britain was first known.[26] Even in 1587 the weighty Holinshed could not avoid the basic outline of the national and universal story. While on close inspection the absence of evidence on which to base the early history is regularly acknowledged, the template set up by Geoffrey of Monmouth and other authorities remains: the chronicle structure, with its reliance on a series of famous incidents and supposedly ancient literary 'moniments', soon reins in any attempt by the chronicler to take a different course.[27]

The dangers of attempting to impeach the integrity of ancient record had been most graphically illustrated by the case of Polydore Vergil, whose history had excited the wrath of Leland, John Bale, and Richard Harvey amongst others.[28] Even Samuel Daniel, a man, like Camden and Selden, convinced that the 'springs' of England's present day civility lay in 'poverty, pyracie, robbery, and violence; howesoever fabulous writers (to glorifie their nations) strive to abuse the credulity of after ages with heroycall, or miraculous beginnings', found it difficult to translate those

---

[24] See John Taylor, *The 'Universal Chronicle' of Ranulf Higden* (Oxford: Clarendon Press, 1966), 44.

[25] On 'ambivalence' see Ferguson, *Utter Antiquity*, 114–33.

[26] See John Hardyng, *The Chronicle*, ed. Richard Grafton, The English Experience, 805 (London, 1543; repr. Amsterdam: Theatrum Orbis Terrarum, 1976), fols. 6ᵇ–9ᵇ (on the island's first inhabitants). Levine, *Humanism and History*, 46, confirms this tendency to report all versions of a story when several are available as a general one. Hardyng's work, incidentally, is an interesting example of politically motivated chronicle rendition: variant versions were produced for Henry VI, Richard Duke of York, and Edward IV in turn.

[27] For example, no chronicle can avoid the tale of Ursula and the 11,000 virgins, the story of King Bladud's disastrous attempted flight, or (in the case of those of Protestant bent) exclude the apocryphal papal letters ceding control of the English church to King Lucius. So too a historical treatment of Hercules forms an inevitable part of histories with a universal dimension.

[28] See May McKisack, *Medieval History in the Tudor Age* (Oxford: Clarendon Press, 1971), 103, and Woolf, *The Idea*, 33.

convictions into a new narrative of national history.[29] In his preface to
The Collection of the History of England, which came out in the same year
as the first instalment of *Poly-Olbion*, Daniel tells us he is 'desirous to
deliver things done, in as even, and quiet an Order, as such an heape will
permit, without quarrelling with the *Beleefe* of Antiquity, depraving the
actions of other nations to advance our owne, or keeping backe those
Reasons of State they had, for what they did in those times' (sig. A3[b]).
Published as late as 1634 'by his last corrected Coppy' this statement is
remarkable for its expression of irreconcilable aims. In his earlier verse
history, *The Civile Wares*, Daniel had stated that he felt himself bound
to maintain 'the general receiv'd opinion' arguing that it would be 'an
impietie, to violate that publike Testimonie we have, with-out more
evident proofe; or to introduce fictions of our owne imagination, in
things of this nature'.[30] Because of this conviction, which was clearly
difficult to square with the poet's beliefs about the realities of Britain's
distant past, Daniel was subsequently forced to drop his plans to start
with 'the beginning of the first British Kings' (sig. B1[a]). For this reason,
too, he relinquished the poetic form which he had already found
problematic in *The Civile Wares*.

Daniel's awkwardness about the early history of his nation proceeded
from the same pressures that we see manifested in the conflicting
prefatory material to Drayton's *Poly-Olbion*, and it resulted in unstable
compromises. As Clark Hulse has shown, Daniel over time began 'to
devalue the ornamental style, to show a growing awareness of the new
historiography, and to evolve the anti-progressive theory of history
which leads to a veneration of the Middle Ages'.[31] Daniel, like Drayton,
harked back to a hallowed medieval age. Yet, like Selden, he also found
his picture of that time beset by new doubts and discoveries. Paradoxically, while one of the most historiographically aware poets of his
day, Daniel came to fashion himself as 'the remnant of another time' in
both the style and the substance of his historical narrative.[32]

---

[29] *The Collection of the History of England* (1634), 1. On these boundaries see also Galbraith,
Architectonics, 77–107.

[30] *The Civile Wares* (1609), sig. A2[b].

[31] Clark Hulse, 'Samuel Daniel: The Poet as Literary Historian', *Studies in English Literature*, 19
(1979), 55–70 (56).

[32] Hulse, 'Samuel Daniel', 68. See also D. R. Woolf, 'Community, Law and State: Samuel
Daniel's Historical Thought Revisited', *Journal of the History of Ideas*, 49 (1988), 61–83; and *The
Idea*, 77–104.

As the case of Samuel Daniel shows, early attempts to construct an alternative national history within existing narrative forms found themselves torn between irreconcilable forces. There were, however, alternative modes through which the past could be addressed. These did not place themselves under the weighty heading of 'History', but this relative marginality could itself be a virtue. Members of the Society of Antiquaries did succeed in conducting investigations into the distant past of their nation. Such investigations, in the shape of short 'discourses', were not printed and inevitably lacked the prestige, or at least the prominence, of the printed chronicles. Such factors, however, also lent greater freedom. The conversational structure of the Society's debates lessened the impact of an exercise which, by definition, implied the existence of differing opinions regarding the past. The modest length and strictly delimited topics of papers, moreover, allowed antiquaries to avoid tackling the past wholesale—facilitating conclusions on the history of specific institutions that were beyond the reach of the unwieldy chronicle. The form of *Poly-Olbion*'s main narrative, likewise, afforded greater scope in which to express the author's individual view. For whilst Drayton used verse chorography to champion the old British legends (as several other verse chorographers had done), its geographically determined narrative also lent itself to more progressive approaches. William Camden, on a more modest scale than Drayton, had also celebrated British myth in chorographic verse (producing the Latin poem *De Connubio Tamae et Isis*). His great work—the *Britannia*—however, had adopted chorography as the appropriate form for the century's most ambitious reconstruction of the distant past.

It is one of the underlying arguments of this book that it was, above all, the choice of *form* that determined and expressed a writer's historiographic perspective—if not always regarding the ultimate facts of history, then certainly the way those facts were approached. It was form, as much as anything else, that provoked the passion of Drayton's preface. His oft-quoted observation that there is 'nothing esteem'd in this lunatique Age, but what is kept in Cabinets' (p. v*) is principally a complaint about poetical fashion. Yet the continuation of that sentence, bewailing the neglect of all that 'savors of Antiquity' also reminds us of the way in which Drayton allies the choice of literary form with a distinct approach to the past. Just as there is more than one historiographic perspective to be found in *Poly-Olbion*, there is also more than one form of history in that volume. Drayton had chosen to write what George

Wither described as a 'Topo-chrono-graphicall Poeme'.[33] Selden, in the 'illustrations' following each of the 'songs', used an approach strongly reminiscent of that found in the cabinets of the Society of Antiquaries. If we include *Poly-Olbion*'s prefatory material, and isolate the portions of Galfridian prophecy that Drayton's poem contains, it becomes apparent just how multivalent the work really is.[34]

Drayton's chorographic verse and Selden's prose commentary may be termed 'forms of history'. As such they are made up of a conjunction of narratological and generic qualities.[35] Chorography, for example, is geographic in structure. Drayton's muse is imagined travelling upon a chariot racing above the nation. As the poet traverses the maps that are included within his volume he tells the stories of landmarks as they loom into view. Hills, rivers, and buildings can all be used as the starting points for individual histories. Antiquarian discourse, in contrast, works in response to questions, implied or actual. 'Was there such a person as King Arthur?', 'what was the nature of this land's first inhabitants?'— such are the starting points of Selden's 'illustrations'. Mustering information from a range of sources, sticking firmly to the matter in hand, and maintaining a careful distance between the time in question and his own, he sets about formulating an even-handed response. None of this would be possible in a chronicle.

If the method of Drayton's or Selden's history is distinct, so too is its substance. In Early Modern history writing these two elements appear to have depended greatly on one another. Although 'truth' was something

[33] Wither's description headed his verse epistle to Drayton, which was included in the 1622 edition. See *Poly-Olbion*, 395.

[34] For an example of Drayton's use of prophecy see *Poly-Olbion*, 98, illustrated by Selden at 107. Chapter 6 of this book discusses the way in which prophecies change their political implications depending on readership. Here what would under Elizabeth have been a classic fulfilment prophecy takes on a critical subtext when delivered during the reign of a Stuart King. See also *Poly-Olbion*, 33 and 44, on 'the *Eagles* prophecies'.

[35] The word 'narratological' here alludes broadly to the thinking set out in Mieke Bal, *Narratology: Introduction to the Theory of Narrative*, trans. Christine van Boheemen (Toronto: University of Toronto Press, 1985; repr. 1988), or Susan Onega and José Angel García Landa (eds.), *Narratology: An Introduction* (London: Longman, 1996). Specifically, it depends on the definitions of *sujet* and *fabula* offered by Meir Sternberg in *Expositional Modes and Temporal Ordering in Fiction* (Baltimore: Johns Hopkins University Press, 1978). As he puts it, 'the *fabula* involves what happens in the work as (re)arranged in the "objective" order of occurrence, while the *sujet* involves what happens in the order, angle, and patterns of presentation actually encountered by the reader' (pp. 8–9). Thus, even if the *fabula* of a chronicle and chorography consisted of the same sequence of events in history, the two would remain 'narratologically distinct' in terms of their *sujet*. The same would be true of an antiquarian discourse or political prophecy based on this same *fabula*. As regards 'generic qualities' we may think of register, audience, medium, etc.

to which almost universal claim was made, it was in practice a malleable quality. For the authors of humanist histories, for instance, truth was often as much instructive or aesthetic as it was factual.[36] Thus, under the influence of Classical models, works such as Sir Thomas More's *Richard III* (1513) granted themselves the licence of imagining speeches or improving stories in the service of greater moral verities.[37] The balance between competing factual, political, or moral 'truths' was—at least in part—a question of genre. The author of an antiquarian discourse (a mode that made little claim for its ethical content) could judge a story on criteria very different from those of a chronicler.

The case of one of the Spenser's contemporaries—John Stow—illustrates this point perfectly. Stow was at the same time an enthusiastic participant in the Society of Antiquaries and a commercial rival of the popular chronicler Richard Grafton. In the year 1598 he consequently produced both *A Survey of London* and another edition of *The Summarie of the Chronicles of England*. The one is an advanced antiquarian text regarded by many as one of the greatest sixteenth-century breakthroughs in the field of history.[38] The other is an entirely conventional if shortened version of the accepted national story.

The radicalism of the *Survey* is not immediately evident at its opening, which repeats the tale of London's foundation by Brutus of Troy in 'about' 1108 BC. This story, however, is immediately marked out as a bid for glory on the part of the 'Welche Historian' Geoffrey of Monmouth. On the following page Stow demonstrates that whatever people inhabited the island at that time were, in fact, incapable of constructing what a reader of the sixteenth century would recognize as a town. In reality such settlements 'were onely thicke and combarsom woodes plashed within and trenched aboute' (p. 3)—the genuine civilization of cities was only to come with the invasion of the Romans. Up to and even after their arrival the Britons were incapable of the construction of brick walls (p. 4). Stow works diligently to uncover the origins of the buildings and place names he finds in the London of his day—he speculates not

[36] See e.g. Peter E. Bondanella, *Machiavelli and the Art of Renaissance History* (Detroit: Wayne State University Press, 1973), which shows the historian's writing to have been governed by literary principles of style and organization often at an accepted cost in terms of factual accuracy.

[37] For text and introduction see *Richard III*, ed. Richard S. Sylvester, in *The Complete Works of St. Thomas More*, 12 vols., ed. Thomas M. C. Lawler, Germain Marc'Hadour, and Richard C. Marius (New Haven: Yale University Press, 1963–81), ii.

[38] See e.g. Ferguson, *Clio Unbound*, 99, which regards Stow's contribution to a developing awareness of change as more significant than Camden's.

only about who built what, but also with whose money and why.[39] It is, as William Keith Hall observes, in part the *Survay*'s structure as a 'perambulation' that allows its author to 'dechronologize' his text.[40] Taking a cue from the practice of Camden's *Britannia*, he undercuts the foundations of Geoffrey's story as he tentatively constructs a new history on the ruins of Britain's genuine ancient past.

Yet while Ferguson is quick to argue that this kind of at-the-coal-face research is 'what really interested Stow' (p. 100), that impression is not one the reader of one of Stow's many chronicle compilations is likely to pick up. Partly as a result of an ongoing battle with Richard Grafton, Stow's prefaces to these works made ever grander claims for their value and integrity. Certainly the careful scepticism about the pre-Roman past displayed in the *Survay* is entirely absent in the *Summarie* of the same date. As in the 1580 *Chronicle* (of which it was an abstract) the ancient Britain it presents is a fusion of the biblical, Classical, and modern. In it pre-Roman kings found universities, build baths and temples, and are subject to plagues or rains of blood.[41] Caesar's observations on the long-haired barbarians he encountered on arrival in Britain—so important in the *Survay*—are here in no way reconciled with the picture of a thriving civilization that Stow presents but a few years before.

Stow's approach may seem inconsistent, but the very fact that a 'summarie' of the national history should have been worth publishing (some sixteen variant editions appeared) reminds us of the continuing importance of this solid outline. The term 'summarie' itself rightly brings across the practical bent of Stow's publication, for the work's arrangement skilfully promotes its utility. It is with some pride, for example, that Stow points his readers to the figures placed beside major events allowing quick access to their dates (sig. A5[a]). Functioning in part as the equivalent to a modern pocket diary, the *Summarie* includes an almanac showing feast days (sig. π8[b]), a rule for the calculation of terms (sig. ¶1[b]), and a set of tables showing 'How a man may journey from any notable towne in England, to the City of London' (sig. 2G7[a]). Woolf rightly speaks of these texts as products performing a considerable number of functions. The long list of these includes 'moral edification', the demonstration of 'the hand of the divine in past times', the preservation of

---

[39] See e.g. *Survay*, 29, on 'Criples gate'.

[40] William Keith Hall, 'A Topography of Time: Historical Narration in John Stow's *Survey of London*', *SP* 88 (1991), 1–15 (6). Hall's term is borrowed from Roland Barthes's 'Historical Discourse', in *Introduction to Structuralism*, ed. Michael Lane (New York: Basic Books, 1970), 147.

[41] *Chronicles* (1580), 22–3.

'information or documents', 'entertainment', the relaying of 'news of recent great deeds' and their preservation for 'posterity'.[42] Crucially, a good number of these are functions with which an antiquarian would not dare meddle.[43]

The practical bent and commercial success of such texts as John Stow's do not detract from the quasi-religious reverence that their authors display for their sources. Most educated Elizabethans would, on one level, have seconded Sir Philip Sidney's assertion that the primary objective of the historian was to teach by example.[44] Certainly, Thomas Blundeville, whose *True Order of Wryting and Reading Hystories* was the first of its kind written in England, is characteristically conventional and derivative in his views on this matter.[45] Like Stow in the *Summarie*, Blundeville is strikingly practical in approach. His book, which was published as an inexpensive quarto, claims on its title-page that the 'true order and Methode' will be 'no lesse plainly than briefly, set forth in our vulgar speach, to the great profite and commoditye of all those that delight in Hystories' (sig. A1ª). Above all, Blundeville stresses the importance of easy access to historical exempla: 'when we finde any such in our reading, we must not onely consider of them, but also note them apart by themselves in such order, as we may easily find them, when soever we shall have neede to use them' (sigs H3ª⁻ᵇ). Stow's *Summarie* is designed to give easy access to this important information. So too Grafton's astrological almanac and marginal dating systems worked efficiently to display a divinely determined pattern to be discovered over time.[46] It is for these complex reasons that Stow tells us he has

---

[42] D. R. Woolf, 'Genre into Artefact: the Decline of the English Chronicle in the Sixteenth Century', *Sixteenth Century Journal*, 19 (1988), 321–54 (323).

[43] William Camden, for example, is exceptionally careful in disclaiming for himself the title of historian. Despite the apparent conflation in Sidney's *Defence* of the character of the antiquarian and the historian, the bulk of Renaissance thinkers were very clear about the distinction between the two disciplines. Most famously, Camden was forced to defend himself against the accusation of the herald Ralph Brooke that he as a 'meere scholler' had pretended to the title of 'historian' in the *Britannia*. It is clear that Camden had no difficulty in separating the two roles, and when he came to perform the latter in producing the history of Elizabeth's reign he was evidently determined to maintain the methodological divides between this and his earlier work. On these events and on the moral, stylistic, structural, and other differences between histories and antiquarian works, see Woolf, 'The Idea', 21–2.

[44] See *The Defence of Poesy*, in *Sir Philip Sidney*, ed. Katherine Duncan-Jones (Oxford: Oxford University Press, 1989; repr. 1991), 221.

[45] *The True Order of Wryting and Reading Hystories*, The English Experience, 908 (London, 1574; repr. Amsterdam: Theatrum Orbis Terrarum, 1979), sigs. F2ᵇ–F3ª, and Woolf, *The Idea*, 3–8.

[46] Richard Grafton, *A Manuell of the Chronicles of Englande* (1565). See also *An Abridgement of the Chronicles of England* (1563; 1564; 1570; and 1572).

'consecrated' himself 'to the search of our famous Antiquities' (sig. ¶6ᵇ). The concluding passage of the 1598 *Summarie* suggests that the commercial decline of the chronicle history has already begun.[47] Despite his concurrent work on the *Survay*, however, Stow's dedication to his task remains unstinted. Stow's desire to preserve and bestow immortality is deep-seated, but grounded in a quite different motivation from that which inspires the *Survay*. The author's self-praise for searching after 'truth' (sig. ¶6ᵇ) in chronicles is noticeably absent in the (in modern terms) more accurate antiquarian text. The 'truth' of the *Summarie*, however, is to a large extent a moral quality. As Annabel Patterson notes, the compilers of the 1587 Holinshed had made the bold claim that 'next unto the holie scripture, chronicles doo carie credit'.[48] It is to that very different kind of truth that the *Summarie* aspires.

Stow had recourse to at least three of the 'forms of history' identified in this book: chronicle, chorography, and antiquarian discourse. Of course, the boundaries between these categories arc ill defined (the *Survay* could be called a 'chorography' but it also contains elements of more pointed antiquarian address). It is not difficult to see, however, that Stow's approach to the past differs markedly in response to the kind of text he is writing. Had he been commissioned to produce a royal pageant, or followed Sir Thomas More in composing a humanist history, these would likewise have delivered a very different representation. Like William Camden it seems Stow had little difficulty making the required shifts when addressing history in new contexts.[49]

What is true of writers appears equally true of readers. Turning again to *Poly-Olbion* we find that here too what is latent in other texts of the period is graphically displayed in prefaces. We find separate addresses to the royal (p. iii*), 'Generall' (p. v*), 'Cambro-Britan' (p. vii*), gentlewoman (p. xiii*) and 'Severe' (p. xiv*) reader, each of whom is directed to specific aspects of the text. Whilst this may at first suggest an orderly stratification, the areas of interest thus defined cannot have been mutually exclusive. Drayton, in dedicating his poem to Henry Prince of Wales, targeted a defined political constituency. Just so Selden must have looked to a group of like-minded scholars, such as that centred on

---

[47] Stow, *Summarie*, 460. On the decline of the chronicle see Woolf, 'Genre into Artefact'.

[48] Holinshed, *Chronicles* (1587), i. 202; Annabel Patterson, *Reading Holinshed's Chronicles* (Chicago: University of Chicago Press, 1994), p. vii.

[49] Camden's *Annales Rerum Anglicarum, et Hibericarum Regante Elizabetha* (Leyden, 1625) was to be written according to principles quite different from those of the *Britannia, De Connubio Tamae et Isis*, or his papers for the Society of Antiquaries.

Cotton's library.[50] Yet the 'severe' reader of antiquarian detail might easily turn his attention to the historical analogies intended for his royal counterpart. And for both the 'gentlewoman reader' might provide a convenient cover under which to enjoy less elevated modes of interpretation.

In *Poly-Olbion*, once more, we find an atomized vision of the past that tells us much about the reading and writing of Edmund Spenser. He too addressed a 'royal' reader. At her court appeals for 'Cambro-Britan' loyalty would find a ready response. Groupings such as that of Leicester House, on the other hand, styled themselves 'severe' readers of more progressive historiography.[51] Of course, such boundaries are ultimately artificial. 'General' readers were able switch readily between interpretative modes. Those at Leicester House could understand Arthurian pageants as easily as they might propagate the theories of Continental humanists. The distant past was a rich source of political narrative. It could be inflected to produce praise, prophecy, and even detailed political programmes. For a poet such as Edmund Spenser—who so instinctively played upon genres of all kinds—it provided an exceptional resource. Given a culture so attuned to the ways in which history could be restructured, it was inevitable that the past in many forms should come to permeate his work.

Forms of History in the Works of Spenser

The thesis of this book is not that Early Modern England had six fixed modes of writing history. Rather, it is that *form* (as a feature of prose and poetry alike) played an instrumental role in the construction of historical meaning, and that 'chronicle', 'chorography', 'antiquarianism', 'euhemerism', 'analogy', and 'prophecy' are useful categories through which to explore the implications of this fact. Each of the following chapters connects Spenser to a particular form of history. The first— looking at chronicles—fixes on the term 'monument'. By exploring the

---

[50] On what Graham Parry calls the intellectual 'oasis' of Cotton's library, see *The Trophies of Time: English Antiquarians in the Seventeenth Century* (Oxford: Oxford University Press, 1995), 5.

[51] Woudhuysen characterizes the group as one that had in common the 'rejection of the myth that the Britons were descended from Brutus and the Trojans' and a respect for writers including Bodin, Tacitus, and Machiavelli. See 'Leicester's Literary Patronage: A Study of the English Court 1578–1582' (unpublished doctoral thesis, University of Oxford, 1980), 76–91. For further discussion of this group see the essays collected in Anderson, Cheney, and Richardson (eds.), *Subject of Biography*.

significance of 'monuments' as physical remains and moral exempla, it draws attention to that term's productive (but also potentially treacherous) polysemy. In a wide range of Renaissance chronicles there is a conflict between the competing demands held together in this term. Tracing the history of Spenser's use of the word, the chapter looks at Spenser's translations of Du Bellay, as well as at his own work in the mould of the French poet: *The Ruines of Time*. At the core of the chapter sits a reading of the 'monuments' in Arthur's chronicle (II. x). Here—as throughout—the chapter argues for the existence of stresses in the Elizabethan idea of 'history': a concept in some ways overburdened by the ideological, moral, and epistemological functions it was made to bear.

The second chapter, on 'chorographies', looks at one possible solution to the problems highlighted at the close of the first. It demonstrates the importance of chorography for both historiographic and political debate. Following an examination of various chorographic texts, it shows how the same structures appear in Books III and IV of *The Faerie Queene* as well as in *Colin Clouts Come Home Againe* and *Prothalamion*. These structures have an unusual capacity for absorbing rival voices. Through the combination of land and history they gave Spenser freedoms not to be found within the confines of chronicle. Readings of Spenser's river passages expose an alliance between historical and political narratives. In particular the poet can be shown to have used rivers with exceptional subtlety to connect ancient history with current colonial endeavour.

The ensuing chapter—concentrating on the discourses of the Society of Antiquaries—establishes the importance of an antiquarian tradition of debate in relation to Ireland. Beginning with Sir James Ware's first published edition of the *View*, which presented the text very much as an antiquarian tract, the chapter argues that this classification has more validity than has hitherto been acknowledged. It looks in detail at the Elizabethan 'College of Antiquaries', showing how much their structured debates on questions of English antiquity have in common with Spenser's *View*. Observing the latent political significance of the work of the society, the chapter proceeds to analyse that tract's transition from exploration of the past to prescription about the future. Closing with the 'Mutability Cantos' it points to structural parallels that further illustrate the significance of 'discourses' as a mode through which to explore past practice and present rights.

Chapter 4—on 'universal' histories—fixes on euhemerism. This intellectual tool allowed Elizabethan historiographers to reach still further back in time. Euhemerism defined pagan myths as allegories, and found in them both moral and historical truths. In effect, it turned mythical tales to unintended 'dark conceits'. Such a method had a curious double status for the 'Poet historical': on the one hand it hailed the first poets as the oldest historians, on the other it condemned them as the original corrupters of truth. By examining a series of episodes (including Book II's fairy chronicle, and the encounters with giants in Books I and V) the chapter sets out Spenser's ambiguous position as both writer and reader of allegory. That position allowed him to forge connections between ancient and modern tyrants, and to construct a truly universal picture of time. It also prompted important questions about the nature of poetry itself.

Chapter 5—on historical analogy—builds on its predecessor and deals with the linkage between Spenser's present-day heroes and the great figures of the past. It examines 'comparison' in contemporary praise and pageantry. Highlighting government suspicions of such parallels, the chapter uncovers the dangers of this two-way construction of history. The writing of historical speeches or pageants meant forming an image of the present as well as the past. Historical 'mirrors' provided a mode through which Elizabethan subjects encouraged, warned, or implicitly criticized their sovereign. Spenser was an adept practitioner of this mode: it may be said to lie at the heart of the justification for his epic. *The Faerie Queene* creates mirrors for Elizabeth, and as the poem grew those mirrors came to reflect a changing political present. The work's second instalment alters the implications of the first—facilitating a play of historical analogues that even the poet himself could not fully delimit.

The study's final chapter looks at attempts made to extend beyond historical endings through the practice of 'political prophecy'. Here, still more so, we are concerned with the changeable reading of old histories. The chapter shows how the 'Briton history', so important in justifying the Tudor dynasty, was also the core narrative of highly subversive manuscript prophecies. Such prophecies multiplied at crisis points in Elizabeth's reign. They were not only themselves culled from existing histories (such as Geoffrey of Monmouth's *Historia*), they also made routine use of history in order to validate their own supposed prognostications. The chapter establishes Spenser's personal contact with those involved in astrological prophecy, and, as a result, forwards a new understanding of the allusive strategies of *The Shepheardes Calender* and the Spenser/Harvey *Letters*. Looking at the prophecies delivered to Britomart in *The Faerie Queene*, Books III and V, the chapter argues that this, ultimately, is the most dangerous form that historical narrative can take.

At the time Spenser coined the term 'Poet historical' even he is unlikely to have envisaged all the forms of history that his work contained. Yet Spenser's instincts were for inclusiveness, and as his output grew the complex morphology of his nation's past inevitably found its way into his writing. The polysemy of his vision was itself the product of a unique juncture in intellectual history—a juncture that he, as poet, was well placed to exploit. For, as he observed in discussing an adjacent matter:

An Historiographer discourseth of affayres orderly as they were donne, accounting as well the times as the actions, but a Poet thrusteth into the middest, even where it most concerneth him, and there recoursing to the thinges forepaste, and divining of thinges to come, maketh a pleasing Analysis of all.[52]

---

[52] 'Letter to Ralegh', *The Faerie Queene*, 738.

CHAPTER 1

'All my Antique Moniments Defaced?': Chronicles and Missing History

Reading Chronicles

If there is one exemplary point in *The Faerie Queene* that foregrounds the reading of history it is in Book II, Cantos ix–x. Here the knights Arthur and Guyon encounter 'An auncient booke, hight *Briton moniments*' and another 'That hight *Antiquitie* of *Faerie* lond' (II. ix. 59. 6, 60. 2). The episode, which has no direct parallel amongst the poet's literary sources, has long been understood to shed light on Tudor historiographical practice.[1] It is, in the first place, intended to give enjoyment to its readers. While present-day students of the poem may be unimpressed by the relentless catalogue that follows, the Queen (who is fulsomely addressed at its opening) is evidently expected to be pleased with it. Certainly Arthur (who generally maintains a very stiff upper lip) is 'quite rauished with delight' (II. x .69. 1). Members of the poet's sixteenth-century audience, too, appear to have shared this enthusiasm for the roll-call of British kings: John Dixon, of whose response we have a detailed record, must have devoted several hours to the annotations that crowd the margins of his copy.[2]

The joy experienced by Spenser's readers stems from good causes. In addition to its encomiastic and patriotic functions the narrative is also didactic: instructing its readers about their past, and inspiring their onward journeys with new-found vision.[3] Bravery is commended, vice reproved, and the dangers of treason and division are repeatedly driven home. As well as these political lessons, the tales also deliver a theological message. For those who seek them, complex numerological patterns

---

[1] Some parallels for Spenser's House of Alma, focusing strongly on the narration of national history, are, however, to be found in a text highlighted by Kathrine Koller. See 'The Travayled Pylgrime by Stephen Batman and Book Two of *The Faerie Queene*', *Modern Language Quarterly*, 3 (1942), 535–41. [2] Hough (ed.), *First Commentary*, 12–15.

[3] On the 'lessons' to be learnt from the historical narrative see Pope, *National History*, 109–36.

express an underlying order to events, and, if read in conjunction, the Briton and fairy histories prove still more revealing.

The *'Briton moniments'* in Eumnestes's chamber, like the prophecy of Merlin discussed in the last chapter of this book, have often been regarded as moments of transcendent vision. More than thirty years ago, S. K. Heninger concluded that it was 'as an apogee in his orgy of adulation' that Spenser cited the lineage of the British kings from Brutus onwards—a history of 'legendary truth' deserving of the deference accorded it by a long series of chroniclers and poets.[4] There is good reason to read the chronicle as part of a providential-dynastic tradition. Numerologists have asserted the importance of the number patterning that Spenser is said to have worked into the passage.[5] Others have pointed to the presence of such embedded histories in the traditions of both Classical and Christian epic.[6] From different perspectives more recent critics have refined these readings by highlighting the chaotic and amoral quality of much of the action, as well as the manner in which the two histories constitute a powerfully symbiotic pairing.[7] As McCabe puts it, whilst Spenser does not ignore 'the problem of pain' his fairy chronicle 'constitutes a fictive image of fortune's ultimate benevolence': once one reads the Briton chronicles 'through' those of fairy 'there is "linear" progress after all'.[8]

The history we read in Canto x takes the form of chronicle: a form whose 'purposes' D. R. Woolf lists as 'entertainment', 'commemoration', 'moral edification', and the demonstration of 'the hand of the divine in past times'.[9] These are tasks that Spenser takes pains to fulfil. The story of the 'vnworthy' King Memprise (II. x. 21. 3) is, for example, followed by that of his successor, Ebranck, whose 'noble deedes' (II. x. 21. 7) are rewarded with foreign conquests—fame and infamy alike are

---

[4] 'The Tudor Myth of Troy-novant', *South Atlantic Quarterly*, 61 (1962), 378–87 (387).

[5] e.g. Mills, 'Spenser and the Numbers', and Maren-Sofie Røstvig, 'Canto Structure in Tasso and Spenser,' *Spenser Studies*, 1 (1980), 177–200, and Røstvig, *Configurations: A Topomorphical Approach to Renaissance Poetry* (Oslo: Scandinavian University Press, 1994), 347–54.

[6] Fichter, *Poets Historical*, and O'Connell, *Mirror and Veil*, e.g. pp. 3–5. That tradition was to be maintained in the vision that the angel Michael affords Adam in John Milton's *Paradise Lost*, Books XI–XII.

[7] Berger, *Allegorical Temper*, 103–14, McCabe, *Pillars*, 103–12, and O'Connell, *Mirror and Veil*, 80–1. Miller, *Poems Two Bodies*, 199, identifies structural parallels between the house of Alma and the chronicles.

[8] McCabe, *Pillars*, 112. Looking back at the tradition of epic catalogues, Joan Warchol Rossi, '*Britons Moniments*: Spenser's Definition of Temperance in History', *ELR* 15 (1985), 42–58, sets out the lessons in temperance to be found in the apparently amoral '*Briton moniments*'.

[9] Woolf, 'Genre into Artifact', 323.

bestowed with confidence. As the example of Thomas Cooper's *Epitome of Chronicles* shows us, these were the staple components of the genre. He, in common with numerous other chroniclers, passed the same moral judgements on these two distant reigns.[10] Spenser, whose Briton history followed its sources exceptionally closely, was in many ways producing a highly conventional narrative.[11]

That fact need not, however, mean that the *'Briton moniments'* are the product of unqualified historical certainty. For what the *Epitome* also shows us, is that the 'Braue moniments' of King Ebranck's triumph (II. x. 21. 9) to which Spenser goes on to appeal were in reality impossible to find. Evidence for the entire history of the Briton's past up to and beyond the supposed reign of Arthur was notoriously elusive. Although the *'antiquitee'* of England 'maye easily contend with any other nacion', Cooper tells us:

By the often civil warres, and invasions of outwarde ennemies, the *monumentes* and remembraunces of the histories passed beyng destrojed, it hath caused no littell ambiguitee and darkenesse to the certayne knowlage of the originall begynnynge thereof. . . . For if there had remained any veritable *monument* of these tymes, surely the worshipful Beda and Gildas, our countreie men, yea and Cesar the conquerour therof, wolde not have omitted them.[12]

For the time before the arrival of the Romans, and for many of the centuries thereafter, there were no documentary records. This admission was to be found in other English chronicles (works that plagiarized each other in this as in so many other ways). In choosing the word 'moniment' to label the work discovered by his hero, Spenser had lighted upon an evocative but also troubling term. For 'monument' was a powerfully ambiguous word in the vocabulary of sixteenth-century England. Its meanings ranged from 'sepulchre' to 'written document', and from concrete 'structure' to enduring 'example'. It could refer to a fragment, 'carved figure', 'statue', 'effigy', or 'legal instrument', as well as to a 'portent' or 'warning'.[13] In its myriad of referents the word provides a curious parallel for the form of chronicle itself—a mode that, as Woolf

---

[10] See Thomas Cooper, *Epitome of Chronicles* (1559), 34, in which the former is reproved for tyranny and unlawful lusts, and the latter credited with the building of York and the castles of Dunbar and Edinburgh.

[11] For details see Harper, *Sources*, 172–85.

[12] Cooper, *Epitome*, 32 (italics mine).

[13] *OED*, 'Monument *sb*', nos. 1–5. I exclude only nos. 3c, 6, and 7, which are not relevant here or for which no citation exists before the second half of the 17th cent. These meanings all derive naturally out of the Latin 'monumentum', i.e. 'that which calls something to mind'.

shows, was already splitting up into other genres in order to perform the contradictory tasks that were demanded of it.[14] Like the 'chronicle of Briton kings' the word 'monument' is torn between two different kinds of truth: that of moral instruction and that of physical evidence. Before returning to Arthur's *'Briton moniments'* at the close of this chapter, it is worth setting out the cultural resonance of the term in Early Modern England as well as its specific significance for Spenser.

Writing Monuments: Foxe, Sidney, and Du Bellay

When the great Tudor martyrologist John Foxe named his life's work the *Actes and Monumentes* he called implicitly upon a great many sources of authority. The individual narratives that went to make up the book were at once warnings and records: edifying tales, but also—as transcribed textual remains—vital pieces of evidence that secured a providential reading of more than one and a half thousand years of history.[15] In writing his work Foxe was *creating* a monument—a physically as well as intellectually imposing text intended to survive long into the future. Within its covers there existed a plurality of monuments in microcosm. Those who had gone to their graves (or into the flames) marked down as heretics were effectively exhumed by Foxe's scholarly spadework only to be reinterred in prose. To be found in each of those architectural monuments to the Christian faith—England's cathedrals—copies of the Book of Martyrs functioned as monuments in their own right: not least as testaments to faith in the recoverability and rightness of history itself.

Not for all individuals, nor for all periods of time, however, was that faith as strong. Most famously, Sir Philip Sidney had dismissed history with rhetorical bravura in his *Defence of Poesy*. For Sidney (at least in the persona he adopts in that tract) several of the senses of the word 'monument' are in conflict. In his satirical portrait we find the historian:

---

[14] 'The chronicle', Woolf tells us, 'did not so much decay as *dissolve* into a variety of genres, such as almanacs (information); antiquarian treatises and classically modelled histories (historical); diaries, biographies and autobiographies (commemorative); and historical drama, verse, and prose fiction (entertainment)' ('Genre into Artifact', 323).

[15] As John N. King, *English Reformation Literature: The Tudor Origins of the Protestant Tradition* (Princeton: Princeton University Press, 1982), 438, says, Foxe's 'concept of texts as witnesses to faith plays upon the different senses of "monument" as sepulchre, written document, and funerary memorial'. Foxe is likely to have modelled his title on Jean Crespin's *Actiones et Monumentes* (Geneva, 1560).

Laden with old mouse-eaten records, authorizing himself (for the most part)
upon other histories, whose greatest authorities are built upon the notable
foundation of hearsay; having much ado to accord differing writers and to pick
truth out of their partiality; better acquainted with a thousand years ago than
with the present age, and yet better knowing how this world goeth than how his
own wit runneth; curious for antiquities and inquisitive of novelties; a wonder to
young folks and a tyrant in table talk, denieth, in a great chafe, that any man for
teaching of virtue, and virtuous actions is comparable to him.

(Defence of Poesy, p. 220)

Although Sidney does not use the word here, 'monuments' in the sense
of 'written documents' clearly surround the historian as he depicts him.
Yet, through the apparently endless deferral from one ancient authority
to another, the concept of monuments as concrete pieces of 'evidence'
becomes a miasma. Worse still, the idea that monuments are moral
examples is actually subverted in proportion to their historical integrity.
As Sidney argues a little further on: 'history, being captived to the truth
of a foolish world, is many times a terror from well-doing, and an
encouragement to unbridled wickedness' (p. 225). Ultimately even the
role of the historian as creator of metaphorical monuments, in the sense
of sepulchres, is usurped as Sidney signs off by directing a light-hearted
curse at the enemy of poetry that 'when you die, your memory die from
the earth for want of an epitaph' (p. 250).

Light-hearted or not, Sidney's critique exposes significant cracks in
the façade of 'providential history' so often ascribed to the Elizabethan
understanding of the past.[16] The rupture is not an overriding one. Sidney
had faith in the history of the biblical texts he so highly praises, and
elsewhere the poet's correspondence evinces respect, above all, for
Tacitus.[17] At the same time Sidney was able to laugh at the Briton

---

[16] This understanding was expressed most strongly in Tillyard's *Elizabethan World Picture* and
Shakespeare's History Plays (London: Chatto & Windus, 1944; repr. Penguin, 1986), 11–76, but
has continued to influence numerous subsequent critics. Henry Ansgar Kelly, *Divine Providence
in the England of Shakespeare's Histories* (Cambridge, Mass.: Harvard University Press, 1970), 298,
provides some significant evidence to qualify these assumptions.

[17] See e.g. *The Correspondence of Philip Sidney and Hubert Languet*, ed. William Aspenwall Bradley,
Humanist's Library, 5 (Boston: Merrymount Press, 1912), 219–23, where, as well as stressing
the need for 'example' (p. 220), Sidney writes revealingly of the cross-over between history and
poetry. On the respect for Tacitus see Woudhuysen, 'Leicester's Literary Patronage', 79. On
the general lack of scepticism in the period about the truth of Classical history see A. D.
Momigliano, 'Ancient History and the Antiquarian,' in *Studies in Historiography* (London:
Weidenfeld & Nicolson, 1966; repr. 1969), 1–39 (first publ. in *Journal of the Warburg and Courtauld
Institutes*, 13 (1950), 285–315).

History as it appeared in the *Breviary of Britain*.[18] And even Foxe repeatedly began editions of his work with expressions of regret that most of the past is 'lost in silence, and some againe misshadowed and corrupted, eyether through obtrectation, or flattery of writers'.[19] In successive editions the martyrologist was forced to respond to those who had criticized his work 'as though there were no histories els in all the world corrupted, but onely this history of Actes and Monumentes'.[20]

Foxe and Sidney stand side by side as key formative influences on Spenser's poetics. Strongly affected by both men, he had access to divergent perspectives on history. 'Monument', or 'moniment' as he more usually renders it, is an important word in the poet's vocabulary. It appears forty-six times in his verse, as well as being the term at issue in a significant exchange in *A View of the Present State of Ireland*.[21] Yet where (at the risk of reductiveness) for Foxe all senses of the word are mutually supportive and for Sidney they work against each other, in Spenser's work its meanings prove to be in constant and productive tension. His interest in the relationship between documentary, architectural, and poetic monuments can be traced from the earliest stages of his poetic career. Already in his teens Spenser had composed translations of Joachim du Bellay's 'Visions' for a work that bore the influence of both humanist aesthetics and Protestant eschatology.[22] Partly because it so

---

[18] *The Complete Works of Sir Philip Sidney*, ed. Albert Feuillerat, 4 vols. (Cambridge: Cambridge University Press, 1912–16), iii. 85.

[19] *Actes* (1563), sig. C1ᵃ, and *Actes* (1570), sig. A1ᵃ.

[20] *Actes* (1583), sig. π6ᵇ. Nor, as recent studies have shown, was the martyrologist himself entirely free of those vices. For varying perspectives on Foxe's use of sources see J. A. F. Thompson, 'John Foxe and Some Sources for Lollard History: Notes for a Critical Appraisal', *Studies in Church History*, *II*, ed. G. J. Cuming (London: Thomas Nelson & Sons, 1965), 251–7; Patrick Collinson, 'Truth and Legend: The Veracity of John Foxe's Book of Martyrs', in A. C. Duke and C. A. Tamse (eds.), *Clio's Mirror: Historiography in Britain and the Netherlands*, Britain and the Netherlands, 8 (Zutphen: Walburg Pers, 1985), 31–54; and T. Freeman, 'Notes on a Source for John Foxe's Account of the Marian Persecution in Kent and Sussex', *Historical Research*, 67 (1994), 203–11. Freeman's recent assessment forces a revision even of the limited claims about the martyrologist's objectivity forwarded by earlier work.

[21] See Charles Grosvenor Osgood, *A Concordance to the Poems of Edmund Spenser* (Washington: Carnegie Institution, 1915), 'Monument' and 'Monuments', 565. The count ought perhaps to be reduced by one as it records both versions of Spenser's translation of the sonnet by Du Bellay. The exchange in the *View* is discussed in Ch. 3 below.

[22] The blank verse renditions of the sonnets of Du Bellay and Petrarch had appeared anonymously in Jan van der Noot's *Theatre for Worldlings* (1569) to which was appended a very Foxeian reading of Revelation; they were to be reworked for publication of the 1590 *Complaints* volume. The way in which Du Bellay's work was internalized and reworked by Spenser throughout his career has been superbly set out by Anne Lake Prescott, 'Spenser (Re)Reading Du Bellay: Chronology and Literary Response', in Judith H. Anderson, Donald Cheney, and

successfully balanced the perspectives found in Sidney and Foxe, the subject matter of these French sonnets was to prove of recurrent interest. Du Bellay, who was passionately concerned with the antiquarian remains of Rome, wrote the poems while resident there. His work considers both the irrecoverable grandeur of that city's glory and the moral lessons to be learnt from its destruction.[23] Given his twin antiquarian and moral concerns it is the paradoxes of historical record that fascinate the creator of the visions. Above all, it is his acute awareness of the unpredictable spikiness of the historical monument that left an enduring impression on the young Edmund Spenser.

The third of Du Bellay's sonnets, concerning the fall of 'une Poincte aguisee' or 'sharped spire', expresses this quality with particular economy.[24] Bearing the ashes of a mighty emperor, the spire (like the temple that precedes it) constitutes an appropriate symbol for worldly vanity. Yet it cannot be dismissed so lightly: it is also a 'Digne tumbeau' or 'worthie tombe' (III. l. 11): itself (like the verse) an attempt to preserve the past. It is a monument in multiple senses: a sepulchre, a public edifice, and a piece of antiquarian evidence. When illustrated, it is even a written record (for the obelisk that appears in the accompanying engraving is emblazoned with archaic symbols). The inscrutability of the hieroglyphics, however, proves emblematic of the more general erasure of the past. Despite the fact that the spire is a 'Digne tumbeau', Du Bellay tells us 'Las rien ne dure au monde que torment!':

> Je vy du ciel la tempeste descendre,
> Et fouldroyer ce brave monument.
> *(Songe*, III. ll. 13–14)

In the original French the conclusion is straightforward: the spire, like other worldly things, is at the mercy of nature (and, behind that, the

David A. Richardson (eds.), *Spenser's Life and the Subject of Biography* (Amherst: University of Massachusetts Press, 1996), 131–45.

[23] For a brief overview of Du Bellay's biography see Anne Lake Prescott, *French Poets and the English Renaissance: Studies in Fame and Transformation* (New Haven: Yale University Press, 1978), 37–40.

[24] For both the *Songe* and *Les Antiquitez* references are to Joachim Du Bellay, *Les Regrets et Autres Œuvres Poëtiques*, ed. J. Jolliffe and M. A. Screech (Geneva: Librairie Droz, 1966). For Spenser's shorter verse—except where otherwise stated—they are to *The Yale Edition of the Shorter Poems of Edmund Spenser*, ed. W. A. Oram *et al.* (New Haven: Yale University Press, 1989). This contains Du Bellay's sonnets both as they appeared in the *Theatre* and in the *Complaints*. In line with that edition's practice, quotations from the former use individual sonnet numbers followed by a line reference in the sonnet. Those to *The Visions of Bellay* use the continuous line numbers. Subsequent references to these editions appear in the text.

mercy of an angry God). In this instance, however, Spenser's translation (which is not generally highly regarded)[25] brings to the fore a paradox only latent in his source. Having no direct equivalent for 'fouldroyer' ('to strike with lightening') the Englishman was forced to deploy his own formulation. Aged around 17 Spenser produced the rather clumsy 'With flushe stroke downe this noble monument' (*Sonets*, 3. l. 14), but when he reworked the piece at a later date the effect was altogether stronger:

> Alas this world doth nought but grievance hold.
> I saw a tempest from the heaven descend,
> Which this brave monument with flash did rend.
> *(Visions of Bellay*, ll. 40–2)

At the moment of destruction a transformation occurs—'rend' having the double sense of 'tearing down' and 'forging anew through splitting or melting'.[26] The word 'monument', which haunts the sonnet through-out but appears only in this last line, is suddenly given the full range of its potential meanings. It is here, finally, that the past really speaks: the obelisk is an archaeological remnant but also a grave; its fall is an endur-ing example but it is also a poetic creation. Even the aphoristic 'Alas this world doth nought but grievance hold' (which is allowed to stand as a single line and sentence) is a candidate for the 'monument' of the last line. By the time this revised version of the sonnet was published, 'monument' had joined that list of special words (like 'salvage', 'aread', and 'antique') which for Spenser remain evocatively multivalent.

The concerns of the *Songe* come to the surface still more clearly in Du Bellay's masterpiece: *Les Antiquitez de Rome*. In the original the 'visions' form a coda to this more ambitious sequence. Spenser, however, came to the work only later—publishing the *Ruines of Rome* as part of the *Complaints* volume. Again, the 'antiquitez' of Du Bellay's title are not restricted to tokens of earthly mutability. As well as betokening destruc-tion, they also enable the intellectual *re*construction of the achievements

---

[25] In the damning words of Alfred W. Satterthwaite, the commission to translate the *Visions* 'brought him a text, on the whole, of better than mediocre quality on which he wrought almost no improvement and which he occasionally debased'; see *Spenser, Ronsard, and Du Bellay: A Renaissance Comparison* (Princeton: Princeton University Press, 1960), 26–7. Prescott's verdict on the translation of the more complex *Ruines of Rome* is scarcely more favourable; see *French Poets*, 48–9. McCabe finds the first translation 'variable' but 'generally accurate' with the second sacrificing some of that accuracy for 'an increased musicality of language and assurance of metrical control' (see *Edmund Spenser: The Shorter Poems* (London: Penguin, 1999), 508 and 639).

[26] *OED*, s.v. 'rend, *v.*¹' versus 'rend. *v.*²'.

of Classical culture.[27] The imperial capital (by absorbing all the cultures and architectures of previous civilizations) constitutes a memorial to both its own and earlier histories:

> Tout ce qu'Egypte en poincte façonna . . .
> Tout ce que l'art de Lysippe donna . . .
> Souloit orner ceste Ville ancienne.
>
> (*Antiquitez*, 29. ll. 1–7)

The 'antiquities' left in the wake of the city's destruction, therefore, have an uncertain status. As Spenser puts it (once more exploiting the word 'monument', which is not there in the original):

> *Rome* living, was the worlds sole ornament,
> And dead, is now the worlds sole moniment.
>
> (*Ruines of Rome*, ll. 405–6)

Whether this makes Rome a museum or a grave remains an open question.

As Thomas Greene's powerful study has shown, Du Bellay's work is 'a labyrinth of ironies', not least the irony that the lessons drawn from a ruined Rome self-consciously echo the words of the ancient poets of the imperial city.[28] Du Bellay allows Rome's literary and architectural monuments to vie for precedence. Initially it seems the former have lasted where the latter crumbled, but ultimately the two become inextricably intertwined. Through the invocation of Orpheus and Amphion the language of buildings and texts becomes interchangeable. Virgil's spirit allows the poet to:

> rebastir au compas de la plume
> Ce que les mains ne peuvent maçonner.
>
> (*Antiquitez*, 25. ll. 13–14)

'Rebastir' and 'maçonner' mark Du Bellay as a builder in verse; conversely the suggestively parchment-like 'vieux fragmens' allow architects to 'Ressusciter ces pouldreuses ruines' (27. ll. 8–14). Texts become

---

[27] The notion of this renaissance had already been forwarded in prose in Du Bellay's poetic manifesto, the *Deffense*. Du Bellay's poetry (and perhaps his tract) had a significant influence on the *Elementarie* of Spenser's headmaster, Richard Mulcaster; see Prescott, *French Poets*, 65–6. On this aspect of the poems see Margaret W. Ferguson, '"The Afflatus of Ruin": Meditations on Rome by Du Bellay, Spenser, and Stevens', in Annabel Patterson (ed.), *Roman Images*, Selected Papers from the English Institute, NS 8 (Baltimore: Johns Hopkins University Press, 1984), 23–50.

[28] T. M. Greene, *The Light in Troy: Imitation and Discovery in Renaissance Poetry*, The Elizabethan Club Series, 7 (New Haven: Yale University Press, 1982), 228.

buildings, buildings become texts. It is with an explicit acknowledgement of this linkage that, at the conclusion of his Sonnet sequence, Du Bellay cautiously considers his own verses as possible 'monuments' (32. l. 6).

Unsurprisingly, the concept of transferring monumentality to verse itself appealed to Spenser. Du Bellay's suggestion is enthusiastically picked up in a coda to the English translation that trumpets him as one who has revived 'Olde *Rome* out of her ashes' (l. 453). By implication, Spenser also placed himself in this line of immortal immortalizers.[29] Poetry as much as stone, however, is a vulnerable medium. If Spenser's *Complaints* volume shares any single theme it is this. Not only are the poems that surround *The Ruines of Rome* concerned with the destructiveness of time, the impoverished state of the arts, and the difficulty of true interpretation, the collection itself is also a kind of 'monument' to poetry's destruction.[30] As the Printer's preface tells us, the volume is made up of but a 'fewe parcels' recovered after considerable effort: the author's shorter poems being 'disperst abroad in sundrie hands, and not easie to bee come by'.[31] Placed alongside aged, partially recovered, and partially inscrutable compositions, the *Ruines of Rome* was afforded another level of irony.[32]

The Ruines of Time

Whilst the translations are suggestive, it is above all the original composition placed at the start of the *Complaints* volume that makes clear the extent to which Spenser has absorbed and adapted Du Bellay's sensi-

---

[29] For an insightful reading of Spenser's position as a translator of Du Bellay, including reference to the concept of '*translatio imperii*', see Ferguson, '"Afflatus of Ruin"', 24. For the argument that the speaker in the sonnets is an ironic persona, see Andrew Fichter, '"And nought of *Rome* in *Rome* perceiu'st at all": Spenser's *Ruins of Rome*', *Spenser Studies*, 2 (1981), 183–92.

[30] Michael McCanles, '*The Shepheardes Calender* as Document and Monument', *Studies in English Literature*, 22 (1982), 5–19, sets out a comparable reading of *The Shepheardes Calender*, in which the archaic work of Colin Clout is framed as a monument within the more modern machinery of E. K.'s explanatory glosses.

[31] William Ponsonby, 'The Printer to the *Gentle Reader*', Spenser, *Shorter Poems*, ed. Oram, 223.

[32] Jean Brink, characteristically challenging the prevailing critical opinion, disputes the evidence that Spenser himself was responsible for the publication and arrangement of the *Complaints*. Whilst caution is always advisable, most of the evidence she considers (the listing of 'lost' Spenserian works, the numerous individual dedications, and the corrections included in later imprints) runs counter to her conclusion. For details, see 'Who Fashioned Edmund Spenser?: The Textual History of Complaints,' *SP* 88 (1991), 153–68.

tivity to 'monuments'. *The Ruines of Time* begins with the poet walking beside the Thames. Here he comes upon a vision that tells him of Verulamium (a Roman city supposedly once built upon the river's banks). After considering the loss of such great architecture, Spenser goes on to contemplate other visions (in particular of literary and religious immortality). In these respects *The Ruines of Time* is very reminiscent of Du Bellay's *Antiquitez*. Spenser does, however, introduce a number of important innovations. For a start, his poem opens by considering the work of William Camden and closes with that of Sir Philip Sidney: an iconic pairing (like that between Foxe and Sidney) that highlights two distinct kinds of monumentality.[33] As Herendeen has argued, Spenser's poem subtly conjoins the scholar's thinking with that of the poet upon whom it concludes.[34] Spenser's praise for the antiquarian is thus complicated by the intrusion of fictions, foremost amongst which is the principal speaker of the first half of the poem. For Spenser puts his praise of England's greatest slayer of myth (Camden) in the mouth of a poetic creation (Verlame: the 'auncient *Genius*' of the Roman city).[35] Camden, Verlame tells us, 'Hath writ my record in true-seeming sort' (l. 168)—a formulation that leaves some room for interpretation. Does 'writ' here stand in contradistinction to 'found'? Is 'seem' intended to raise questions it so often triggers in *The Faerie Queene*? The ensuing stanza provides no clear-cut answers to these questions. Indeed, its statements appear to be deliberately confusing *non sequiturs*:

> *Cambden* the nourice of antiquitie,
> And lanterne unto late succeeding age,
> To see the light of simple veritie,

[33] Positioning the *Ruines* as a 'deliberately transitional' text, Richard Danson Brown, '*The New Poet*': *Novelty and Tradition in Spenser's 'Complaints'*, Liverpool Texts and Studies, 32 (Liverpool: Liverpool University Press, 1999), argues that the poem (in both its form and content) enacts a conflict between 'traditional complaint' and a 'new poetry' (p. 110).

[34] Wyman H. Herendeen, 'Wanton Discourse and the Engines of Time: William Camden— Historian among Poets-Historical', *Renaissance Rereadings: Intertext and Context*, ed. Maryanne Cline Horowitz *et al.* (Urbana: University of Illinois Press, 1988), 142–58 (145). As Herendeen recognizes, even in his own right Camden is a complex figure. He is an antiquarian, but also the author of a mythologically rich river poem. For a reconstruction of *De Connubio Tamae et Isis*, fragments of which were worked into the *Britannia*, see Jack B. Oruch, 'Spenser, Camden, and the Poetic Marriages of Rivers', *SP* 64 (1967), 606–24. As Oruch notes, Spenser need not necessarily have known that the fragments were part of Camden's poem (p. 617).

[35] Verlame's name, as observed below, is itself a fascinating conundrum. It is Spenser who identifies her as 'th'auncient *Genius* of that Citie brent' (l. 19), the speaker describes herself only as the *former* Verlame and now a nameless entity (l. 41). For the sake of clarity, however, 'Verlame' here refers to Spenser's fictional speaker, and 'Verulamium' to the historical city.

Buried in ruines, through the great outrage
Of her owne people, led with warlike rage,
Cambden, though time all moniments obscure,
Yet thy just labours ever shall endure.
(*Ruines of Time*, ll. 169–75)

Camden's 'light' appears to have two functions. It is envisaged as a beacon exemplifying 'just labours' for all eternity—a light that will continue to shine 'though time all moniments obscure'. Yet the lantern is also an investigative tool, allowing scholars to discover still more history 'Buried in ruines' (in one sense obscured by them but in another inherent in their very substance). Verlame's praise is thus equivocal. For especially given the earlier claims about her loss of name and substance, the city's 'genius' remains uncertain whether Camden has created or discovered her past.

Through Camden (and more obviously through a contrast between him and Sidney) Spenser is juxtaposing two rival understandings of the word 'moniment'. The two perspectives inhere in the very title of *The Ruines of Time* which can be read as a statement of loss or discovery.[36] Ultimately, the poem, like Du Bellay's Roman work, ends in poetic and religious vision, praising a pantheon of lost nobility whom Spenser aspires to immortalize. In this desire to preserve the recent past, however, the poet displays an anxiety not there in his Continental model. For while Du Bellay is concerned with ruin, the notion of the complete loss or erasure of the past does not figure.

In *The Ruines of Time*, Spenser transposed Du Bellay's Roman experience to Britain and Verulamium, and, in a characteristically Spenserian way, exacerbated rather than reconciled the tensions existing in his model.[37] For if Rome is archetypally a city of monuments, Verulamium is *archetypally* a city without them. Camden, whom Verlame credits as the only writer of her record (ll. 166–8) noted that the city had been 'turned into fields'. The bulk of his discussion is concerned specifically with the systematic erasure of its physical remains.[38] Almost from the date of its

---

[36] On this double quality see Millar MacLure, 'Spenser and the Ruins of Time', in *A Theatre for Spenserians*, ed. Judith M. Kennedy and James A. Reither (Manchester: Manchester University Press, 1973), 3–18 (4).

[37] For another example of this characteristic shift towards a point of tension, see the discussion in Ch. 2 on Spenser's adoption of the river marriage form in Book IV of *The Faerie Queene*.

[38] William Camden, *Britain*, trans. Philemon Holland (1610), 412. All subsequent quotations in the text are to the 1610 translation. In order to facilitate examination of the Latin text to which Spenser had access footnotes (where necessary) also give page numbers for the 1586 edi-

foundation, Verulamium has been assaulted and plundered—a process that runs seamlessly from military attack to civilian excavation. For the story of that destruction Camden is forced to rely 'upon the credite of an ancient *Historiographer*' (p. 411). That source tells how tenth-century monks 'overthrew' all the ancient vaults of Verulamium, blocked its strong arches ('the lurking hooles of whores and malefactours'), and drained and filled with earth its large fishpool ('an evill neighbour' to 'the monastery'). This last is no incidental detail, as anchors dug up on the site of the city, combined with a corrupt passage in the work of the historian Gildas (a monument in a different sense), led many to the erroneous conclusion that the river Thames once flowed past the city. (Physical remains, even where they do survive, prove to be fallible aids in the construction of historical record.)

According to Camden's source, the next abbot continued the 'work' begun by his predecessor. The second stage in the destruction of old Verulamium proves to be still more emblematic of the equivocal testimony of both textual and architectural monuments. Thus, when the abbot's men razed the foundations of a palace 'in the hollow place of a wall as it were, in a little closet' they discovered, along with 'vessels . . . of glasse containing the ashes of the dead' a set of ancient books 'whereof one contained the life of Saint Albane written in the British tongue' (p. 411). In a nice inversion, the text recovered through the destruction of the walls in turn inspires their reconstruction. For (presumably as a devout response to this inspirational find) 'out of these remaines of Verulam' the abbot 'built a new Monasterie to Sainte Albane' (ibid.).

The transformation of stone through text in this tale from the *Britannia* invites parallels with Du Bellay. The suspicious neatness of this reversal, however, also leads us to question further the testimony of textual monuments. Camden does not pass judgement on the veracity of the story, but his subsequent transcription of Latin verses by a one-time resident of Verulamium again brings to the fore the mythology that surrounds this place. It tells of '*Arthurs* Syre *Pendragon*' and offers high praise to the activities of its monks. This piece of encomiastic history must have fuelled still further Spenser's fascination with the poetics of 'preserving' a past that was, in reality, already lost.

Camden's *Britannia* forms a remarkably fertile source for *The Ruines of Time*. From the start Spenser's treatment of Verulamium fixes upon a

tion. The 1586 section on Verulamium is to be found on pp. 219–22, with the above quotations on p. 222.

multiform insubstantiality. Already in the opening lines we are witness to a curious act of misplacement.[39] For, if Camden has told us anything it is that the city's ruins are not to be sought by the Thames—it is almost as if Du Bellay were to have contemplated the disappearance of Rome whilst scanning the banks of the river Po:

> It chaunced me on day beside the shore
> Of silver streaming *Thamesis* to bee,
> Nigh where the goodly *Verlame* stood of yore,
> Of which there now remaines no memorie,
> Nor anie little moniment to see,
> By which the travailer, that fares that way,
> This once was she, may warned be to say.
>   (*Ruines of Time*, ll. 1–7)

The location in which Spenser here places the upcoming exchange makes what follows still more provocative. If neither 'memorie', 'moniment', nor warning exists, how is the speaker able to make any claims about Verulamium? Verlame, at her first appearance, makes this same self-contradictory claim: 'Name have I none (quoth she) nor anie being' (l. 34). Her sepulchre, too, is a self-denying conundrum: the speaker telling us she has 'in mine owne bowels made my grave' (l. 26), and that she lies 'in mine owne ashes' (l. 40). The irony of her position as monument-less monument is played upon repeatedly as her lament progresses. Even as she describes her final overthrow under Saxon assault, Verlame seeks out and then denies monumentality:

> And though at last by force I conquered were
> Of hardie *Saxons*, and became their thrall;
> Yet was I with much bloodshed bought full deere,
> And prizde with slaughter of their Generall:
> The moniment of whose sad funerall,
> For wonder of the world, long in me lasted;
> But now to nought through spoyle of time is wasted.   (ll. 113–19)

Building to a crescendo of negatives, she tells us the Saxon grave 'And all the rest that me so honord made':

> Is turnd to smoake, that doth to nothing fade;
> And of that brightnes now appeares no shade.   (ll. 123–4)

---

[39] Charles G. Osgood, 'Spenser's English Rivers', *Transactions of the Connecticut Academy of Arts and Sciences*, 23 (1920), 65–108 (97), attributes the river's mislocation to a combination of carelessness and credulity.

Even smoke is too substantial; former brightness leaves not even its opposite. As a final token of her abandonment, Verlame returns to the Thames, which has been the poem's starting point. 'That gentle River', she tells us:

> for great griefe
> Of my mishaps, which oft I to him plained;
> Or for to shunne the horrible mischiefe,
> With which he saw my cruell foes me pained,
> And his pure streames with guiltles blood oft stained,
> From my unhappie neighborhood farre fled,
> And his sweete waters away with him led.   (ll. 141–7)

Rivers, in chronicle history, are frequently the monument of last resort —where all else has disappeared, there is in them at least a linguistic trace of past events.[40] Yet for Verlame it seems the opposite has occurred: it is not just that her name has failed to take root in the landscape, it is that the Thames (the 'river of time' that witnessed her past) has itself abandoned her.[41]

The fleeing Thames both creates and removes a monument. For the more the city's genius denies her own substance, the more she comes into focus in Spenser's art. In a paradox familiar from Du Bellay, the greater her physical erasure the closer she comes to being a monument to worldly vanity. Appropriately, straight after identifying herself as a warning (in particular to the unnamed Lord Burghley), she herself vanishes with 'dolefull shrikes' (l. 471). Verlame cannot be understood as the subject of unqualified mourning. The image of the fleeing Thames— with associated fish and fishermen—is less than edifying. Especially given the fact that the river of whose absence she complains was in fact a 'fishpool' there is some justice in the very last of the speaker's complaints, that 'me no man bewaileth, but in game' (l. 162).

The two-way movement that governs *The Ruines of Time* questions the integrity of both historical and poetic memory. Verlame's claim that poetry can 'rehearse' past heroes and make them 'live for ever' (ll. 253–5)

---

[40] Monmouth's history, as Lewis Thorpe puts it, is 'larded with toponymic conundrums'. The river Humber, for example, functions as the geographical *tabula rasa* on which is marked the record of that general's death. Events following Locrine's defeat of Humber also result in the naming of the Severn after the king's illegitimate daughter. Such myths are adopted in almost all subsequent chronicles. See Lewis (ed.), *History*, 23 and 75–7.

[41] McCabe, discussing *Prothalamion*, has marked the Thames as the river of 'tempus' or time (*Shorter Poems*, ed. McCabe, 729). On the significance of land and rivers to history see Ch. 2.

is also compromised—especially as Spenser so pointedly contrasts it with the eternity of heaven once she has disappeared. In Rasmussen's view her despair at the destruction of earthly pomp associates her with the 'wicked spirits' of the Old Testament, and even what he calls 'her delusion that heaven is poetic fame' leads Verlame into 'dark waters'.[42] There is something disturbing about the dead Verlame's pride in being the object of the blood sacrifice of a Saxon general, and her desire for 'faire temples' and 'sacred supulchers' is, likewise, questionable (ll. 92–4). The line between reverence for ancient monuments as remnants of the past and the worship of monuments, in the sense of idols, is a fine one: antiquities (and antiquaries) liberated by the Reformation provoked diverse responses—on the one hand of intellectual rapture, and on the other of hostility.[43] In Verlame's mouth 'antique moniments' (l. 179), of whatever kind, are not necessarily to be trusted.

In *The Ruines of Time* we find Spenser responding with subtlety not just to poetic sources, but to historical ones as well. In locating the action of the poem by the Thames he did not—as has previously been asserted—show a disregard and ignorance of innovative historical works such as that of Camden. Rather, he showed a detailed and critical awareness of it. The details—factual and otherwise—of Spenser's account of Verulamium are to be found in the pages of the *Britannia*, and so too is the form through which a physical location becomes the meeting place for myth and history. The poet was fascinated by the combination of all these elements: stories, fragments, and historical truths. In his repeated use of the word 'moniment', Spenser drew attention to the competing claims to which he was subject in rendering an account of his nation's past. Verlame—placed on the featureless banks of the Thames (the river of time)—offers a powerful emblematic vision of the condition of the 'Poet historical'.

---

[42] See Carl J. Rasmussen, '"How Weak Be the Passions of Woefulness": Spenser's *Ruines of Time*', *Spenser Studies*, 2 (1981), 159–81 (163 and 171).

[43] See MaryClaire Moroney, 'Spenser's Dissolution: Monasticism and Ruins in *The Faerie Queene* and *The View of the Present State of Ireland*', *Spenser Studies*, 12 (1998), 105–32. On the ambiguous attitude towards icons in Spenser see Kenneth Gross, *Spenserian Poetics: Idolatry, Iconoclasm, and Magic* (Ithaca: Cornell University Press, 1985). Joan Evans, *A History of the Society of Antiquaries* (Oxford: Society of Antiquaries, 1956), 5, and *DNB* observe how John Stow's interest in the contents of monastic libraries aroused the suspicion of some in government.

In Eumnestes's Chamber

The work of the *Complaints* volume problematizes the veneration of monuments in Eumnestes's chamber. As observed at the opening of this chapter, even popular compilations such as Cooper's *Epitome* acknowledged the absence of textual and architectural remains through which to substantiate early history. To those familiar with Britain's chronicles the scene in Alma's castle must have struck an equivocal note. Eumnestes is 'halfe blind, | And all decrepit in his feeble corse, | Yet liuely vigour rested in his mind' (II. ix. 55. 5–7); the records that surround him are 'incorrupted' yet 'all worm-eaten, and full of canker holes' (II. ix. 56. 7, 57. 9). As 'th'hindmost' of the three faculties of the sensitive soul Eumnestes is characterized by an uncomfortable mixture of Phantastes's restlessness and his neighbour's tranquillity: 'Tossing and turning' his records 'withouten end' he is 'set' in his chair 'vnhable them to fet' (II. ix. 58. 1–3).[44] In all, though a venerable sage, he is rather reminiscent of Sidney's satirical portrait of the historian.[45]

Setting aside the description of Eumnestes, there are other reasons to question the chronicle of Canto x. For from whatever perspective one regards them, its narrative and that of the text in Alma's castle fail to align. The *'Briton moniments'* kept by Eumnestes and *'chronicle of Briton kings'* announced thereafter are simply not the same thing. Not only is the history contained in Canto x explicitly directed to the sovereign rather than Prince Arthur (a fact made clear by a lengthy, and hitherto unprecedented, mid-book address to Elizabeth), its subject matter too is

---

[44] McCabe, *Pillars*, 51, argues that the middle figure represents an ideal and that 'in the world of art, the "poet historical" sits like Reason between Phantastes and Eumnestes "recoursing to the thinges forepaste, and diuining of things to come"'. The inhabitants of the chambers are usually taken to represent Imagination, Reason, and Memory. On Renaissance physiological psychology and for a specific reading of this episode see Michael C. Schoenfeldt, *Bodies and Selves in Renaissance England: Physiology and Inwardness in Spenser, Shakespeare, Herbert, and Milton*, Cambridge Studies in Renaissance Literature and Culture, 34 (Cambridge: Cambridge University Press, 1999), 40–73. For a succinct overview of this mechanistic conception of the brain see also Lawrence Babb, *The Elizabethan Malady: A Study of Melancholia in English Literature from 1580 to 1642* (East Lansing: Michigan State College Press, 1951), 1–3.

[45] In a benign way Eumnestes might even be said to echo the restless Mammon. With his rusted coat and numismatic tendencies (collecting coins either 'withouten moniment' or stamped with 'antique shapes') the god is himself a kind of demonic antiquary (II. vii. 5. 7–9). Certainly, as Judith H. Anderson recognized in 'The Antiquities of Fairyland and Ireland', *Journal of English and Germanic Philology*, 86 (1987), 199–214 (211), there is a slippage here from 'antickes' (meaning 'fantastic figures') to 'antique' (meaning 'agéd') (II. vii. 4. 6, 5. 9). On the limitations of Eumnestes see also David Lee Miller, *The Poem's Two Bodies: The Poetics of the 1590 Faerie Queene* (Princeton: Princeton University Press, 1988), 186–205.

significantly different. The '*Briton moniments*', the poet had clearly stated, 'of this lands first conquest did deuize, | And old diuision into Regiments, | Till it reduced was to one mans gouernments' (II. ix. 59. 7), but this is not at all the story we end up reading. Hamilton's gloss on the last line—'i.e. Arthur's'—is unsatisfactory.[46] Barring its initial occupation by giants, the chronicle with which we are presented has England ruled by 'one mans gouernments' right from the moment of conquest. It contains no information about an evolutionary progression from conquest through regional division on to national monarchy. Nor is it presented as the product of the kind of document-shuffling we witness in Eumnestes's chamber. What we find in Canto x is not the '*Briton moniments*' but instead '*A chronicle of Briton kings, | From Brute to Vthers rayne*' (II. x. Argument). While in the world of romance Eumnestes may find all the material he needs, this is not accessible for Spenser or his sovereign in England.[47]

That a development from individual 'Regiments' (II. ix. 59. 8) towards single rule had occurred was far from being beyond the comprehension of the English Renaissance historian. Most prominently it was Spenser's younger contemporary, Samuel Daniel, who was to insist upon the reality of a pre-Roman British history based on 'a multitude of petty regiments, without any entire rule, or combination'.[48] But the notion already had considerable currency at the time that Spenser was writing his poem. Whilst Daniel may have been the first chronicler to fully concede that 'God in his providence ... barres us out from long antiquity, and bounds our searches within the compasse of a few ages', reticence about the validity of historical testimony was widespread.[49] In numerous popular chronicles, including those of Stow, Grafton, Cooper, and Holinshed, the 'Briton Chronicle' constituted a necessary but also an uncomfortable and unwieldy presence set apart from the main body of the text, much in

---

[46]   Hamilton (ed.), 258 n. or 2nd edn. (2001), 246.

[47]   Andrew King's '*The Faerie Queene' and Middle English Romance* discusses this concept at length. King notes the way in which matter in Eumnestes's chamber encompasses the physical and textual 'in a very medieval view of the creation of work as an almost physical thrusting together or regurgitation of different volumes' (p. 1). On the authority of Eumnestes's records see also Judith H. Anderson, '"Mine actour": Spenser's Enabling Fiction and Eumnestes's "immortal scrine"', in George M. Logan and Gordon Teskey (eds.), *Unfolded Tales: Essays on Renaissance Romance* (Ithaca: Cornell University Press, 1989), 16–31.

[48]   *Collection of the History of England*, 2. Daniel's analysis of what he terms 'the progresses in the affairs of mankinde' (sig. B2ᵇ) is remarkably astute. For earlier formulations of this notion see Ch. 3 below.

[49]   Ibid. 1. Daniel's use of the word 'providence' here is a bold move, as its working was often found precisely in histories that did span that 'long antiquity'.

the way of Spenser's. In bringing Arthur (at once the most acclaimed and the most disputed 'monument' of national greatness) face to face with the 'moniments' of British history Spenser brought the different senses of that word into productive conflict.

As a reader of the past Arthur has notable affinities with Verlame. Both are (to use Spenser's term) historical fictions: creations based upon reality which is famously difficult to retrieve.[50] Both too, look upon 'moniments' of the past that are notoriously irrecoverable. Finally, both prove in themselves to be moral monuments, not least as testaments of the failure to record history itself. Transferred to Rome, Arthur's outburst at the conclusion of the chronicle ('Deare countrey, O how dearely deare' (II. x. 69. 3)) could come as easily from the mouth of Verlame.

The way Spenser has moved away from the substance of *'Briton moniments'* as they exist in Eumnestes's chamber is apparent from the opening of the chronicle. What we read is all too clearly not the magic-ally preserved record of one who knew Mathusalem in his infancy:

> The land, which warlike Britons now possesse,
>   And therein haue their mightie empire raysd,
>   In antique times was saluage wildernesse,
>   Vnpeopled, vnmanurd, vnprou'd, vnpraysd,
>   Ne was it Island then, ne was it paysd
>   Amid the *Ocean* waues, ne was it sought
>   Of marchants farre, for profits therein praysd,
>   But was all desolate, and of some thought
> By sea to haue bene from the *Celticke* mayn-land brought.   (II. x. 5)

This opening stanza describes the island entirely in terms of what it is not.[51] Especially when we add ensuing line ('Ne did it then deserue a name to haue') it is more than a little reminiscent of Verlame's opening

---

[50] The observation that Arthur was a worthy man 'overloaden' with fictions is a recurrent one in Elizabethan chronicles. Stow tells us that 'of this King there be many fabulous reportes, but certayne, he was a Prince (as *Malmesberie* saith) more worthy to have advancement by true Histories, than false Fables' (*Chronicles* (1580), 85 [mispaginated '81']). Holinshed, likewise, declares that 'woorthie was he doubtlesse, of whom feined fables should not have dreamed, but rather that true histories might have set foorth his woorthie praises' (*Chronicles* (1587), 'History', i. 92). See, also, Grafton, *Abridgement* (1563), fol. 21ᵃ. Foxe, speaking of the Britons, declares that 'the merciful providence of almighty God, raised up for them King *Arthure*, the sonne of *Uter*: who was then crowned after him and victoriously raigned' (*Actes* (1583), 113). At the same time, however, he considers the deeds attributed to him 'more worthy to be joyned with the *Iliades* of *Homere*, then to have place in any Ecclesiasticall hystorie' (ibid.).

[51] This observation is made in Miller, *Poem's Two Bodies*, 193.

act of self-erasure. Above all, the chronicle's progression from an absence of praise to an absence of name is of a piece with Verlame's message to the reader.

As with the early geography of the land, the origins of the 'saluage nation' of 'hideous Giants, and halfe beastly men' (II. x. 7. 1–2) who populate it is a matter of acknowledged uncertainty (II. x. 8. 1–2). In Holinshed's *Chronicles*, too, we are told that the history of what precedes Brutus is highly doubtful—the accepted narrative being based 'onelie upon the authoritie of *Berosus*, whom most diligent antiquaries doo reject as a fabulous and counterfet author' (i. 6). Like Holinshed, Spenser both reports and reproves the stories of how the island came to be inhabited. It is as much the inaccuracies of history as the creatures themselves that are 'monstrous'. The fact of their presence on the island is not questioned:

> But whence they sprong, or how they were begot,
>   Vneath is to assure; vncath to wene
>   That monstrous error, which doth some assot,
>   That *Dioclesians* fiftie daughters shene
>   Into this land by chaunce haue driuen bene,
>   Where companing with feends and filthy Sprights,
>   Through vaine illusion of their lust vnclene,
>   They brought forth Giants and such dreadful wights,
> As farre exceeded men in their immeasurd mights.   (II. x. 8)

After an expression of doubt, Spenser's verse runs smoothly onwards, and it is all too easy to be swept along. The 'monstrous error, which doth some assot' is, however, not the transgression of the women but that of the reader or writer of history. For the story of the daughters, although it appears as a matter of course in English chronicles, is the product of a notorious chain of speculative leaps and misunderstandings. As so often in Spenser's work, 'error', as much as anything else, is an act of misreading.

The arrival of Brutus in the next stanza marks the beginning of the chronicle proper. Yet, the contrast between the uncertain early history of the island and the accepted catalogue of British monarchs that follows is not as absolute as it initially appears. For, whilst the 'monstrous error' of the preceding narrative stands in contradistinction to the providentially inspired 'fatall error' of Brutus's journey (II. x. 8. 3, 9. 8) the echo of that earlier sense remains. Certainly it is soon apparent that the authority that underpins this report rests in 'moniments' that exist outside the text. Having moved from monuments in the plural in Eumnestes's chamber to an individual chronicle, we move out to non-textual monuments as they exist in Elizabeth's England. In support of Brutus's conquest of the island and defeat of the giants living therein, for example, Spenser tells us:

> That well can witnesse yet vnto this day
> The westerne Hogh, besprincled with the gore
> Of mightie *Goëmot*, whom in stout fray
> *Corineus* conquered, and cruelly did slay.   (II. x. 10. 6–9)

As in the *Ruines of Time*, the record of past events is sought not in the written word but in the supposed material evidence of conflict or through the immortality conferred by place names. In the case of Corineus's contribution to Brutus's victories:

> In meed of these great conquests by them got,
>   *Corineus* had that Prouince vtmost west,
> To him assigned for his worthy lot,
>   Which of his name and memorable gest
> He called *Cornewaile*, yet so called best.   (II. x. 12. 1–5)

Whereas the Thames apparently flees Verulamium, in the chronicle of Canto x witnesses rush to the fore. Even where there are no precedents in existing chronicles, Spenser blithely spawns myths of origin. A certain '*Debon*' is allotted his 'shayre' in '*Deuonshyre*' and an equally fictitious '*Canute*' receives land which 'he cald *Canutium*, for his hyre; | Now *Cantium*, which Kent we commenly inquire' (II. x. 12. 7–9). False etymologies, a well-known affectation of old chronicle writers, are here taken to what seems like demonstrative excess. As the distinguished keeper of British Antiquities in the British Museum observed, 'nobody had heard of Debon and Canutus before' making their presence 'signals' that 'the British History was in detail such nonsense that almost any liberties could be taken with it'.[52]

Not only do place names ('Albania', 'Camber', 'Humber', 'Seuerne', 'Cairleill') and the supposed physical remnants of conflict ('The western Hogh', an 'ample Pit', 'three monstrous stones') become the self-validating staging posts of history, the land itself is anthropomorphized to become the repository of knowledge.[53] Ebranck's 'noble deedes', are,

---

[52] Kendrick, *British*, 128–9.
[53] *The Faerie Queene*, II. x. 14. 3, 14. 4, 16. 7, 19. 8, 25. 3; 10. 7, 11. 1, 11. 5. If Randi Eldevik is right, the 'stoure' (II. x. 19. 5) too should be added to this list—the word, which would then

it is claimed, registered in Henault in Belgium, where 'Braue moniments remaine, which yet that land enuies' (II. x. 21. 9). Likewise, in the case of the second Brutus's victories, Spenser appeals directly to rivers, towns, and other witnesses:

> Let *Scaldis* tell, and let tell *Hania*,
>   And let the marsh of *Estham bruges* tell,
>   What colour were their waters that same day,
>   And all the moore twixt *Eluersham* and *Dell*,
>   With bloud of *Henalois*, which therein fell.   (II. x. 24. 1–5)

On the one hand these are the confident tones of patriotic encomium, but on the other they are akin to Verlame's desperate appeals. The watery flux of rivers and marshes offers no historical stability, and Elversham and Dell once more appear to be Spenserian additions.[54]

Again and again as he relates the history of the line of Brutus Spenser defers authority to elements that exist outside the world of the poem. As the poet chronicles the demise of the dynasty, however, he watches it crumble like a 'sharped spire':

> Here ended *Brutus* sacred progenie,
>   Which had seuen hundred yeares this scepter borne,
>   With high renowme, and great felicitie;
>   The noble braunch from th'antique stocke was torne
>   Through discord, and the royall throne forlorne:
>   Thenceforth this Realme was into factions rent,
>   Whilest each of *Brutus* boasted to be borne,
>   That in the end was left no moniment
> Of *Brutus*, nor of Britons glory auncient.   (II. x. 36)

The manœuvre is a familiar one. Even as he denies the survival of one kind of 'moniment' Spenser affirms the existence of another. For the regrettable fact that no record of Brutus remains is made to stand as a monument, in the sense of a warning or lesson, of the dangers of discord. Paradoxically the very glory of the dynasty's record excites the rivalry that brings about its destruction. From the work of Du Bellay Spenser must have gained a sensitivity to the way in which such contra-

denote both an 'emotional tumult' and the stream in which a notorious killing occurred, would constitute a particularly intriguing self-confirming monument. See '*The Faerie Queene* II.x.18–19', *Spenser Studies*, 12 (1998), 207–14.

[54] Harper, *Sources*, 68.

dictions inhere in this history. The collapse of the original Briton line, like the collapse of the palaces of Du Bellay's Rome, is a moment that poses significant questions about the preservation and status of distant history.

This awareness about the vulnerability of monuments comes not only from poetic precedents. Spenser's admission of uncertainty about the island's giants coincides with the end of Book I of Holinshed's *Chronicles* and comes to the same conclusions. Holinshed too mourns the disappearance of the 'history' he has just recalled. The pattern is repeated for Book II, where Spenser's stanza bewailing the destruction of evidence for 'Britons glory auncient' once more matches Holinshed in its lament for the 'loss' of its own story (*Chronicles*, i. 15). Indeed, the end of Holinshed's third book (looking back at an account of over a thousand years) comes very close to rejecting that entire testimony.[55]

Once more, there are parallels with Spenser who, like Holinshed, proceeds from the reign of King Lud to the Roman conquest. Lud's reign in the *Chronicles* remains a peculiar island of certainty. While the previous chapter wrestles with conflicting chronologies (i. 22) and the one that follows it begins to confront discrepancies between reports on the social make-up of the island, Lud's time remains one of 'princelie dooings' and 'the advancement of the common wealth by studies' (i. 23). In Spenser's chronicle Lud's reign is a similar high point. The stanza that immediately precedes Caesar's invasion contains the most positive and comprehensive use of the word 'moniment' in the entire chronicle. Lud, we are told:

> Left of his life most famous memory,
> And endlesse moniments of his great good:
> The ruin'd wals he did reædifye
> Of *Troynouant*, gainst force of enimy,
> And built that gate, which of his name is hight,
> By which he lyes entombed solemnly. (II. x. 46. 2–7)

As the restorer of ruined walls, as the builder of a structure that immortalizes his name, and as one who 'lyes entombed solemnly' beside

[55] At the end of Book III Caesar's report of a country governed not by 'one sole prince' but a number of regional chieftains is compared to that which 'the British histories report of this matter'. The compilers do not entirely abandon the earlier narrative: though they 'admit' Caesar's report to be true, 'yet may it be, that in the beginning, after Brute entered the land, there was ordeined by him a monarchie, as before is mentioned, which might continue in this posteritie manie yeares after' (i. 31). Yet, if this is so, there are no monuments to prove it.

his own creation, Lud is assuredly the source of 'endlesse moniments'.[56] Yet the secondary meaning of that phrase (suggesting 'purposelessness') proves prescient. For the king's solid achievements are soon to be transformed from physical remains into moral monuments of earthly transience. As with the collapse of Brutus's dynasty earlier, Spenser makes the paradoxical assertion that it was 'the Britons blazed fame' (II. x. 47. 8) that provoked its destruction. Likewise, the oft-repeated lesson that 'Nought else, but treason, from the first this land did foyle' (II. x. 48. 9) is brought to the fore.

The arrival of the Romans, which marks such a major transition in Holinshed, does not correspond with an equivalent rupture in Spenser's rendition. Whereas in the *Chronicles* Lud's reign is the last to be described in unquestioning terms, in Spenser it is just one in the ongoing succession. Yet the stanza that separates Lud from '*Kimbeline*' (or 'Cymbeline' as we are more likely to recognize him) is momentarily suggestive. At the point at which Holinshed inserts a chapter assessing the conflicting claims of the Briton and Roman histories, Spenser tells us:

> *Cæsar* got the victory,
> Through great bloudshed, and many a sad assay,
> In which him selfe was charged heauily
> Of hardy *Nennius*, whom he yet did slay,
> But lost his sword, yet to be seen this day.
> Thenceforth this land was tributarie made
> T'ambitious *Rome*, and did their rule obay,
> Till *Arthur* all that reckoning defrayd;
> Yet oft the Briton kings against them strongly swayd.   (II. x. 49. 1–9)

Whilst the chronicle reports the Roman victory with the best possible slant on British resistance, it does nevertheless hint at the existence of rival narratives. The above lines deliberately contrast historical fact (Caesar's conquest) and patriotically desirable myth (Arthur's supposed requital).[57] Indeed, the stanza is unique within the chronicle for its con-

---

[56] As Stow reports, there was indeed a 'Ludgate' amongst the gates of London. The image of Lud that adorned it was, however, placed there in the 28th year of Elizabeth's reign (i. 33). The gate (its name, in Stow's opinion, being a corruption of '*Fluds* gate' (i. 32)) was in all likelihood built in the year 1215—a belief he backs up not only by means of contemporary records but also through an astute archaeological account of the make-up of the stones themselves.

[57] This observation has been made by John Curran who also notes three other moments at which this contrast is made. See Curran 'Poets Historical', 79, and also 'Spenser and the Historical Revolution: Briton Moniments and the Problem of Roman Britain', *Clio: A Journal of Literature, History, and the Philosophy of History*, 25 (1996), 273–92.

tinuous see-saw movement: Caesar got the victory, *but* was 'charged heauily' by Nennius, *yet* the Roman general slew his opponent, *but* he lost his sword, *yet* the Romans triumphed, *but* the Briton kings 'against them strongly swayd'. Like the battle described immediately before it, the stanza is governed by the swinging pendulum of historical fortune.

It is noteworthy that the stanza should include the mention of a monument, in the shape of Caesar's lost sword 'yet to be seene this day'. Such objects appear at numerous points in the first instalment and are almost invariably misleading historical markers. In Book I, for example, we have been told of 'ruefull moniments' that misleadingly identify Redcrosse as an experienced warrior (I. vii. 19. 8): 'forlone reliques' to which Una (twice in the same stanza) appeals as a 'record' of that knight's deeds (I. vii. 48). In the same section we find reference to Arthur's 'shield, and sword, and armour', which disbelievers in the Prince's historicity are invited to inspect in 'Faerie lond, where yet it may be seene, if sought' (I. vii. 36. 6–9). Caesar's sword (which Monmouth cites as proof of valiant Briton resistance) is, like Arthur's, famous for having disappeared with the death of its last owner: it is no more to be seen 'this day' than that of the Briton Prince.[58]

Finally, 'this day' is itself a provocative phrase to introduce into the chronicle. For, right at this moment, we encounter the Briton Prince as a historical figure: the '*Arthur*' who 'all that reckoning defrayd' (II. x. 49. 8). This intrusion of the chronicle's supposed reader further problematizes the status of its narrative. 'Defray', in general Tudor usage, means to 'expend' or 'settle' in the financial sense, but also carries the additional sense of 'rub off or away'.[59] Most obviously, Arthur's supposed colonization of Europe settles the account in military terms by conquest. In a more contentious reading, however, the line may also bring us closer to Arthur as reader. For if 'defray' means 'erase', Arthur's response to Rome's challenge is as much a textual as a military intervention. Certainly, there is a considerable gap between the history we are told we will hear and the narrative that unfolds in the subsequent stanzas. If 'Thenceforth this land was tributarie made' (II. x. 49. 6) there is precious little evidence of this in the history. Despite Holinshed's injunction that

---

[58] Monmouth's *History* (p. 110) reports its burial alongside the knight who won it from the Emperor. King, *'Faerie Queene' and Middle English Romance*, 160–88, shows how Spenser transforms Geoffrey of Monmouth's strategy of referring to 'things still there' by transplanting them to Fairyland.

[59] *OED*, s.v. 'Defray *v.*1' versus 'Defray *v.*2 *Obs*'.

the roll-call of Briton Kings that follows the Roman invasion 'is more easie to be flatlie denied and utterlie reprooved, than either wiselie defended or trulie amended' (i. 36), the next stanza of Spenser's chronicle continues without any sense that a significant change has occurred in Britain's circumstances. Spenser never acknowledges the by then widely accepted fact of Roman supremacy and works hard at suppressing all mention of rival British or Saxon kings. If Arthur has 'defrayd' the record of Roman hegemony he has done a thorough job.

The final section of the chronicle, from Caesar's arrival to the reign of Pendragon, once more depicts a single line of British leaders, including a notable 'moniment of womens prayse' in Boadicea (II. x. 56. 1). It repeats the established pattern, however, by ending on the treacherous slaughter of Vortigern's men, 'Whose dolefull moniments who list to rew, | Th'eternall markes of treason may at *Stonheng* vew' (II. x. 66. 8–9). Stonehenge, looked upon as at once a surviving structure, a grave, and an imprint of 'Th'eternall markes of treason' should constitute the perfect monument. In reality it was also the cruellest irony of all: a monument that has physically survived but whose message to posterity remains a famous mystery.[60] Spenser is likely to have known of Camden's verdict on the stones. The antiquarian relates the story of the Briton slaughter by means of '*Alexander Necham*, a Poet of no great antiquitie . . . having his instructions out of *Geffreys* British historie'.[61] For himself he tells us 'about these points I am not curiously to argue and dispute, but rather to lament with much griefe that the Authors of so notable a monument are thus buried in oblivion' (p. 253). As a set of structural remains without a written history Stonehenge constitutes a tragic inversion of the fate of Verulamium.

Camden's phrase 'Authors of so notable a monument' again exposes the dual status of monuments as architectural remnants and texts—a duality with which Spenser too is concerned. After this final and most solid of monuments, we return with Arthur to a demonstrably textual incarnation of history (even the detail of its punctuation is made clear to us):

---

[60] Although the theory that Stonehenge marks the mass grave containing the victims of Saxon treachery is a popular one reproduced in numerous chronicles it was also frequently acknowledged as questionable. Harrison reports the story but notes its doubtfulness (Holinshed, *Chronicles* (1587), i. 129) and the usually credulous Drayton can offer no explanation as to who built it, making its description the occasion for an oration upon the failures of historical record (*Poly-Olbion*, 49–50).

[61] *Britain* (1610), 253; *Britannia* (1586), 119.

> After him *Vther*, which *Pendragon* hight,
> Succeding There abruptly it did end,
> Without full point, or other Cesure right,
> As if the rest some wicked hand did rend,
> Or th'Authour selfe could not at least attend
> To finish it.   (II. x. 68. 1–6)

Teasingly Spenser returns us to the '*Briton moniments*' as a physical text just at the moment when the reader comes upon a torn, or perhaps abandoned, final page. The '*chronicle*' and the '*moniments*' literally meet at a vanishing point. Spenser's own wording—'Succeding There'— matches the grammatical oddity described in the text Arthur is reading. Nowhere else in *The Faerie Queene* do we find a capitalized adverb not preceded by a full stop. Both Arthur's book and Spenser's verse chronicle end 'without full point or other Cesure right'. All that they share is that missing punctuation mark. As we exchange the massy Stonehenge for a collection of papers we find that the historical substance of both eludes us.

In the following stanza Arthur goes on to deliver a thumping endorsement of the reverence due to history. Yet even as he describes Arthur's rapture, the poet recognizes the elusiveness of the true Briton history. It is with a telling pun on 'British' that Spenser has Arthur intone:[62]

> How brutish is it not to vnderstand,
> How much to her we owe, that all vs gaue,
> That gaue vnto vs all, what euer good we haue.   (II. x. 69. 7–9)

That, regretfully, was indeed the British predicament. Like the translations of Du Bellay and the *Ruines of Time*, the Briton history of II. x presents a moment of moral vision that acknowledges its own historical unreliability. As we read a monument in one sense, we lose sight of it in another. The effort of reading the Briton chronicles requires precisely that act of simultaneous engagement and disengagement. At the point the histories move towards an expression of providence their constituent parts blur into fictions so that, just as at the conclusion of *The Ruines of Time*, we move from 'moniments of earthlie masse' (l. 419) to a literary 'moniment' of praise (l. 682). Ultimately, the episode in Eumnestes's chamber is very much concerned with that transition.

The '*Briton moniments*' and the poems of the *Complaints* volume are concerned with *absences* in the historical record. The resulting mixture of

---

[62] On this punning exposure see also Baker, *Between Nations*, 169–73.

playfulness, scepticism, and regret (to an extent that has been under-emphasized by critics of *The Faerie Queene*) is a vital component of Spenser's art. The diverse influences of Foxe, Sidney, Camden, Holinshed, and Du Bellay all helped to shape the poet's response to chronicle. Like his contemporaries, Spenser could not avoid the relentless narrative drive of the form. Nor did he fail to exploit its moral and encomiastic potential. He understood it as an inscriber of providence. Yet there was inevitable friction between chronicle and other forms of history. Elizabethans such as Holinshed catalogued the great deeds of the ancient Britons only to allow other historical voices to intrude. Thus, at such moments as Julius Caesar's landing in Britain forms of history collided, leaving ruptures in the fabric of the past. For chronicle writers these were deeply troubling. Yet, for Spenser, absence could also become an eloquent presence. Loss in one sense could forge new material in another. In his poetry 'monuments' as verses, documents, remains, or moral lessons took part in a system of exchange. By turns regretful, parodic, and visionary, Spenser's work contains all these elements at once.

CHAPTER 2

'The Stream and Current of Time':
Chorography and the Presence
of the Past

'Topo-chrono-graphicall' Narrative

The tribute paid to William Camden in *The Ruines of Time* came by way of form as well as content. For, by taking ruins and a river as the starting point for a story about the past, Spenser replicated the essential features of the narrative mode Camden adopted for his great project. In the preface to the *Britannia* its author had complained that to engage with the myths of the island of Britain was to 'strive with the streame and currant of *Time*'.[1] The river metaphor through which Camden expressed his impotence, however, also gestured towards the form that allowed his empowerment. For there was an aspect of the *Britannia* that made its encounter with the distant past significantly different: it was a chorography.

Scepticism about the substance of British history remained restricted to the margins of chronicle. Although evidence might indeed be missing, men such as Samuel Daniel or Edmund Spenser were still reluctant to quarrel in this form with the '*Beleefe* of Antiquity'.[2] The attitude was all but ubiquitous amongst sixteenth-century thinkers. Even Camden was eager to assure his public that he had 'impeached no mans credit, no not Geoffray of Monmouth whose history (which I would gladly support) is held suspected amongst the judicious'.[3] To attack the *Historia*, was 'to struggle against opinion commonly and long since received'. Yet the structure of the *Britannia* meant that the 'currant of *Time*' could be diverted. Whilst the word 'chorography' did not of itself necessitate a

---

[1] *Britain* (1610), 6; these exact words did not appear in 1586.
[2] Daniel, *The Collection*, sig. A3ᵇ.
[3] *Britain* (1610), sig. π5ᵇ; *Britannia* (1586), sig. A6ᵃ.

concern with the past, in practice the form proved well suited for the conjunction of physical and historical description.[4] Characterized by its use of land as the organizational template governing its narrative, proceeding region by region, landmark by landmark, it delivered its account of the past in response to individual concrete objects. One of its defining attributes was a tendency to work from the basis of the physical and historical *present* (the 'here' of specific architectural remains and the 'now' of the moment of narration). It is the present, in both senses of that word, that becomes a springboard to the past: a ruin encountered by the narrator, for example, allowed him to describe a castle that once was, or an event that once occurred. When the *Britannia* (or any other chorography) encounters a region, river, or ruin it moves from the present to the past.

By moving spatially across the nation as it described its history, chorography not only allowed the antiquarian to circumvent the established staging-posts of the Briton history, it also avoided some of the ideological pressures associated with it. Although boundaries were beginning to blur, no late sixteenth-century Englishman, not even Camden himself, considered the work of the antiquary to be history.[5] In part because the antiquary avoided the rhetorical, moral, and structural characteristics of more explicitly high-minded 'histories' and 'chronicles', he was able also to eschew the established conclusions that accompanied them. The new antiquarian movement was able not only to question the principal elements of the mythical history, but also to replace that history with an entirely different model for the development of civilization.

In the absence of a fully developed tradition of academic dispute, chorography facilitated an escape from the dictates of chronicle that did not require either outright conflict or the establishment of a complete alternative national history. At times it seems that antiquarians were themselves not entirely aware of the advantages that the newly popular

---

[4] *OED*, s.v. 'Chorography', nos. 1–3, refers to the description of a particular region or district without specifying the presence of a historical element. The sixteenth- and seventeenth-century texts that the *OED* mentions, however, almost all combine geographic and historical description. The work of Greek and Roman writers (including Strabo, Varro, and Seneca) to which the term was attached shares these same qualities, as does that of the great Italian antiquarian Flavio Biondo. For surveys of the form see also Helgerson, *Forms*, 131–9, Galbraith, *Architectonics*, 113–21, and Anthony Grafton, *Bring Out Your Dead: The Past as Revelation* (Cambridge, Mass.: Harvard University Press, 2001), 31–61.

[5] See Woolf, *The Idea*, 18–22, and also Introduction, n. 43.

form gave them. Harrison complained in the 'Description' attached to Holinshed's *Chronicles* that the task of compiling it had drawn him away from his unfinished 'Chronologie', 'whose crums as it were fell out verie well in the framing of this Pamphlet' (sig. A4ᵃ). Yet the contrast between the innovation of the 'Description' and the conventionality of the chronicle that followed it clearly illustrated the intellectual freedom afforded by the apparently 'lower' form.[6]

Of course, as the example of *Poly-Olbion* shows us, the genre was by no means tied to a 'progressive' position on the status of Monmouth's history. Humphrey Lhuyd was to use a chorographic structure (as well as a 'discourse' using some advanced linguistic scholarship) to mount a prose attack on Polydore and the other doubters; and Thomas Church-yard's *The Worthines of Wales* was but one of several verse chorographies that defended the old story.[7] Instead, chorography—which, as a form, flourished during precisely that period identified as one of intellectual transition—provided an outlet for a multiplicity of historiographic perspectives: from Drayton's nostalgia to Camden's new thinking. At the time the first instalment of *Poly-Olbion* was published and (more importantly) throughout the period Edmund Spenser was writing, new historiographical and political perspectives were nascent and of critical concern. Chorography was to prove itself perhaps uniquely capable of holding these developing perspectives, as it were, in suspension. Spenser —throughout his literary career—was to draw on all these qualities of the form.

---

[6] The 'Description' and the Chronicle's respective treatment of the first habitation of the earth provide a clear example. The opening chapter of the 'Description', concerning 'the division of the whole earth after the flood' (i. 1), sets out a significantly different picture of the island's beginning from that offered by the Chronicle proper. In it Harrison struggles valiantly with the problems resulting from the gaps in Genesis concerning the repopulation of the earth. Finding himself torn between recent discoveries (particularly in the New World) and the dictates of ancient authority, he tells his readers he is both determined 'not to remooue the credit of that which antiquitie hath delivered' and 'loth to continue and maintaine any corrup-tion that may be redressed' (i. 1). Ultimately, however, Harrison is bold enough to put aside the testimony of antiquity in order 'to give foorth a new division more probable, and better agree-ing with a truth' (i. 1). This is precisely the 'reforming' the Chronicle declines to do.

[7] *The Breviary of Britayne*, trans. Thomas Twyne (1573); *The Worthines of Wales* (1587; repr. London: Thomas Evans, 1776). Lhuyd's defence of the British History, whilst comprehensive, is generally cautious in its pronouncements. Instead of a passionate defence of Monmouth's integrity, it is an attempt to bolster the events reported in his history with corroborative linguistic and historical evidence.

The Faerie Queene *(1590):* 'Deheubarth *that now South-wales is hight'*

At first sight, the epic romance form of *The Faerie Queene* suggests that its adoption of the ancient Monmouth framework is inevitable, and Spenser's choice of Prince Arthur as the poem's principal hero would seem to confirm that view. The play of opposing voices is, however, one of the poem's most intriguing features and in dealing with the Briton history Spenser utilizes this quality with effect. As Jonathan Goldberg's sensitive reading of the work's first Proem has shown, from the moment of *The Faerie Queene*'s opening, the poet frustrates the reader's attempts to determine with any certainty the exact nature of either his muse or his much vaunted sources.[8] When, in the second stanza of the Proem, Spenser invokes the assistance of the 'holy Virgin chiefe of nine' we cannot be certain as to whether this is a reference to Clio or Calliope—a confusion heightened when her 'euerlasting scryne' and 'antique rolles' turn out to concern on the one hand the potentially historical 'Briton Prince', but on the other the decidedly unhistorical tale of his love for 'fairest *Tanaquill*' (I. Proem. 2. 1–6).

In Book II chronicles are initially encountered as physical objects by Spenser's questing knights. In this, the romance form of the poem effectively replicates some of the qualities of chorography; indeed, it may be said that a chorographic element is latent within all romances. The fact that his errant knights traverse the landscape of Fairyland in a manner that frees them from the dictates of a single linear plot line allows Spenser to parcel up the narrative of Britain's past with a very similar freedom to that used by Camden. From this perspective the embedded narratives of the poem resemble the fragments so important to antiquarian research. While much of this potential is already there in Spenser's most important Renaissance model, Ariosto's *Orlando Furioso*, it was the English poet who appears to have been the first to seize upon this capacity inherent in the Italian form. On numerous occasions, Spenser grasps opportunities to recontextualize the material from ancient history that he has transplanted into the world of his poem. From the worm-eaten parchments found in Eumnestes's chamber (II. ix. 57) to the Saxon weaponry and armour that King Ryence has kept 'for endlesse moniments' (III. iii. 59. 3), *The Faerie Queene* evinces a concern

---

[8] *Endlesse Worke: Spenser and the Structures of Discourse* (Baltimore: Johns Hopkins University Press, 1981), 12–24. See also Galbraith, *Architectonics*, 4–6, and Anderson, "Mine actour".

with the remnants of history that is evocative of the pages of Camden's *Britannia*.

Camden's text (as we have already begun to see) proceeds by attaching stories to objects and places. In his chapter on Dorset, for example, Camden reaches Shaftsbury, telling us that 'most famous is this place, by occasion of a pretty fable that our Historians doe report of *Aquila* prophesing here of the conversion or change of the Britans Empire'.[9] This Prophecy of the Eagle is the basis of claims that, as Camden mockingly puts it, 'this place is of greater antiquitie than Saturne himselfe' (p. 214). In reality, he tells us, 'most certaine it is, that it was first built by *Alfred*'—a claim he proceeds to substantiate by citing an inscription 'translated from the ruines of the wall into the *Chapter house of the Nuns*' (ibid.). The inscription, which the antiquarian renders in capitals and sets apart from the main body of his work, effectively anchors his claims in the physical ruins of the place he describes. The fact that (as with the reported antiquities of Verulamium) Camden's authority for this inscription itself rests on the word of a centuries-old historiographer seems almost incidental. For him it is the link between narrative and place that is crucial, and in the more lavish and extensive 1610 translation such fragments become still more prominent. It is by reconstructing their text and context that Camden gradually fleshes out his groundbreaking depiction of early Britain.

It would be excessive to claim that Spenser in any way 'fleshes out' an accurate depiction of Arthurian England. Yet the encounters with the fragments of history that he engineers do, for a moment, open vistas onto a very different past. At such moments Spenser's knights are still firmly rooted within Fairyland; at significant points, however, the poet also tells us of places that lie outside it, and it is at these times that his narrative can come to resemble chorography more closely.[10] Barring the 'Mutability Cantos', by far the longest section of the poem dealing with a land outside Fairyland is to be found in Book III, where we encounter an instance of analepsis—a return to a time before the moment of

---

[9] *Britain* (1610), 214; *Britannia* (1586), 93–4.

[10] For the most detailed examination of those places outside Fairyland, see Wayne Erickson, *Mapping 'The Faerie Queene': Quest Structures and the World of the Poem*, Garland Studies in the Renaissance, 3 (New York: Garland Publishing, 1996). A rewarding reading of 'the boundaries between poetry and history' in Fairyland is offered by Galbraith, *Architectonics*, 11–17. Early modern conceptions of the land are also discussed in Garrett A. Sullivan, Jr., *The Drama of Landscape: Land, Property, and Social Relations on the Early Modern Stage* (Stanford, Calif.: Stanford University Press, 1998).

narration.[11] Spenser, in the second canto of Book III brings the reader back to '*Deheubarth* that now South-wales is hight' (III. ii. 18. 4). It is there that he describes the beginnings of Britomart's quest for Artegall. Even compared to Fairyland, Britomart's childhood home has an air of antiquity about it. In the first place, Deheubarth is beset by serious inter-racial warfare; whereas in Fairyland Britomart (a Briton) and Redcrosse (a Saxon) appear, like the Elizabethans themselves, to be either unaware of, or unconcerned about, their own origins, these tensions are alive and well in the wars of the lady knight's homeland. Deheubarth is part of an island that has yet to develop into two single, more or less centralized, states: instead of the near-universal loyalty of the knights of Fairyland towards the Fairy Queen, Deheubarth forms part of a world of regional monarchs (of whom Britomart's father is one). In addition (whilst one would not wish to overestimate Elizabethan achievements in the area of manners) there are signs that at least some of the inhabitants of Deheubarth are just plain uncouth: Glauce, certainly, blithely performs strange cures involving face-spitting which, one feels, would meet with a frosty reception from the urbane knights who populate Spenser's main narrative.[12] If the past is a foreign country, that country is Deheubarth.

It is not only the past that comes into sharper focus in these sections of the poem: for the moment of analepsis is simultaneously one of prolepsis—as well as moving back in time to the distant Deheubarth 'As it in bookes hath written bene of old' (III. ii. 18. 3) the narrator moves his readers forward to the present: the 'now' of 'South-wales' under Elizabeth.[13] In contrast to the palimpsest past/present of Fairyland, Spenser's treatment of Deheubarth momentarily allows a different dynamic to emerge: one that shifts from a distinct Elizabethan present to a shady half-reconstructed Briton past. This simultaneous analepsis and prolepsis is characteristic of chorography. In the *Britannia*, too, we find 'South-wales' and the 'Deheubarth' of 'Posteritie' falling within the

---

[11] For a definition of the term see Paul Ricœur, *Time and Narrative*, trans. Kathleen McLaughlin and David Pellauer, 3 vols. (Chicago: University of Chicago Press, 1983–5), ii. 83.

[12] This last, originating in the psuedo-Virgilian *Ciris*, ought perhaps to be dismissed as a straightforward imitation. Carme's strange rituals (transferred onto Glauce), do, nevertheless, add a kind of period colour. It is difficult to say whether, in having Britomart spit on her face rather than her own bosom, Spenser has accentuated or lessened the indecorousness of the episode. See *Virgil*, trans. H. Rushton Fairclough, 2 vols. (London: William Heinemann, 1918), i. ll. 371–3.

[13] For a definition of the term 'prolepsis' see Ricœur, *Time and Narrative*, ii. 83.

same sentence.[14] Spenser's practice replicates Camden's, the only difference being that the direction of the comparison is reversed: instead of moving from a present site to an ancient story, we move from past to present, from Deheubarth *to* South Wales.

When, a canto later, Britomart and her nurse Glauce arrive at the mouth of Merlin's cave in order to seek advice from the prophet this shift from past to present is once more in evidence. Following directly on from the poet's address to Clio, these lines provide a subtly different introduction to the history that follows:

> Forthwith themselues disguising both in straunge
>> And base attyre, that none might them bewray,
>> To *Maridunum*, that is now by chaunge
>> Of name *Cayr-Merdin* cald, they tooke their way.   (III. iii. 7. 1–4)

The description continues in a manner entirely characteristic of chorography:

>> There the wise *Merlin* whylome wont (they say)
>> To make his wonne, low vnderneath the ground,
>> In a deepe delue, farre from the vew of day,
>> That of no liuing wight he mote be found,
> When so he counseld with his sprights encompast round.

> And if thou euer happen that same way
>> To trauell, goe to see that dreadfull place:
>> It is an hideous hollow caue (they say)
>> Vnder a rocke that lyes a little space
>> From the swift *Barry*, tombling downe apace,
>> Emongst the woodie hilles of *Dyneuowre*:
>> But dare thou not, I charge, in any cace,
>> To enter into that same balefull Bowre,
> For fear the cruell Feends should thee vnwares deuowre.
>>> (III. iii. 7. 5–8. 9)

Nowhere else in *The Faerie Queene* does Spenser address the world of sixteenth-century England in this way. The Merlin of whom we first hear is presented not as a character in the romance plot, but as a legend whose tale emerges in response to a geographical feature. Indeed, the mysterious Merlin of myth and rumour presented here is scarcely to be

---

[14] *Britain* (1610), 659; *Britannia* (1586), 380. Camden tells us that 'when Wales was subject to three Princes' the region was 'called in their tongue De-heu-barth, that is, The part lying on the right hand'.

reconciled with the chirpy figure who makes his appearance in Stanza 14. The seven stanzas that separate the two Merlins are concerned at once with the geographical Cayr-Merdin of the late sixteenth century and the legends of the magician Merlin which are still attached to that place. The poet's description repeats many of the features, including the 'ghastly noise of yron chaines' (III. iii. 9. 2), noted by chorographical texts of the period. Spenser's probable source, William Harrison's 'Description of Britaine' (which formed part of Holinshed's *Chronicles*) included the material under the heading 'Of the marvels of *England*' and insisted that 'such as have written of the woonders of our countrie in old time, have spoken (no doubt) of manie things, which deserve no credit at all' (i. 128). Harrison presents the matter as an antiquarian curiosity: having listed a number of peculiar English landmarks, ranging from Stonehenge to a wind-generating cave in the Peaks, he tells us:

> Besides these foure marvelles, there is a little rockie Ile in Aber Barrie (a riveret that falleth into the Saverne sea) called Barrie, which hath a rift or clift next the first shore; whereunto if a man doo laie his eare, he shall heare such noises as are commonlie made in smiths forges, to wit, clinking of iron barres, beating with hammers, blowing of bellowes, and such like: wereof the superstitious sort doo gather manie toies, as the gentiles did in old time of their lame god Vulcans pot.[15]

Harrison does not deign to tell us what those superstitions are, and Camden, who presents a similar description in italics as the report of Giraldus, fails even to mention that such stories exist.[16] Spenser, of course, cannot fail to relate the myth concerning the origin of the sounds, but his prominent use of a 'they say' formula (which appears four times over the stanzas) likewise stresses that what follows is the folklore attached to a particular region. What we hear of Merlin in this 'chorographic' introduction to his cave is, furthermore, well in excess of what we see of him in the main narrative. The Merlin of Cayr-Merdin of whom we are told, could, amongst other things, 'call out of the sky | Both Sunne and Moone, and make them him obay: | The land to sea, and sea to maineland dry' (III. iii. 12. 1–3). Spenser concludes his description with the most disputed of all claims made about Merlin: 'men say that he was not the sonne | Of mortall Syre, or other liuing wight, | But wondrously begotten, and begonne' (III. iii. 13. 1–3). This claim, which bordered on the heretical, was rejected even by the stri-

---

[15] Harrison, 'Description', *Chronicles* (1587), i. 129.
[16] *Britain* (1610), 643; *Britannia* (1586), 366–7.

dently pro-Monmouth Drayton (pp. 101–2). It was rejected too, in the notes that accompanied the later translation of Spenser's primary literary source for the episode: Ariosto's *Orlando Furioso*.[17] Spenser, in combining geography with folklore, is able to present a significantly different perspective on Merlin from that available to the writer of chronicle.

The way in which Spenser transformed the Merlin episode as found in Ariosto confirms the degree of consideration that underlies his antiquarian exactitude—an exactitude absent in *Orlando Furioso* whose description of Merlin's tomb John Harington found it necessary to shadow with a marginal note reminding us that it is 'poeticall licens' on the Italian's part to 'faine' Merlin's cave to be in France (p. 18). Spenser, who for most of his poem abandons the familiar European geography of Ariosto's work in favour of Fairyland, is clearly making a deliberate choice when he makes an exception for Merlin. As Barbara Reynolds observes, Spenser's decision to place his description of Merlin's cave in Book III Canto iii of *The Faerie Queene* is 'a pretty piece of coincidental effrontery' designed to demonstrate the extent to which the former 'overgoes' his predecessor, who had dealt with the cave in Canto iii of his poem.[18] One of the areas in which Spenser intends to overgo the Italian is, it seems, in antiquarian sophistication.

In point of fact Spenser's description is not quite accurate, but his minor error about the proximity of 'the woodie hilles of *Dyneuowre*' (III. iii. 8. 6) appears, paradoxically, to be a testament to his desire for precision (Osgood suggests that it is the result of a misreading of Harrison).[19] It is no wonder that John Selden should so approvingly have cited a very similar Spenserian stanza as further evidence for his own reading of the poet. Describing the precise geographical setting of this same '*Caer-Merdhin*', he tells us:

Hence questionles was that Fiction of the Muses best pupil, the noble *Spenser*, in supposing *Merlin* usually to visit his old *Timon*, whose dwelling he places

> *low in a valley greene*
> *Under the foot of* Rauran *mossie hore*
> *From whence the River* Dee *as silver cleene*
> *His tumbling billows rols with gentle rore.*   (*Poly-Olbion*, 210)

---

[17] Harington, *Orlando Furioso*, 22. In line with this reading, Harry Berger's *Revisionary Play*, 101, marks Merlin as a product of 'the popular imagination which may have once been a fresh and significant cultural force but can no longer be taken seriously'.

[18] See Ludovico Ariosto, *Orlando Furioso*, trans. Barbara Reynolds, 2 vols. (London: Penguin, 1973), i. 81.

[19] Osgood, 'English Rivers', 100. See Harrison, 'Description', 76.

The antiquarian notes the poet's geographical detail with enthusiasm: 'for this *Rauran-Vaur* hill is there by in *Merioneth*'. Like Harington with Ariosto, however, Selden nevertheless over-anxiously stresses that we may 'permit it, only as Poeticall, that he makes K. *Arthur* and this *Merlin* of one time'. Selden need not have been so concerned. By appropriating the language and matter of chorography, Spenser had done his work for him—making his Arthur and Merlin the product of very different times. The world of Deheubarth and Maridunum is made to stand con-spicuously apart from that of either Elizabethan England or the rest of the poem. Working directly from the chorographic texts of his time, Spenser imported the same double perspective that they afforded. Long before *Poly-Olbion*, he used chorography to twin the past and present, incorporating both Drayton's myth and Selden's scepticism.

The Faerie Queene *(1596): The Marriage of Thames and Medway*

The narrative delivered by Merlin in Book III, forming the second half of the national history embedded within the first instalment, takes the form of prophecy rather than chorography. These catalogues, with their concomitant concerns with empire, origins, providence, and teleology, constitute important focal points of the first three books of the poem. We do not find the same kind of material in the 1596 instalment. Along with the thematic concerns of the first half of the poem it is, to some extent, set aside when Spenser embarks on the second instalment of *The Faerie Queene*. The chorographic element identified in the 1590 text, how-ever, is not absent. Indeed, if the chronicle of Briton kings functions as an embodiment of a particular kind of history, the 'Marriage of the Thames and Medway' may be said to perform that same representative role for chorography. Like the semi-independent chronicle section of Book II, the 'Marriage' is especially noteworthy because it functions as a text within a text; both the chronicles and the 'Marriage', in fact, are strongly suspected of being distinct compositions only later incorpo-rated into the larger work.[20] Just as on previous occasions, Spenser

---

[20] For evidence that the sections on British history may have been composed before the poem had been started see Harper, *Sources*, 189. For a discussion of the evidence that the 'Marriage of the Thames and Medway' may in some way be an adaptation of Spenser's lost or projected poem *Epithalamion Thamesis*, see Oruch, 'English Rivers', 613–22; Josephine Waters Bennett, *The Evolution of 'The Faerie Queene'* (Chicago: University of Chicago Press, 1942), 155, 174–5, and 276; and also Osgood. The last of these argues for the likelihood that *Epithalamion Thamesis* was never completed, or perhaps begun, but that the material for it had been assem-bled.

explicitly alerts the reader to a change in authorial persona. Even the appeals to Clio, 'noursling of Dame *Memorie*' (IV. xi. 10. 2), and the 'moniments of passed times' (IV. xi. 17. 6) are repeated.

The 'Marriage of the Thames and Medway' (a pageant witnessed in Proteus Hall by Marinell before he slips away for a moment from his mother's obsessive care) is a classically chorographic poem. Its place in a tradition of English and European river poetry has been adumbrated over a number of scholarly books and articles. Osgood, in 1920, described Spenser's river verses (in *The Faerie Queene* and elsewhere) as 'specimens of a type not uncommon in their time', in particular pointing to parallels with Leland's *Cygnea Cantio*, Camden's *De Connubio Tamis* (fragments of which are distributed over the *Britannia*) and Vallans's *A Tale of Two Swannes*.[21] The last two, he pointed out, may themselves have been inspired by Spenser's lost or projected work *Epithalamion Thamesis*, but Leland's Latin work clearly provided the earliest English example. Oruch, in 1965, collected and corrected the observations of a number of his predecessors—detailing the *Epithalamion*'s relationship to Camden and sketching out something of their collective indebtedness to Italian river poetry. Braden, two years later, reminded readers of Spenser's own acknowledgement of the passage's roots in the tradition of epic catalogues.[22] Finally, Herendeen, in 1986, brought out a wide-ranging work about the river's place in literature from antiquity into the seventeenth century, of which a discussion of Spenser forms a part.[23] His broad-brush conclusion was that, to an extent that did not obtain elsewhere in Europe, the river in England was inseparable from history and myth (p. 183).

Repeatedly Spenser's pageant moves from rivers 'present' at the marriage to old and new histories: the Thames which once bore 'famous Troynouant' (IV. xi. 28. 8) on its back, the Tyne 'along whose stony bancke | That Romaine Monarch built a brasen wall' (IV. xi. 36. 1–2), and the Granta beside which Spenser himself was once a Cambridge student (IV. xi. 34. 5–9).[24] The rivers (with their associated regions and

---

[21] Osgood, 'English Rivers, 101.

[22] Gordon Braden, 'Riverrun: An Epic Catalogue in *The Faerie Queene*', *ELR* 5 (1975), 25–48.

[23] Wyman H. Herendeen, *From Landscape to Literature: The River and the Myth of Geography* (Pittsburgh: Duquesne University Press, 1986). See also Herendeen, 'The Rhetoric of Rivers: The River and the Pursuit of Knowledge', *SP* 78 (1981), 107–27. For a wide-ranging interpretation of the 'Marriage' see David Quint, *Origin and Originality in Renaissance Literature: Versions of the Source* (New Haven: Yale University Press, 1983), 133–66.

[24] Parallels with other chorographic writing are strong—as William Keith Hall says of the

peoples) who mingle at the marriage banquet that Marinell attends provide us with a very different perspective on national histories from that presented in the earlier chronicle sections of the poem. Spenser's inclusion of all the great rivers of the earth (a feature absent from his immediate models)[25] also dilutes the narrative of Briton greatness with the rival streams of other peoples. As we find that the likes of the 'Nile', 'Rhodanus', 'Scamander', and 'Tybris' carry their own famous races and legends (IV. xi. 20–1), it is easier for us to look upon the English stories too as the kind of boasts that might do the rounds at a wedding party.[26]

As with the chorographic entry points dealing with the mythology of Merlin in *The Faerie Queene*'s first instalment, chorography in the 'Marriage of Thames and Medway' works to attach myths to places (and therefore potentially questions them). Spenser, however, was willing to use the conjunction of 'story' and 'place' in other ways. In Herendeen's assessment his effort as chorographer was always to harmonize the two. 'Characteristically', he concludes, 'Spenser's landscapes subsume history in what we have called perceptual myths—imaginative constructs which organize the meaning of landscape' (p. 251).

There is a good evidence to back up this position, which echoes almost all the studies that precede it. In Roche's words, Spenser's treatment of the marriage is 'orderly in the extreme'.[27] As a focal point in the legend of friendship it is undeniable that the joining of the Thames and Medway is intended to contribute to the prevailing theme of concord, which is to find its ultimate expression in the union of Marinell and Florimell (whose anticipated marriage echoes that of the rivers). Poetical unifying, however, also exposes actual divisions. To state but one glaring fact: in geographical reality the Thames and Medway never really do

---

Britannia's treatment of the Thames: 'in a manner of speaking, the river *moves* into and out of history, winding through the ruins of antiquity into the narrator's present'. See 'From Chronicle to Chorography: Truth, Narrative, and the Antiquarian Enterprise in Renaissance England' (unpublished doctoral thesis, University of North Carolina, 1996), 210.

[25] For Leland's *Cygnea Cantio* and Vallans's *A Tale of Two Swannes* see Thomas Hearne (ed.), *The Itinerary of John Leland the Antiquary*, 3rd edn., 9 vols. (Oxford: James Fletcher & Joseph Pote, 1770), ix. 1–106, and v. pp. v–xx. Fragments of Camden's *De Connubio Tamae* are distributed (in their most complete form) over the 1610 translation of *Britannia*. See Oruch for an attempt to reconstruct the poem in its entirety.

[26] The notion that the various foundation myths of the Spaniards, French, Irish, and English are indeed but misguided boasts is forwarded by Irenius in Public Record Office manuscript of the *View*. See *View*, 86n.

[27] Thomas Roche, Jr., *The Kindly Flame: A Study of the Third and Fourth Books of Spenser's 'Faerie Queene'* (Princeton: Princeton University Press, 1964), 178. Helgerson is one of many who echo this emphasis on unity in the 'Marriage' (see *Forms*, 141–2).

marry.[28] Instead of the uncontroversial union of Thames and Isis (which formed the subject of Camden's poem) the poet chose to transfer the site of marital union to the ambiguous meeting place of two rivers and a sea—a place of uncertain boundaries and origins.

As well as concord or scepticism, Spenser could use the chorographic mode to inscribe localized grievance and broad territorial ambition. The tales that circulate among the guests in Proteus Hall are far from being entirely laudatory—indeed, Spenser's most prominent additions to his sources carry messages that are anything but comforting. In particular, the last of the non-British rivers—the 'Oranochy' and the Amazon— provide the occasion for an admonitory address:

> And shame on you, O men, which boast your strong
> And valiant hearts, in thoughts lesse hard and bold,
> Yet qualle in conquest of that land of gold.
> But this to you, O Britons, most pertaines,
> To whom the right hereof it selfe hath sold;
> The which for sparing litle cost or paines,
> Loose so immortall glory, and so endlesse gaines.   (IV. xi. 22. 3–9)

The conflation of up-to-the-minute geography ('but knowen late' (IV. xi. 21. 7)) and ancient mythology ('warlike Amazons' (IV. xi. 21. 9)) is, once again, entirely characteristic of chorography. Ralegh's *Discovery of Guiana* (entered in the Stationers Register only months after the second instalment of *The Faerie Queene*, and itself a travel history with a strong chorographic element) presented the Orinoco to the English public with a very similar mixture of the mythical and geographic.[29] Ralegh's narrative, which like Spenser's stanza is very much directed at promoting the colonization of Guiana, intercuts the description of the Orinoco and its

---

[28] This fact is noted by Braden, who goes on to make a number of convincing observations about the passage's exploration of the disorder of origin. Berger reaches a similar conclusion in his essay 'Two Spenserian Retrospects: The Antique Temple of Venus and the Primitive Marriage of Rivers', *Texas Studies in Literature and Language*, 10 (1969), 5–25 (repr. in *Revisionary Play: Studies in the Spenserian Dynamics* (Berkeley: University of California Press, 1988), 195–214).

[29] Sir Walter Ralegh, *The Discoverie of the Large, Rich and Bewtiful Empire of Guiana* (1596). For the registration dates of *The Faerie Queene* and *The Discovery*, see Edward Arber (ed.), *A Transcript of the Registers of the Company of Stationers of London: 1554–1640 AD*, 5 vols. (London: privately published, 1876), iii. 7 and 9. The two works were registered on 20 January and 15 March respectively. On the new 'worlds' of Spenser's fiction see Roland Greene, 'A Primer of Spenser's Worldmaking: Alterity in the Bower of Bliss', in Patrick Cheney and Lauren Silberman (eds.), *Worldmaking Spenser: Explorations in the Early Modern Age* (Lexington: University of Kentucky Press, 2000), 9–31. For speculation about the Spanish dimension of Spenser's epic see David Read, *Temperate Conquests: Spenser and the Spanish New World* (Detroit: Wayne State University Press, 2000).

tributaries with tales old and new—of the great Spanish explorers and their paths to riches, and of the rumoured 'Great and Golden City of Manoa (which the spaniards call El Dorado)' (sig. A1ᵃ). The conjunction of land, myth, and history inherent in chorography constitutes a subtle means through which Ralegh and Spenser promote political, and particularly colonial, agendas. Spenser's treatment of the Orinoco is but the first of several instances at which these connections are made.

For whilst the historical matter borne by the English rivers who attend the Marriage of Thames and Medway, like that of the world rivers preceding the Orinoco, is entirely conventional, there are a number of less comforting stories circulating amongst the wedding guests.[30] As on the previous occasion (with the newly discovered Amazon and Orinoco) there are latecomers to the pageant. With the English rivers already ushered off 'toward *Proteus* hall', the introduction of a party of guests from overseas comes as something of a surprise. The late arrivals are fairly distant relations (certainly neither Camden nor Vallans had seen fit to invite them to their river marriages). Admittedly, it is easier for Spenser to accommodate non-English rivers within his less geographically restricted pageant. But, from the manner in which he introduces them, it is evident that he is not quite comfortable with their presence:

> Ne thence the Irishe Riuers absent were,
>   Sith no lesse famous then the rest they bee,
>   And ioyne in neighbourhood of kingdome nere,
>   Why should they not likewise in loue agree,
>   And ioy likewise this solemne day to see?
>   They saw it all, and present were in place;
>   Though I them all according their degree,
>   Cannot recount, nor tell their hidden race,
> Nor read the saluage cuntreis, thorough which they pace.   (IV. xi. 40)

Spenser's question, 'Why should they not likewise in loue agree, | And ioy likewise this solemne day to see?', appears at first glance merely rhetorical—prompting a rejoinder cheerfully affirming the love and joy of the Irish rivers. The lines that follow, however, by merely insisting again on a presence of which we were already aware, leave room for a very different reading. The rivers suddenly shift from the past to the political present, so that the question is no longer rhetorical but genuine.

---

[30] Hadfield, *Irish Experience*, 142–5 and 158–9, and also Hadfield, 'Spenser, Drayton', 588, has drawn attention to these stories. A number of the points about the Irish rivers made below are already to be found in his analysis. See also McCabe, 'Poet of Exile', 95–6.

Asked why the Irish rivers should 'not likewise in loue agree, | And ioy likewise this solemne day to see' the more knowing Elizabethan reader would surely pause to question why these streams had, in reality, proved so reluctant to pay tribute to the Thames. As with the Orinoco, the wealth of the Irish rivers leads naturally into an exhortation in favour of a full English conquest—this time, however, that step is more politically dangerous. The history encoded within this landscape is neither easy nor entirely comforting to read: Spenser is at once forthcoming and strangely reticent about the stories that these rivers have to tell: all were present, yet he 'Cannot recount, nor tell their hidden race, | Nor read the saluage cuntreis, thorough which they pace' (IV. xi. 40. 8). The double meaning of the word 'race'—offering at the same time a geographic and ethnographic reading—already gives us something of the double vision of chorography.[31] Why is it that Spenser 'Cannot recount'? Is it merely that he has no time or does not know? Or is there a suggestion that he is not allowed to tell—that the tales they hold within them will be ill received amongst the coterie of rivers so flatteringly in attendance on the Thames? Does the Thames, for a moment, function as synecdoche for the court in London, or even the monarch? Certainly, the possibility of this reading is strengthened when we come to the last of the rivers mentioned in Spenser's report. As Hadfield has noted, despite the assurances to the contrary, the unwelcome message about the 'saluage cuntreis' and their 'hidden race' begins to leak out.[32] At first the stanza suggests that all is well with the rivers of Ireland:

> There also was the wide embayed Mayre,
>> The pleasaunt Bandon crownd with many a wood,
>> The spreading Lee, that like an Island fayre
>> Encloseth Corke with his deuided flood;
>> And balefull Oure, late staind with English blood:
>> With many more, whose names no tongue can tell.
>> All which that day in order seemly good
>> Did on the Thamis attend, and waited well
> To doe their duefull seruice, as to them befell.   (IV. xi. 44)

The river that runs through the middle of this stanza cuts a fissure that ultimately threatens the triumphal conclusion to the pageant. For the

---

[31] A 'race' can be a rush of water or an ethnic group (*Faerie Queene*, n. 516). This combination appears repeatedly in Camden's *Britannia*, which tends to work by associating pre-Roman tribes with specific rivers.

[32] Hadfield, *Irish Experience*, 159.

description of the bloodstained Oure not only shocks us with a sudden dramatic change of scene, with typical chorographic prolepsis it also punningly wrenches the reader away from the mythological past to face the harsh reality of our present 'hour'. The 'balefull Oure' is an allusion to Glenmalure: the valley into which Lord Grey had (at the beginning of his Irish campaign) sent half his men, only for them to be routed—an event at which Spenser may well have been present, and of which he would certainly have had intimate knowledge.[33] As with the earlier pun on 'race', the poet's wording here plays astutely on the form and content of chorography. For the way in which the 'balefull Oure' is both a location and a moment in time opens the stanza to a very different reading. The 'many more, whose names no tongue can tell' can now also be read to refer to the other bloodstained Irish rivers, or to the other English soldiers who have died.[34] Those 'which that day in order seemly good | Did on the Thamis attend' may be either men or rivers; either way, their service has come at a terrible cost. The shock of this secondary meaning is extraordinary. Ending as it does with another suggestive pun (in 'befell'), this stanza potentially transforms our reading of the Irish landscape: exposing not only a savage geography, but a savage history as well. In this double capacity for rendering both place and action we find a key feature of the chorographic mode.

Much more than a way of putting local myth and history in perspective, chorography provided Spenser with a tool for exploring his nation's geographical and historical integrity. Yet, writing and reading in an Irish context, the results of that exploration would have been increasingly disquieting. In *The Ruines of Time* the poet has responded with fascination to the *Britannia*: mimicking its chorographic structure to explore the ways in which history and myth mark the English landscape. So too in the 1590 *Faerie Queene* he had offered a physical setting for the mythology of Wales. But in 1596, to an English resident of Ireland, the *Britannia* would have been a less comfortable read, not least because a form that by nature expressed geographical and historical connection could also draw attention to a genuine divide.

This aspect of the *Britannia* was to become graphically evident in the

---

[33] See Alexander C. Judson, *The Life of Edmund Spenser* (Baltimore: Johns Hopkins University Press, 1945), 88. The incident is also related in the continuation of the History of Ireland by Hooker. See *Chronicles* (1587) ii. 169–70.

[34] For Grey's complaints about the lack of support for his mission see e.g. Judson, *Life*, 87 and 94.

frontispiece of the 1607 edition (which, of course, appeared after Spenser's death). The map at its centre displayed not only a physically marginalized Ireland (pushed beyond the edge of the frame) but also a historically denuded one (missing the kind of ethnographic specificity inscribed upon the landscape of Britain). Ireland's rivers did not have the names of ancient tribes engraved alongside them, and instead of reaching to the heart of the nation they stopped short just a little way in from the coast.

Already in 1586, the neat one-word title of the *Britannia* obscured not only a multiplicity of local histories, but also a geographical and historical divide between Great Britain and Ireland. Camden had decided to write his book on England, Wales, Scotland, and Ireland. Yet Ireland had never formed part of the Roman 'Britannia' that had given Camden's book its name and structure. Because of this, the section on Ireland was conspicuously thin, and had an entirely different aspect from that on England and Wales. Instead of an ordered Roman framework interlaced with native legends (which was the pattern elsewhere), the section on Ireland alternated between foreign myth and more recent political history. Local conflict like that at Spenser's 'balefull Oure' feature prominently in this portion of the text. Here, for Camden, there was no ancient civil infrastructure and no patchwork of local literary myth. The sea dividing Britain and Ireland was thus both historically and geographically dominant. As if anticipating the later frontispiece, the 1586 edition of the *Britannia* even physically divided the sections on Britain and Ireland by placing between them a separate essay devoted to the sea (p. 489). On the page, as in reality, a stretch of water divides two lands and histories.

The uncomfortable tales and doubtful unions of Spenser's 'Marriage of Thames and Medway' owe much to the form in which the episode is cast. Reading Camden's text the poet would have found a description of Ireland that explicitly acknowledged its strangeness to an English audience. Unlike the native British tribes, its ancient inhabitants had not been successfully mapped or civilized by Roman invaders. In the 1610 edition Camden was himself to voice what was implicit in the version that Spenser knew, declaring what a 'blessed and happy turne had it beene for Ireland, if it had at any time been under [Roman] subjection' (p. 66). In that edition, too, Camden was to commend the extraordinary cruelty of Spenser's employer Lord Grey in his treatment of Irish rebels (p. 75)—thus adding still further to the litany of recent violence that already marked this portion of his text. The way in which the Irish rivers are strangers at Spenser's marriage banquet—their unrecorded peoples, obscure legends, unknown landscapes, and unmentionable recent troubles—all find expression in the chorography that he used as a source. These features are shared by *Colin Clouts Come Home Againe*—a work in which chorography has a more marginal, but also a still more incisive, presence.

Colin Clouts Come Home Againe *(1595)*

Of all Spenser's works, the one whose treatment of Ireland bears the most obvious parallels to the 'Marriage of the Thames and Medway' is *Colin Clouts Come Home Againe*. Indeed, in the 'Marriage' (which, as a part of the second instalment of *The Faerie Queene*, appeared a year after *Colin Clout*) Spenser refers back explicitly to his earlier creation and its role in setting Irish rivers on the literary map (IV. xi. 41. 9). Like its successor, *Colin Clout* structures itself around an encounter between river and ocean; in it too we find a profusion of streams and stories. Following the reintroduction of the pastoral mode and characters familiar from the *Shepheardes Calender*, Colin's own narrative immediately establishes for itself a geographic position tied to his own river (in reality the Irish Awbeg).

> One day (quoth he) I sat, (as was my trade)
> Under the foote of *Mole* that mountaine hore,
> Keeping my sheepe amongst the cooly shade,
> Of the green alders by the *Mullaes* shore:
> There a straunge shepheard chaunst to find me out.
> *(Colin Clout*, ll. 56–60)

That shepherd turns out to be 'The shepheard of the Ocean by name' (l. 66), and it is across the ocean (or least the sea) that he is soon to draw the river-loving Colin. Once he has arrived at his destination, moreover, Colin is to pay tribute to Cynthia, who is characterized as the ruler of the sea.

Chorographic meeting points, as was already apparent in the conjunction of the Thames and Medway, have the capacity to become a locus for the expression of ambiguities beyond the geographical. One may go so far as to call the meeting of river and ocean a recurrent motif of Spenser's writing, for as well as the 'Marriage', the chorographic complexities of *Colin Clout* pre-empt those that appear in the oft-quoted final stanza of Book VI's Proem. Here, at the close of his address to the Queen, Spenser abandons the mirror metaphor he has for so long been using and opts for an altogether more ambiguous alternative:

> Then pardon me, most dreaded Soueraine,
>   That from your selfe I doe this vertue bring,
>   And to your selfe doe it returne againe:
>   So from the Ocean all riuers spring,
>   And tribute backe repay as to their King.
>   Right so from you all goodly vertues well
>   Into the rest, which round about you ring,
>   Faire Lords and Ladies, which about you dwell,
> And doe adorne your Court, where courtesies excell.   (VI. Proem. 7)

As Catherine Bates has shown, the stanza presents a picture of the 'cycle of reciprocity' that should exist between poet and sovereign.[35] What is pertinent to *Colin Clout*, however, is that Spenser has once more used an imperfect chorographic description to convey his own political unease—in his punning transition from geographical tributary to courtly 'tribute' the poet works to expose the gap between the ideal and the actual. Just as the Thames and Medway, in geographical reality, never really do marry, so too 'all riuers' do *not* 'from the Ocean' spring.

While these passages from Books IV and VI undoubtedly have much in common with *Colin Clouts Come Home Againe*, neither can match the earlier work in its sustained concentration on chorographic complexities. Colin's song is not merely sung beside a river, it also tells of rivers and is itself structured like one. It is no surprise that the first of several interjectors should himself be borne along by this pervasive metaphor:

> There interrupting him, a bonie swaine,
> That *Cuddy* hight, him thus atweene bespake:
> And should it not thy readie course restraine,
> I would request thee *Colin*, for my sake,
> To tell what thou didst sing, when he did plaie.
>   (*Colin Clout*, ll. 80–4)

The 'readie course' of Colin's tale, it soon becomes clear, *is* restrained by the diversion that Cuddy puts upon it. The tale of 'my river *Bregogs* love' (l. 92) which follows is almost as 'deceitfull' (l. 118) and 'secret' (l. 146) as

---

[35] Catherine Bates, *The Rhetoric of Courtship in Elizabethan Language and Literature* (Cambridge: Cambridge University Press, 1992), 14.

that river itself. Colin's claim that he will not sing 'of my love, nor of my losse' (l. 88) is only half true. For the love 'That made me in that desart chose to dwell' (l. 91) alludes not only to Rosalind, but also to the Queen who has left her greatest poet 'quite forgot' in the 'waste' that is Ireland (l. 183). Nor are that royal love and the love of the Bregog river as far removed as one might assume: because the story of the river's illicit underground journey 'into the *Mullaes* water' (l. 144), and the subsequent punishment inflicted by the mountain 'old *Mole*' (ll. 146–55), constitute a political allegory of Ralegh's fall from Elizabeth's favour.[36]

The entire first section of the poem, dealing with the meeting of the two 'shepheardes' and their journey to see the Queen has a strong chorographic element, the tone of which is already established at the beginning of Colin's story. Despite its up-to-date political content it is a tale that he describes, tongue firmly in cheek, as being 'No leasing new, nor Grandams fable stale, | But auncient truth confirm'd with credence old' (ll. 102–3):

> Old father *Mole*, (*Mole* hight that mountain gray
> That walls the Northside of *Armulla* dale)
> He had a daughter fresh as floure of May,
> Which gave that name unto that pleasant vale;
> *Mulla* the daughter of old *Mole*, so hight
> The Nimph, which of that water course has charge,
> That springing out of *Mole*, doth run downe right
> To *Buttevant*, where spreading forth at large,
> It giveth name unto that auncient Cittie,
> Which *Kilnemullah* cleped is of old:
> Whose ragged ruines breed great ruth and pittie,
> To travailers, which it from far behold.   (ll. 104–15)

The combination of myth and geographic detail, the rendition of etymological fables, the reference to the old name for an ancient city, the description of ruins, the mention of present-day travellers—all are features of chorography. The subsequent unrecorded song of the 'Shepheard of the Ocean' appears to continue this strain of myth and history, being 'all a lamentable lay, | Of great unkindnesse, and of usage hard, | Of *Cynthia* the Ladie of the sea' (ll. 164–6).

---

[36] It is not quite clear whether the poem initially referred to Ralegh's secret marriage with Elizabeth Thockmorton, or to an earlier more minor indiscretion. Certainly, when published in 1595, it would be hard to imagine anyone reading the episode as referring to anything other than the 1592 marriage. See Carmel Gaffney, '*Colin Clouts Come Home Againe*' (unpublished doctoral thesis, University of Edinburgh, 1982), 13.

After Colin and the Shepherd of the Ocean have exchanged tales, the latter persuades the former through 'hope of good, and hate of ill' (l. 192) to leave the 'waste' where he is 'quite forgot' (l. 183) and travel to see the now apparently bountiful Cynthia. The two cross 'A world of waters heaped up on hie, | Rolling like mountaines in wide wildernesse' (ll. 196–7) that is described by means of a consistent geographic analogy. As the pair approach the British Isles the distinctive perspective of the chorographic muse comes once again to the fore:

> We *Lunday* passe; by that same name is ment
> An Island, which the first to west was showne.
> From thence another world of land we kend,
> Floting amid the sea in jeopardie,
> And round about with mightie white rocks hemd,
> Against the seas encroching crueltie.   (ll. 270–5)

Spenser's move here from the eye-level perspective of the Shepherd Colin to the overview of the shape of Cornwall is strongly reminiscent of Camden, who at several points describes the difficult travels of his 'ship of Antiquity'.[37] Even the antiquarian's analysis of the etymology of the name of the peninsula is repeated:

> The first to which we nigh approched, was
> An high headland thrust far into the sea,
> Like to an horne, whereof the name it has,
> Yet seemed to be a goodly pleasant lea:
> There did a loftie mount at first us greet,
> Which did a stately heape of stones upreare,
> That seemd amid the surges for to fleet,
> Much greater then that frame, which us did beare:
> There did our ship her fruitfull wombe unlade,
> And put us all ashore on *Cynthias* land.   (ll. 280–9)

Colin's landing place, the south coast of Cornwall, like the 'Marriage of Thames and Medway' and the ocean-emptying rivers of the Proem to Book VI, is a geographical oddity. It requires a wind-blasted journey at least as terrible as the one the Shepherd describes. Whatever the likelihood of Colin's place of disembarkation, there is good reason to believe Spenser had motivation beyond the exigencies of maritime travel for his

---

[37] Camden, *Britain* (1610), Scotland, Ireland, and the British Ilands, 201 (sig. 4R5ᵃ); *Britannia* (1586), 525. The navigational metaphor is also deployed at the close of Camden's work: *Britain* (1610), 233 (sig. 4V3ᵃ); *Britannia* (1586), 556.

choice. In the first place the move from Ireland to Cornwall involves a transition from Spenser's to Ralegh's land (the knight's position as 'Lord Wardein of the Stanneries, and Lieutenant of the Countie of Cornwall' being prominently advertised in the poem's dedication). It is an exchange that, like the earlier exchange of songs, allows Spenser to compliment his friend and patron.[38] By landing in Cornwall, however, Colin also takes the first step of that great journey set out in Camden's *Britannia*—thereby sending out significant signals about the tradition in which he is writing.

As Camden tells us, Cornwall is 'the first of all Britaine': the inevitable starting point for a chorographic survey—constituting both the geographical and historical beginning of the nation.[39] It is in the treatment of Cornwall that the chorographic topoi of geography, myth, and antiquarian enquiry fall most easily together. As well as being the westernmost part of the island of Britain (the natural entry-point for a geographical reading of the nation), Cornwall is, first, the supposed landing place of the Trojans (a myth that, in the 1610 *Britannia*, Camden presents only in the form of a quotation from 'a late-borne Poet') and, second, the repository of the earliest remains of the land's ancient inhabitants.

In different ways, both the *Britannia* and the later *Poly-Olbion* treat Cornwall as the birthplace of the nation that they attempt to encapsulate. For Camden, Cornwall is a repository of ancient humans as well as artefacts, being 'inhabited by that remnant of Britans, which Marianus Scotus calleth *Occidentales Britones*, that is Britans of the west parts, who in the British tongue (for as yet they have not lost their ancient language) name it *Kernaw*'.[40] For Drayton the region is a fecund mythological source—a place of strength and fertility the roots of which lie both in geography and early history ('A Husband furthering fruite; a Midwife helping birth').[41] Cornwall is the birthplace of the nation, and beginning with it the *sine qua non* of national chorography. It is appropriate, then, that Colin's ship should unload its 'fruitfull wombe' in precisely this loca-

---

[38] For a brilliant reading of *Colin Clouts*' claims on patronage and assertion of material possession see Louis Adrian Montrose, 'Spenser's Domestic Domain: Poetry, Property, and the Early Modern Subject', in Margreta De Grazia, Maureen Quilligan, and Peter Stallybrass (eds.), *Subject and Object in Renaissance Culture*, Cambridge Studies in Renaissance Literature and Culture, 8 (Cambridge: Cambridge University Press, 1996), 83–130.

[39] *Britain* (1610), 183; *Britannia* (1586), 67.

[40] *Britain* (1610), 183; *Britannia* (1586), 67.

[41] *Poly-Olbion*, I. l. 262 (8). Drayton, in this passage as elsewhere, is building upon mythology and more general speculation to be found in the *Britannia*.

tion (l. 288). The landing of Spenser's shepherd replicates the moment of Britain's first settlement—the Shepherd, like the first Briton colonists, travels over the sea to a land of 'fruitfull corne, faire trees, fresh herbage' and 'all things else that living creatures need' including rivers 'No whit inferiour' to those of the home country, Ireland (ll. 298–300).

Here, however, the geography of homecoming becomes complicated—as Colin moves away from his supposed land of origin (Ireland) the poet moves *towards* his (England). Home is a place of both beginnings and returns, but the question of which home we are considering remains problematic throughout the poem.[42] The 'again' of the poem's title draws attention to this problem. Are there two homecomings, or even more? Colin, in his role as narrator, has come home to Ireland after his trip to visit Cynthia. But the poet who is shadowed in him (Edmund Spenser) would initially have returned home to England, only to find himself returning home 'again' to Ireland—a location that has earlier been described as a 'waste' and place of banishment. The tale of what is obviously the shepherd's first sea journey, full of naïve terror, is irresistibly evocative of how we might imagine the poet's first journey from his native land (to Ireland). As in the 'Marriage of Thames and Medway', Spenser exploits the uncertainties that surround the division between England and Ireland. The landscape of Ireland should be as familiar as that of England, but it is not; we ought not to be surprised at the presence of the Irish rivers at the wedding, but we are.

Colin's narrative deals with arrival in Cynthia's land (i.e. England) in a way reminiscent of Ralegh's arrival on the distant coast of Guiana, whose riches he is at great pains to describe. Like Guiana, Cynthia's land is dealt with as a foreign country. Yet if the tropes are familiar, the direction of movement is not. That conspicuous oddity is made still more so by the interventions of Colin's audience:

> What land is that thou meanst (then *Cuddy* sayd)
> And is there other, then whereon we stand?
>   Ah *Cuddy* (then quoth *Colin*) thous a fon,
> That hast not seen least part of natures worke:
> Much more there is unkend, then thou doest kon,
> And much more that does from mens knowledge lurke.
> For that same land much larger is then this,
> And other men and beasts and birds doth feed:

---

[42] On Spenser's position in Ireland, and in particular its depiction within *Colin Clouts Come Home Againe*, see McCabe, 'Poet of Exile' (esp. pp. 89–94) and Montrose 'Domestic Domain'.

> There fruitfull corne, faire trees, fresh herbage is
> And all things else that living creatures need.
> Besides most goodly rivers there appeare,
> No whit inferiour to thy *Funchins* praise,
> Or unto *Allo* or to *Mulla* cleare:
> Nought hast thou foolish boy seene in thy daies.   (ll. 290–303)

The return to the Irish rivers of the poem's opening—the Funchin, Allo, and Mulla—highlight the reversal still more strongly: instead of familiar English rivers being used as a measure against which to judge alien ones, it is unknown Irish rivers that are described as familiar where the English rivers are strange.[43] The reversal raises troubling questions strikingly similar to those that precede the description of the Irish rivers in Book IV of *The Faerie Queene*. Why is it that the Shepherd knows nothing of Cynthia and her dominion? Why is the Queen absent from Ireland? Cuddy, like a parody of the audience greeting the New World explorer (or of the English reader of Camden's *Britannia*), declares himself amazed that there should be a land other than that he stands on. Colin's response takes on the tone of one patronizing an unknowing yokel; his praise for Cynthia's land, however, gradually becomes a more and more open assault on the shortcomings of Ireland:

> Both heaven and heavenly graces do much more
> (Quoth he) abound in that same land, then this.
> For there all happie peace and plenteous store
> Conspire in one to make contented blisse:
> No wayling there nor wretchednesse is heard,
> No bloodie issues nor no leprosies,
> No griesly famine, nor no raging sweard,
> No nightly bodrags, nor no hue and cries;
> The shepheards there abroad may safely lie,
> On hills and downes, withouten dread or daunger.   (ll. 308–17)

As our reading progresses, the hints about what kind of Ireland this is become gradually stronger. The famine, raging sword, night-raids, and 'hue and cries' finally bring us unmistakably to the Ireland of Spenser's day. As with the 'Marriage of Thames and Medway', Irish rivers bring with them troubling political history. In a sense Spenser's presentational strategy here is the reverse of that which he was to employ for the

---

[43] Oruch, 'Spenser, Camden', 622–3, makes the point that Spenser's personal names for the Irish rivers complicate what, for a London audience, would already be obscure details.

'Marriage'. If in *The Faerie Queene* the Irish rivers are too little known for the poet to 'tell their hidden race', here they are all too familiar. The effect, however, is the same: in both cases an encomiastic account of English landscape is given a critical edge by means of implied contrast with Ireland. Undeniably there is a strong element of union. In the 'Marriage' and *Colin Clout* alike, rivers are conjoined at the court of a ruler of the seas (Proteus and Cynthia share the same sphere of government). As well as a medium for unification, however, the ocean is also something that divides. When at the end of *Colin Clouts Come Home Againe* its protagonist is once more in Ireland under 'glooming skies' (l. 954) that sense of division remains all too apparent.

Colin Clout is not consistently chorographic (indeed, one of the poem's great strengths is its immense generic diversity).[44] It does, however, illustrate the effectiveness with which Spenser allied land, myth, and history. Many times over the course of the poem he attaches stories to rivers, seas, and landscapes, allowing the narrative of chorography to expose or forge connections. That narrative worked all the more effectively in combination with others (such as that promising immortality through verse). Its mixture with other genres was a recurrent feature of Spenser's art looking at least as far back as *The Ruines of Time*. The material of that poem was, in various ways, revisited by the poet—not just in *Colin Clout* and the 'Marriage of Thames and Medway' but also after the publication of these two pieces. In *Prothalamion*, published towards the end of 1596, Spenser was to return to the Thames itself as a source for what was to be his most consistently chorographic poem.[45]

Prothalamion *(1596)*

Prothalamion draws together many of the qualities of Spenser's earlier river works. As an engagement song it has obvious affinities with the 'Marriage of Thames and Medway'—not least in its depiction of order and union. As a riverine discourse that pays tribute to a controversial public figure (and that follows the speaker's disillusioned departure from

---

[44] Gaffney, 'Colin Clouts', 12–26, argues that Colin's journey is to be seen as a conflation and parody of numerous literary forms, most prominently that of romance.

[45] *Prothalamion*, in *Shorter Poems*, ed. Oram. All subsequent references appear in the text and are to this edition. McCabe, whose more recent edition arranges the shorter poems into order of publication, places *Prothalamion* last and observes it must have been composed 'sometime between mid-August, when the Earl of Essex returned from the Cadiz expedition, and 8 November when the wedding took place at Essex House' (*Shorter Poems*, ed. McCabe, 727–8).

court), it presents notable parallels with *Colin Clout*. Furthermore, as in *The Ruines of Time*, the 'Themmes' around which it is structured is itself the river of '*tempus*' or time.[46] That river, in common with the Cam and Irish Awbeg, flows through a place which the poet can call home— London being the 'kindly Nurse' of Spenser's youth (l. 128). The fluvial character of this 'native sourse' (l. 129) is characteristic of the tradition in which he is writing, and as our reading progresses the conventionality of *Prothalamion* becomes more and more apparent.

Unlike Spenser's earlier work, *Prothalamion* makes explicit and consistent use of a chorographic focalizer.[47] Thus, as the swans on which the poet's attention is fixed follow the river to the edge of the metropolis, they encounter sites of both past and present significance. First the birds come to 'those bricky towres, | The which on *Themmes* brode aged backe do ryde':

> Where now the studious Lawyers have their bowers,
> There whylome wont the Templer Knights to byde.   (ll. 134–5)

The Temple—'now' the workplace of the bridegrooms celebrated in the poem, 'whylome' the site of a suspected martial-monastic order—offers the familiar double perspective of chorography.[48] The site that neighbours it is likewise described in terms of its past and present. Here, however, the past is closer, not only to the time at which the poet is writing, but also to the person of Spenser himself:

> Next whereunto there standes a stately place,
> Where oft I gayned giftes and goodly grace
> Of that great Lord, which therein wont to dwell,
> Whose want too well, now feeles my freendles case.   (ll. 137–40)

The 'stately place' of which Spenser speaks (the first major building to

---

[46] *Shorter Poems*, ed. McCabe, 729—as McCabe notes, the river's journey takes us from sunlight to starlight.

[47] A focalizer, through which the narrator 'sees' the objects about which we are told, is always implicit in chorographic narrative. In verse chorography it is generally more conspicuous—Vallans's *A Tale of Two Swannes* used precisely this device to describe the same journey. On the term 'focalizer' see Bal, *Narratology*, 100–14.

[48] As both the victims of corrupt Papal persecution and an embodiment of supposed monastic degeneracy, the Knights Templar offer a double lesson to the Protestant poet. Spenser, however, seems to consider them only as a further example of decay through pride. For a recent history of the order see e.g. Nicholas Best, *The Knights Templar* (London: Weidenfeld & Nicolson, 1997) or Helen Nicholson, *The Knights Templar: A New History* (Stroud: Sutton, 2001). Gregory Wilkin, 'Spenser's Rehabilitation of the Templars', *Spenser Studies*, 11 (1990), 89–100, claims great significance for the place of the Templars in Spenser's art.

greet the down-river traveller, as well as the most westerly point on which to begin a chorographic reading of the city) is Leicester House. It is a point of considerable resonance for the poet: its very name—conjoining a historic personage with an extant physical edifice—evokes the characteristic past–present of the form he employs. As the home of Spenser's former patron (Robert Dudley, Earl of Leicester) the house triggers plaintive retrospection. 'Yet', as with the Temple, the decay of the old has made way for new inhabitants:

> therein now doth lodge a noble Peer,
> Great *Englands* glory and the Worlds wide wonder,
> Whose dreadfull name, late through all *Spaine* did thunder.   (ll. 145–7)

Now inhabited by the Earl of Essex (the new object of Spenser's national and personal ambitions) the house also offers hope for a joyous future.[49] Following his recent triumph at Cadiz, the Earl had become *the* icon for proponents of a more proactive foreign policy. His home—first 'Leicester' and now 'Essex' House—provides an exemplary site for the operation of chorography.

The last three stanzas of *Prothalamion* illustrate more than ever the dynamic perspective on time that chorography affords: in them, the temporal focus of Spenser's poem changes at least a dozen times. The distant past of the Knights Templar; the recent past of Spenser's youth; the fictional past of the swans' journey; and the immediate past of Essex's victory—all are described in relation to the enduring present of London itself. At the conclusion of his penultimate stanza, however, Spenser sings no longer 'Against' the bridal day but 'Upon' it (l. 161)— thus extending the time-frame of his poem still further.[50] The present continuous with which the poet opens his final stanza—'From those high Towers, this noble Lord issuing' (l. 163)—thus leaves the reader quite unable to place the event described with anything beyond geographical precision. Essex, recently returned from his Atlantic adventure, descends from the great House to the river 'Like Radiant *Hesper* when his golden hayre | In th'*Ocean* billowes he hath Bathed fayre'

---

[49] Patrick Cheney, *Spenser's Famous Flight: A Renaissance Idea of a Literary Career* (Toronto: University of Toronto Press, 1993), 225–45, reads *Prothalamion* as a 'meta-allegory of the poet's ongoing career' (p. 244).

[50] Spenser has, once before, at the end of Stanza 6, used 'Upon' in place of 'Against'. In that stanza the nymph too looks forward to a successful future, and the visions of sexual and political consummation in the two stanzas are clearly intended to complement one another. In other cases, with the exception of 'Even' in Stanza 4, Spenser uses 'Against'.

(ll. 164–5). Is this the future of the Earl's anticipated glory, the present of Essex House as the swans approach it, or the past of a remembered engagement ceremony? There is simply no way of knowing. In lines that exploit the qualities of historical chorography, the poet allows multiple 'moments' to coexist in one place. By this point the Earl was already contemplating other journeys, and Spenser, whilst picturing himself beside the 'silver streaming *Themmes*' (l. 11), inevitably directed his inner gaze at them.[51] For him this most localized of forms seems always to have had a tendency to stray over national borders, not least across the Irish sea.

When, further into the final stanza, the poet does fix on a specific moment of time, it comes as a surprise to the reader. With the emergence of 'Two gentle Knights . . . forth pacing to the Rivers side' (ll. 169, 175) it becomes apparent that Spenser has shifted the frame of his narrative: it is not swans that they find there but 'those two faire Brides, their Loves delight' (l. 169).[52] In the final lines it is the betrothal ceremony of Elizabeth and Katherine Somerset on which Spenser centres. 'Birdes' become 'Brides' and mythology makes way for history.[53] Looking ahead at 'th'appointed tyde' (l. 177) of the marriage ceremony, Spenser once more punningly asserts the temporal elasticity of the chorographic mode.

Prothalamion was probably Spenser's last published poem. Looking back at earlier works it is possible to see just how longstanding the poet's engagement with chorography had been. As the work closest to the model established by Leland, *Prothalamion* also offers a reference point through which these earlier creations may be assessed. It shows how local legend can be brought into proximity with current affairs, and how poetical fiction interrelates with history. Grand chorographic collections such as the *Britannia* and *Poly-Olbion* demonstrate how inclusive the form can be. In both we find that one historical discourse pays host to another (Camden, as an antiquarian, collected a mass of poetic frag-

---

[51] At the concluding stages of the *View* Irenius speaks of the need for 'a Lorde Liuetennante of some of the greatest personages in Englande suche an one I Coulde name uppon whom the ey of all Englande is fixed and our laste hopes now rest' (p. 228).

[52] Spenser, as McCabe observes, has finally converted the signifier into the signified: through a seamless act of linguistic slippage birds become brides; see *Shorter Poems*, ed. McCabe, 733.

[53] In the first half of the 16th cent. 'Bryde' appears to have been a fairly common spelling for 'bird'—Tindale, for example, refers to 'the bryddes of the aier'. See *OED*, s.v. 'bird *sb.*' no. 2, and 'bryd(de)'.

ments; Drayton, as a poet of legend, included detailed historical commentary). Using chorographic works as sources as well as models, Spenser adopted a comparable openness. By introducing specific locations he also set free a host of histories. Having taken his place beside a river, the poet could cast himself as an observer of the past and present. Above all, it seems to have been the diversity of the historical landscape that drew him to this form.

CHAPTER 3

'Written Dialogue-Wise':
Antiquarianism and Ireland's
Conquest

Spenser's View *and Ware's* Historie

If chorography tended towards inclusiveness, the opposite is true for discourses at the Society of Antiquaries. Here Camden, Stow, and others worked on a smaller scale to determine answers to specific questions. While their opinions may not have changed absolutely from one form to another, the way in which they expressed them certainly did. In these unprepossessing oral submissions, put forward as part of an orderly debate, such men probably came closest to formulating their own private opinions. The unique structure through which they did so facilitated intellectual developments that only gradually found expression in published literature. Even if antiquarians ultimately presented their ideas by way of other modes (including chorography) it is clear that the practice of ordered dispute had played a vital role in their original formation. From the mid-1580s to the early years of King James's reign, the Society of Antiquaries provided the debating chamber in which new thinking about historical evidence and cultural change gradually took hold.

It is a curious fact that when Spenser's aggressive colonial tract *A View of the Present State of Ireland* came to be printed, its seventeenth-century editor presented the work as if it were the product of this English historical movement. For in 1633 a respected antiquarian and government official named Sir James Ware published the *View* as part of *The Historie of Ireland, Collected by Three Learned Authors.*[1] Printed in Dublin by means of the Society of Stationers, this volume was part of an attempt to emulate for Ireland the success of the antiquarian movement that had

---

[1] For Ware's biography see *DNB* and also T. W. Moody, *A New History of Ireland*, 10 vols. (Oxford: Clarendon Press, 1976–), iii (1987), 568.

flourished a generation earlier on the other side of the Irish Sea. In the 'Preface to the Subsequent Histories' Ware tells us that England 'hath had the happines that some parts of her Historie have bin lately excellently performed' (sig. ¶3ᵃ). William Camden and Sir Robert Cotton are mentioned specifically, and even some of that nation's chroniclers are said to provide a useful source for Irish history.[2] In Ware's footnotes John Selden and other current English luminaries add their voices, so that as a whole the volume conveys an impression of collective scholarly endeavour. It was in this company that *A View of the Present State of Ireland* first appeared in print.[3]

The other 'Learned Authors' whom Ware collected to produce *The Historie of Ireland* were also English imports. Although their contributions are but 'tastes' of what future research on Ireland will yield, it is evident that Ware intends us to approach them as contributors to the antiquarian tradition. His title-page presents the texts almost as if they were the product of a joint enterprise. The first two (Edmund Campion's *History of Ireland* and Meredith Hanmer's *Chronicle*) are unlikely to raise eyebrows, but Spenser's (at least to modern eyes) seems out of place in such academic company. Yet there are few signs that Ware regards Spenser's work as differing significantly from those that precede it. If the 1633 *Historie* showcases a culture of antiquarian

---

[2] Ware, sig. ¶3ᵃ⁻ᵇ. The English authors of earlier times mentioned as possible sources for work on Ireland are the 13th-cent. chroniclers John Wallingford and Thomas Wykes. Ware also mentions 'the right honorable *Francis* late Viscount of St. Alban' and 'the right Reverend *Francis* Lo: Bishop of Hereford'. The Bishop of Hereford in question was Francis Godwin, who was a friend of Camden and who accompanied him into Wales in search of antiquities. He is best known for his *Catalogue of the Bishops of England* (1601), and died in April 1633. The Viscount of St Albans, Francis Bacon, is presumably cited as the author of the *History of Henry the Seventh* (1621–2), although the remains of several other historiographic projects survive. Bacon had died in 1626, Camden in 1623, Cotton in 1631. For details see respective entries in *DNB*.

[3] In the last few years the bibliographical assumptions surrounding Spenser's *View* have been challenged. Jean Brink and Andrew Hadfield have noted the lack of evidence for the work's suppression, although Hadfield notes that such suppression is quite possible. For details see Jean R. Brink, 'Constructing the *View of the Present State of Ireland*', *Spenser Studies*, 11 (1994), 203–28, and Andrew Hadfield, 'Was Spenser's *A View of the Present State of Ireland* Censored? A Review of the Evidence', *N&Q*, 139 (1994), 459–63. Brink has suggested the work is unfinished and even questions its attribution to Spenser. While doubts over Spenser's authorship are worth raising they should not be overstated. Willy Maley's response to Brink's article strongly defends the original attribution (see *Salvaging Spenser: Colonialism, Culture, and Identity* (Basingstoke: Macmillan, 1997), 163–94). Brink's article does serve to remind us of the instability of the *View* as a text: no discussion of the work can ignore the presence of a number of variant copies or fail to mention their uncertain provenance. In the opening stages of this article references are to the title-pages and editorial machinery of Ware's 1633 edition of Spenser's text, thereafter they are to the text in *Works*, ed. E. Greenlaw, references to which appear in the text.

learning, Spenser is presented as one of its chief exponents. As Ware says in his preface, the poet's 'proofes (although most of them conjecturall) concerning the originall of the language, customes of the Nation, and the first peopling of the severall parts of the Iland, are full of good reading, and doe shew a sound judgment'.[4] In the annotations that appear in the margins of Spenser's prose, Ware's own comments are intermingled with those of other antiquaries, so that even where the commentary is critical it works to assimilate Spenser into a community of learned discourse.[5]

Following the text of the *View* itself, we find a further set of endnotes providing detailed commentary on such topics as 'the first originall of this word Tanist and Tanistry' or 'of the ancient Bards or Poets'.[6] Beyond these the collection concludes with 'Certaine verses of Mr. Edm. Spenser's' (sig. L1ª). Both major pieces are typical of the kind written and collected by English antiquarians. The first is the portion of the 'Marriage of the Thames and Medway' that catalogues the Irish rivers. The second, from the Mutability Cantos, deals with the myth and recent history of another Irish landmark: Arlo Hill. Describing the site of the debate between Jove and the Titaness Mutabilitie, it gives us a mythical tale of the hill's transformation to its current state. With the addition of a few occasional poems directed by Spenser to figures of authority in Ireland, Ware brings his volume to a close.

Ware's presentation of the *View* is generally regarded as an exercise in damage limitation. As its most recent editors put it, Sir James 'clearly felt uneasy about Spenser's text, including it in a selection of antiquarian works when, despite its wealth of detailed comment on Irish genealogy, its main thrust is towards an analysis of contemporary Irish society'.[7] Ware's choice of accompanying works, his annotations, his prefaces, even his reduced title for the *View*, have all been seen as attempts to disguise the political extremism of the text he edits. Thus, as Willy Maley puts it, by dropping the word 'present' he: 'elevated the past, but

---

[4]   *View*, in *Historie* (1633), sig. ¶4ª. Of the first two titles Ware admits that 'it cannot be denyed, that the judicious eye may discerne, especially in *Campion*, many slips, through want of necessary instructions' (sig. ¶2ª).

[5]   The *Historie*'s construction of conjoined narratives is reminiscent of what Steven Shapin calls 'the gentlemanly constitution of scientific truth'; see Shapin, *A Social History of Truth: Civility and Science in Seventeenth-Century England* (Chicago: University of Chicago Press, 1994), pp. xxi and 310–54.

[6]   *View*, in *Historie* (1633), 121.

[7]   *A View of the State of Ireland*, ed. Andrew Hadfield and Willy Maley (Oxford: Blackwell, 1997), p. xxiv.

as something of interest only to antiquarians. Indeed, he replaced the 'present' with the past, with antiquity'.[8]

The editors of the 1997 reprint are undoubtedly right to be sceptical about the fit of its antiquarian clothing. The way in which the *View* appeared in 1633 was, in fact, far from being inevitable. As both his statements and the appearance of the text testify, Ware's annotations were an afterthought. The first forty or so pages of Spenser's text had been printed without annotations, so that, as the editor explains, the notes for that section needed to be tacked on as an appendix.[9] The editor's last-minute change of heart about the desirability of annotations (presumably while the copy was already at the press) is symptomatic of a more deep-seated ambivalence already in evidence in the preface provided for that work. Upon closer inspection, Ware's preface to Spenser's text accords it a dual status. His 'proofes' about ancient societies are indeed the subject of praise. There is, however, a second (contradictory) way in which the *View* tells us about earlier times. For, especially 'when these our halcyon dayes are compared with the former turbulent and tempestuous times, and with the miseries (of severall kindes) incident unto them' (sig. ¶2ᵃ), it becomes apparent that in some senses the *View* is itself an antiquity—a relic from a more barbarous age. The aspersions that the *View* casts on specific families and on the Irish nation as a whole, as well as some of its more extreme proposals for reform, are characterized as the product of those times rather than of Spenser as a person. Had he lived to see 'the good effects which the last 30. yeares peace have produced in this land' Ware suggests he would have omitted them (sig. ¶3ᵇ). In the absence of such self-control from the author, the editor himself stepped in, pruning not just the *View*'s title, but its most extreme anti-Irish sentiments as well.[10]

Ware's title-pages, like the annotations, both expose and obscure the underlying tensions that exist between the three works collected. While the final version of the general title-page suggests an inspired collective enterprise, an earlier state (which included only Campion and Hanmer)

---

[8] Maley, *Salvaging*, 171. On Ware's presentation of the text, and the way in which it differed from the predominant manuscript versions, see also Sheila T. Cavanagh, '"Licentious Barbarism": Spenser's View of the Irish and *The Faerie Queene*', *Irish University Review*, 26 (1996), 268–80. Significantly, Maley suggests that 'in fact, Spenser's text may have been read in manuscript as an antiquarian text', but that 'once in print it was a stick of dynamite' (p. 173).

[9] For Ware's statements about the annotations see *View* (1633), sig. ¶4ᵃ and 121.

[10] For a summary of the alterations made between manuscript versions and the printed text, see Greenlaw *et al.* (eds.), *View*, 519–23.

shows the fragility of that construct. Not only did Spenser's text in fact have no place in the original *Historie* (so that the 'Preface to the Subsequent Histories' did not originally refer to it), the remaining pairing of Campion and Hanmer likewise proves unstable. Ware's earlier title-page had listed first the older Campion and then Hanmer. In the later version the order was reversed. This change was a result of the intervention of Hanmer's son-in-law, who (furious that the Doctor in divinity's name had appeared below that of a Catholic traitor against whom Meredith Hanmer twice directed publications) demanded a reversal of their respective billing. The authors who appear so amicably alongside one another in Ware's collection were in fact bitter enemies, and that enmity was still remembered by at least some members of the 1633 readership.[11]

The conjoining of Spenser and Campion in a single title-page was perhaps still more provocative, and here too what was probably an earlier state (with Spenser's text alone appearing) suggests that such a pairing might not immediately have seemed a natural one. Certainly Spenser's tract does not miss out on the opportunity to direct jibes at Campion's friend and fellow Catholic Richard Stanyhurst, whose despised (but still much-used) *Description of Ireland* had in large part been adapted from Campion's *Historie*.[12] Spenser uses his interlocutors Eudoxus and Irenius 'dialogue-wise' both to refute and to level contempt at Stanyhurst.[13] When Irenius responds to Eudoxus's scoffing criticism of the antiquarian by saying mockingly 'youe knowe not *Eudoxius* howe well mr *Stan*: Coulde see in the darke . . . but well I wote he seethe not well the verye lighte in matters of more weighte', it appears that the elevated 'discourses' of antiquarianism have descended to the level of petty sectarian squabbling (p. 104).

---

[11]   See F. R. Johnson, in *A Critical Bibliography of the Works of Edmund Spenser* (Baltimore: Johns Hopkins University Press, 1933), 51–3. As Johnson tells us, Hanmer's son-in-law, Matthew Manwaring, was no doubt particularly incensed because Meredith Hanmer had been the author of perhaps the most important of the Protestant attacks upon Campion's *Decem Rationes*, having published in 1581 a quarto pamphlet entitled, *The great bragge and challenge of M. Champion, a Jesuite . . . aunswered by Meredith Hanmer, M. of Art and student in Divinitie* (p. 52). Hanmer had also published *The Jesuites Banner . . . With a Confutation of a late Pamphlet . . . written in Answeare to M. Champion's offer of disputation* (1581).

[12]   For Stanyhurst's involvement with both Campion and the Holinshed project, see Colm Lennon, *Richard Stanihurst the Dubliner, 1547–1618: A Biography with Stanihurst's Text 'On Ireland's Past'* (Blackrock: Irish Academic Press, 1981), 38–40. As Lennon shows, at the time Spenser composed the *View* Stanyhurst was in exile, openly a Catholic, and working with the Spanish to promote rebellion in Ireland. For evidence of the *View*'s indebtedness to the 'Description', see Willy Maley, 'Spenser's *View* and Stanyhurst's *Description*', *N&Q*, 241 (NS 43) (1996), 140–2.

[13]   Hanmer too writes mockingly of his fellow antiquarian—telling us that '*Stanihurst* stammereth, writing one thing in English, another thing in Latine' (*Historie*, 67).

Despite all this, there is a coherence to the eventual form of the 1633 text that demands to be given deeper consideration. What could have induced Ware to present, and perhaps understand, Spenser's text as an antiquarian tract, or to believe that a passionate Protestant divine such as Meredith Hanmer and the Jesuit priest Edmund Campion could be united with it in a collective academic enterprise? Was Ware's edition *merely* an attempt to present Spenser's text as something it wasn't? Was the antiquarian project, in any case, quite as apolitical as such a role would imply? The acrimony underlying the pairing of Campion's and Hanmer's texts suggest it was not. As much as anything, the biographies of the writers of these works should indicate that any simple separation between antiquarian and political purpose is misleading. There are reasons to be sceptical about the degree to which the *View*, in its own right, ought to be approached as an antiquarian text. All the same, the understanding of Ware's editorial practice (and Spenser's antiquarianism itself) as deliberately obfuscatory also has limitations. In particular, the belief that Spenser's *View* is a 'sustained exercise in bad faith' needs to be questioned.[14] Such ire is understandable, but by dismissing the tract's dialogue form and antiquarian discussions as mere decoys it nevertheless risks unduly simplifying Spenser's text. For all the questions surrounding Ware's presentation, key facts remain. The *View* was the product of a period during which the English antiquarian project flourished. Its presentation of the Irish was both indebted to, and a contribution towards, the developing understanding of primitive cultures. Most strikingly, its use of the dialogue format was highly suggestive of the discourses conducted by the Society of Antiquaries on descents of inheritance, common law, and the nature and origin of early societies.

We need not reach as far forward as Ware's edition of 1633 to find an example in which these features of Spenser's text are expressed through editorial practice. An unfinished manuscript of the *View* to be found in the Bodleian Library, believed to have been produced in Spenser's lifetime, again draws attention to all of these elements.[15] Like Ware's, the

[14] The view is forwarded by Ciarán Brady, 'Spenser's Irish Crisis: Humanism and Experience in the 1590s', *Past and Present*, 111 (1986), 17–49 (41).

[15] Bodleain MS Gough Ireland 2. The title-page is reproduced in the Variorum *View*, 43 n. Ray Heffner, 'Spenser's *View of Ireland*: Some Observations', *Modern Language Quarterly*, 3 (1942), 507–15, presents arguments for assigning an early date to the manuscript. Its condition, he states, 'makes it absolutely certain that it was designed for publication' (p. 510). A very limited examination of annotations in manuscript versions of the *View* tends to confirm the assessment that their antiquarian element was of concern to readers. Cambridge University Library, MS

text comes with numerous marginal notes giving summaries and references. Its title-page—beginning with the words 'Irelands Survey or A Historical Dialogue and View of ancient and modern times wherein is discoursed the Ancient Originalls of the Irish Nation'—places almost all its emphasis on the description of the island's cultural history. Ray Heffner's judgement on the manuscript—in line with the later views of Hadfield and Maley—is that 'although the publisher expected Spenser's *View* to be read as a treatise on the antiquities of Ireland . . . the main purpose, to him at least, was a practicable solution of the English difficulties in that island' (p. 511). The labels attached to Spenser's text, however, suggest that historical and dialogic elements of the work were, in fact, far more fundamental to its make-up than has hitherto been recognized. The title-page's enumeration of features such as the 'Ancient Originalls of the Irish Nation', 'the Antiquity of their Letters, Characters, and Learning', 'their Tenures and Ancient and Modern Laws and Customes', and 'their Habitts Armes Soldiers and manner of Fights Lyveings and evill Usages' places this work very much within the genre of antiquarian discourse. The page's conclusion on 'the Authors opinion out of long employment and experience there how that Realme may be reduced to Obedience and Civillity' seems not so much the surreptitious revelation of a 'real' purpose as the logical conclusion of the analysis that has preceded it. The way in which Spenser's Irish tract first appeared in print reveals more than is commonly thought. Not just the context of antiquarian scholarship, but also the presence of Spenser's verse compositions on Ireland, make Ware's publication an illuminating starting point for an enquiry into the place of history in *A View of the Present State of Ireland.*

The Antiquarian View

The details of Spenser's connections with the antiquarian movement of the late sixteenth century remain hard to establish, but that they existed in some form is indisputable on the basis of internal evidence from the *View* itself. When Spenser accompanied Ralegh to court in 1590, the Elizabethan Society of Antiquaries would have been a flourishing insti-

---

Dd.14.28.1 contains three marginal annotations, each of which refers to matters of antiquarian interest (Brehon Law: fol. 3ᵃ; Tanistry: fol. 4ᵃ; The first King of Ireland: fol. 9ᵃ). Those in Gonville and Caius, Cambridge, MS 188.221 correct historical errors and fill in missing details (Edward II: fol. 17ᵃ; Edward le Bruce: fol. 22ᵃ).

tution. Sir Henry Spelman's list of the members of that society includes Ralegh; but although Van Norden's study found him to be one of the few plausible candidates for whom no contemporary record exists, his is nevertheless likely to be an ornamental addition to the roll-call.[16] In reality, the Society's members appear to have come from somewhat less exalted circles: most were gentlemen leasing or owning manors, almost all were university educated, some were poets, many were involved with the law or other state institutions, several were directly involved with the administration of Ireland, none came from the church, and few held the very highest government positions.[17] In general, their social profiles match very closely that of Spenser himself. It is more likely, then, that Spenser would have encountered antiquarian thinking through a university or Irish connection. William Camden himself is also a possibility. Camden was acquainted with Sir Philip Sidney and Spenser's collective praise of the two in *The Ruines of Time* may suggest the poet knew them together.[18] Certainly, that poem attests to Spenser's knowledge of and enthusiasm for the great antiquarian's work. It proves that by 1591 Spenser was familiar with the *Britannia* and aware of its central place in an intellectual revolution that was reclaiming a past seemingly 'Buried in ruines' for all time.[19]

Whether directly or not, the new thinking about the past we find in the *View* must be traced back to the Society of Antiquaries—the formal gathering of Elizabethan and early-Jacobean antiquarians centring on Camden, Spelman, and Cotton (to all of whom Ware's edition refers).[20] This body had been the spearhead of what has been called 'an heroic age

[16] See Linda Van Norden, 'The Elizabethan College of Antiquaries' (unpublished doctoral dissertation, University of California at Los Angeles, 1946), 229.

[17] Van Norden, 'College', 266–87.

[18] H. R. Woudhuysen's study of the Leicester House circle concludes that, whilst Camden was an opponent of the Earl, the antiquarian would have had contact with a number of those under his patronage, amongst whom he numbers Edmund Spenser (see 'Leicester's Literary Patronage', 75–8). Roland M. Smith, 'Spenser, Holinshed, and the *Laebhar Gabhála*', *Journal of English and Germanic Philology*, 43 (1944), 390–401 (390), stresses Spenser's indebtedness to Camden.

[19] *Ruines of Time*, l. 172. As noted in the Introduction to this book, the concept of 'intellectual revolution' needs to be severely qualified, but does hold within it an important element of truth.

[20] Van Norden, 'College', remains the key authority from which most subsequent works take the lead. On the more widespread culture of antiquarianism, however, see also Woolf, *The Idea*, and Woolf, *Reading History*; Stan A. E. Mendyk, *Speculum Britanniae: Regional Study, Antiquarianism, and Science in Britain to 1700* (Toronto: University of Toronto Press, 1989); Parry, *Trophies of Time*; Joan Evans, *A History of the Society of Antiquaries* (Oxford: Society of Antiquaries, 1956); Ferguson, *Clio Unbound*; Piggott, *Ancient Britons*; and Kendrick, *British Antiquity*.

of English scholarship'.[21] Inaugurated by the publication of Camden's *Britannia*, it met regularly between the years 1586 and 1607.[22] Its conventions, which appear to have been rigorously adhered to, demanded regular assemblies at the Herald's Office for the exchange of pre-prepared 'discourses' on antiquarian matters as part of what one of them described as 'a courte of Morespeach'.[23] All members, it seems, were required to contribute something to the discussion, with the strongest submissions, in the words of Spelman, being 'enter'd in a Book; that so it might remain unto Posterity'.[24] Fortunately this confidence was not misplaced. Over a century and a half after its last meeting a substantial number of the Society's manuscripts were still in existence, so that one of a new generation of record keepers, Thomas Hearne, was at last able to publish them as *A Collection of Curious Discourses Written by Eminent Antiquaries*.[25] One of the two extant summonses for meetings of the Society, calling for opinions 'Of the antiquitie, etimologie, and priviledges of parishes in England' and 'Of the antiquitie of armes in England', gives a representative snapshot of the issues that came under discussion.

Purely on an organizational level there are significant similarities between the *View* and the *Curious Discourses*. Although Spenser's text inherits a number of its structural qualities from a non-antiquarian tradition of English works on Ireland, the exchanges of the Society must be counted as an additional influence.[26] In particular, the *View*'s use of the dialogue is important. The assembly and exchange of views stood at the core of the Society's being; Van Norden's analysis shows that very few of its speeches are self-sufficient enough to be understood as anything but a series of answers to implied questions—in a great many of them we

---

[21]   Van Norden, 'College', 2.

[22]   For a discussion of the probable dates between which the Society was active see Van Norden, 'College', 74–109.

[23]   The member mentioned is Arthur Agard (Ayloffe, I, no. LVII, 184, sig. Z4ᵃ; quoted from Van Norden, 141) who was, in fact, somewhat critical of the lack of judicial rigour in the proceedings.

[24]   From Sir Henry Spelman's 'The Occasion', quoted in full by Van Norden, 'College', 74.

[25]   *A Collection of Curious Discourses Written by Eminent Antiquaries Upon Several Heads in Our English Antiquities*, ed. Thomas Hearne, 2 vols (London: W. and J. Richardson, 1771). Subsequent references to Hearne's edition appear in the footnotes credited to their contributor as '*Discourses*'.

[26]   For an outline of the English tradition of dialogues on Ireland, see Willy Maley, 'Dialogue-wise: Some Notes on the Irish Context of Spenser's *View*', *Connotations*, 6 (1996–7), 67–77. On the cultural context of dialogue in Ireland see also Nicholas Canny, *Making Ireland British, 1580–1650* (Oxford: Oxford University Press, 2001), 1–8.

find mention of 'the question put'.[27] In its exchanges about the past the *View* reflects not just the practices of the Society, but also something in the nature of all antiquarian discourse. The footnotes, prefaces, and conjoined narratives of Ware's 1633 volume share that quality, giving voice to an emergent intellectual practice which we also find in its component texts. Meredith Hanmer's *Chronicle* (a more progressive study than Campion's) assembles such writers as Harrison and Camden not as authorities but as the exponents of evidence-based arguments. His text, like Ware's collection in general, marks a step in the halting movement from what Woolf calls a 'focus on rhetorical *restatement* of the past' towards a 'more modern structure involving controversy, dispute and debate'.[28] The major causes to which he attributes that shift are pertinent to the *View*, one is the gradual absorbtion of antiquarian knowledge, the other is the 'catalyst' of ideology (p. xii).

Unlike, for example, the 'virtually interchangeable' interlocutors of Richard Beacon's *Solon his Folie* (one of a number of English dialogues on Ireland), Spenser's speakers in the *View* have significantly different opinions on matters of historiographical fact and methodology.[29] Although most antiquarian insight comes from Irenius, Eudoxus is not without his contributions—providing a number of English counter-examples, such as the observation that 'in Englande theare are in manye places as lardge Customes as that of *Coigny* and Liverye' and showing considerable interest (as well as faith) in the proceedings of the Westminster Parliament.[30] Eudoxus's interventions (which repeatedly insist upon a reliably signposted discussion, moving from 'evills' to the 'redressinge of them', and from 'Lawes' to 'Customes' to 'religion') have more than a little of the Society's self-consciousness.[31] In his frequent praise of his interlocutor too, Eudoxus follows the practice of the antiquaries. Spelman tells us that after each of the Society's meetings the most memorable contributions would be copied down for future reference, and that a new set of questions would be set 'to be handled at

[27] Van Norden, 'College', 315.

[28] Woolf, *The Idea*, p. xii.

[29] Richard Beacon, *Solon His Folie; or, A Politique Discourse Touching the Reformation of Common-weales Conquered, Declined or Corrupted*, ed. Vincent Carey, Medieval & Renaissance Texts & Studies, 154 (Binghamton, NY: Medieval & Renaissance Texts & Studies, 1996); the assessment is Carey's (p. xlii).

[30] *View*, 79 and 48.

[31] This outline for the discussion, the second half of which is of Irenius's design, is consistently present in Eudoxus's contributions. For its initial delineation, see *View*, 45.

the next that followed'.[32] In his last speech in the *View* Irenius likewise informs us he has 'thoughte good to set downe a remembraunce' of his 'simple opinion' (p. 230)—his companion responding with a reminder of his half-promise 'that heareafter when we shall mete againe uppon the like good occacion ye will declare unto us those your observacions which ye have gathered of the Antiquities of Ireland' (pp. 230–1). Eudoxus's adoption of the plural, and his stipulation about the subject to be addressed at their subsequent meeting, may well prompt questions as to what that 'like good occacion' is intended to be.

The conversational approach, the lack of ornament, and the unobtrusive but ever-present structure of the *View* are all characteristic of what we know of the proceedings of the Society of Antiquaries. Ultimately, however, it is the *View*'s understanding of indigenous cultures that presents the most telling parallel. It is, for example, notable that Irenius's explanation of the ancient tanist system and its ceremonies should be, as Gottfried tells us, 'fuller and more complete than that of any English contemporary' and 'corroborated by modern archaeology in almost every detail'.[33] T. D. Kendrick, still one of the major authorities on the subject, called Spenser 'a serious antiquary' and the *View* a work of 'noteworthy sagacity'.[34] Arthur Ferguson's more recent study goes so far as to describe Spenser's work as a major contribution to the understanding of early societies, noting that the anthropological evidence linking these with the native cultures encountered by sixteenth-century settlers came especially from 'the Irish experience of men like Edmund Spenser'.[35]

Spenser's interest in primitive cultures is most immediately evident in the *View*'s lengthy disquisition upon the Scythians, whose dress, immoderate wailing, and other characteristics Irenius traces in the 'mere Irish' (pp. 82–110). In Hanmer's *Chronicle* too we find such a discussion, again based on the delineation of cultural and linguistic parallels (pp. 20–3). Although the *View*'s conclusions on this and other matters are riddled with errors, there can be no doubt that its methodology was very much up to date.[36] In his linguistic exploration Spenser follows, among

---

[32] Cited by van Norden, 'College', 74.

[33] Rudolf B. Gottfried (ed.), *View*, in *Works*, 282–3 n. It should be noted that R. A. McCabe's forthcoming study *Spenser's Monstrous Regiment* (Oxford: Oxford University Press, 2002) is set greatly to complicate this picture of Ireland's culture. The degree to which Spenser relied on his own observations (rather than other written texts) remains open to question.

[34] *British Antiquity*, 126–7.

[35] *Clio Unbound*, 110.

[36] A number of these errors were corrected in Ware's 1633 edition. F. F. Covington, in

others, the highly regarded Jean Bodin, who in his chapter on the
'criteria by which to test the origins of peoples', had stated: 'I will explain
only this one thing our writers about origins have not made sufficiently
plain, that is, the linguistic traces in which the proof of origins chiefly
lies, as well as in the character of the lands occupied'.[37] This search for
'traces'—linguistic, cultural, textual, and physical—was the primary
activity of the Society of Antiquaries, and lies at the heart of Irenius's
reconstructive enterprise.[38]

If Irenius is the (ultimately dominant) voice of a particular body of
English colonists, he is at the same time the embodiment of a groundbreaking understanding of history: it is through him that Spenser
channels his knowledge of, and enthusiasm for, antiquarian research.
When Eudoxus expresses doubts about his companion's use of the
'moste fabulous and forged' (p. 84) dross of Irish chronicles, his accusation elicits from Irenius a defence of antiquarian practice that is worth
citing at length:

Trewlye I muste Confesse I doe soe, but yeat not so absolutelye as ye doe

'Spenser's Use of History in the *View of the Present State of Ireland*', *University of Texas Bulletin,
Studies in English*, 4 (1924), 5–38, is critical of Spenser's use of chronicle material. Roland M.
Smith in 'The Irish Background of Spenser's *View*', *Journal of English and Germanic Philology*, 42
(1943), 499–515, and 'Spenser, Holinshed, and the *Laebhar Gabhála*', concludes (via Covington)
in the second of these articles that 'it seems likely, in view of Spenser's 'characteristic uncritical
use of his material, of hasty reading, and . . . of defective memory', that he was not without the
help of a competent guide trained, no doubt, in the bardic traditions' (p. 400). Clare Carroll,
'Spenser and the Irish Language: The Sons of Milesio in *A View of the Present State of Ireland, The
Faerie Queene*, Book V and the *Laebhar Gabhála*', *Irish University Review*, 26 (1996), 281–90, makes
some additions to knowledge about Spenser's familiarity with Irish-language material, and
argues for his ambivalence about using it. Andrew Hadfield, in 'Briton and Scythian: Tudor
Representations of Irish Origins', *Irish Historical Studies*, 28 (1992–3), 390–408, notes the
selectiveness of Spenser's scepticism about certain elements in mythical history. David J. Baker,
'Spenser and the Uses of British History', *Worldmaking Spenser: Explorations in the Early Modern
Age*, Studies in the English Renaissance, ed. Patrick Cheney and Lauren Silberman (Lexington:
University of Kentucky Press, 2000), 193–203, argues for a conflict between Spenser's
researches into British history and his belief in enforcing an English identity. Thomas Scanlan,
Colonial Writing and the New World, 1583–1671: Allegories of Desire (Cambridge: Cambridge
University Press, 1999), 86, argues that a nebulous English identity stands in disconcerting con-
trast to a more fixed Irish one.

[37] *Method for the Easy Comprehension of History* (1565), trans. Beatrice Reynolds (New York:
Columbia University Press, 1945), 337. Bodin's programme in the *Method*, whilst it provides
considerable intellectual justification for antiquarianism, is not itself primarily antiquarian.
Other elements of Bodin's thinking, e.g. on the importance of numerology, also find their way
into Spenser's work. On Bodin's influence on Spenser, see Andrew Hadfield, 'Spenser, Ireland,
and Sixteenth-Century Political Theory', *The Modern Language Review*, 89 (1994), 1–18.

[38] The importance of etymology is immediately evident to a reader of the *Discourses*; see also
van Norden, 'College', 369.

suppose do I hearein relye uppon those Bardes or Irishe Cronicles, thoughe the
Irishe themselves thoroughe theire Ignorance in matters of Learninge and deper
judgement doe moste Constantlye beleve and Avouch theym, But unto them
besides I add myne owne readinge and out of them bothe togeather with comparison of times likenes of manners and Customes Affinytie of wordes and
names properties of natures and uses resemblaunces of rightes and Ceremonies
moniments of Churches and Tombes and manie other like circumstances I doe
gather a likelyhode of truethe, not certainlye affirminge anye thinge but by
Conferringe of times nacions languages monimentes and suche like I doe hunte
out a probabilitye of thinges which I doe leave unto your Judgement to beleeve
or refuse. (*View*, 84–5)

Irenius's repeated use of the term 'moniments' is especially instructive.
Eudoxus's claim that 'no monument remaynethe' (p. 84) of Ireland's
beginnings is gently refuted by his companion's adoption of the term in
the plural. For Eudoxus the word is still monumental—his search is for
the single, truth-telling narrative. Irenius, by contrast, uses it to denote a
plethora of ambiguous traces: fragments of manuscripts, the ruins of
buildings, and even the remains of arcane customs and languages. After
a number of illustrative sorties from Irenius, the newly pliant Eudoxus
becomes enraptured by this innovative and adventurous form of historical enquiry:

Surelye *Iren*: I have in these fewe wordes hearde that from youe which I woulde
have thoughte had bene ympossible to have bene spoken of times so remote
and Customes soe anciente with delighte, wheare of I was all that while as it
weare entraunced and Carried so far from my selfe as as [*sic*] that I ame now
righte sorie that yee ended so sone. (*View*, 109)

Eudoxus's outburst is a reflection of the passion that the antiquarian
movement aroused—we might, in passing, refer back to Verlame's
acclaim in *The Ruines of Time* for '*Cambden* the nourice of antiquitie, | And
lanterne unto late succeeding age' (ll. 169–70). What Eudoxus calls 'this
rippinge up of Ancestries' (p. 95) heralds an escape from the dictates
of established authorities—figures who are not abandoned but newly
interrogated and anatomized. Of course, as Stan Mendyk's study of the
movement cautions us, the antiquarian account of the past itself 'often
straddled the fine line between myth and reality' (p. 3), and certainly
Irenius's story is often to be found straying onto the wrong side of that
line. Eudoxus's ecstatic reaction is, nevertheless, testimony to the kind
of near-mystical revelation to which such accounts at times laid claim.

As Mendyk says, 'whenever such a story-teller wove together an accurate account by linking local historical study with topography, antiquarianism, and, later on, science, his tale was transformed—as if by magic— into a *speculum* or 'looking-glass' into the *theatrum* of British history' (pp. 3–4). Ware presented the *View* as just such a speculum. That he was able to do so reflects significant aspects of the text as it was originally constructed.

Of all the parallels that may be drawn between the speeches collected in Hearne's *Curious Discourses* and those of the *View*, perhaps the most illuminating concerns the discussion on ancient laws that open both works. The first discourse in the *Collection* is an oration by William Hakewill upon 'The Antiquity of the Laws of this Island' (p. 1). Although it can in no sense be considered a source, it bears a particularly striking resemblance to Irenius's analysis.[39] According to Hakewill, there are two ways in which the age of Britain's laws may be assessed. The first considers 'the ancient grounds, from whence they have been derived', including the degree to which they 'agree with the written law of God' (ibid.). In this respect the island's statutes are on a par with those of almost any nation. The second examines 'the long time, during which they have been used within the same state or kingdom' (ibid.), and in that sense the bulk of the nation's laws are relatively recent arrivals. It is in terms of this latter *antiquarian* perspective that 'the question is put'. From this point of view the laws of a kingdom are the product of two factors: partly they reflect the condition of a people, but principally they inscribe a history of conquest.[40] Hakewill dismisses the claims of others for the great antiquity of the present law as based on the 'motive' of promoting 'honor to our nation' (a formulation itself indicative of a sophisticated understanding of history-making).[41] Instead, he is 'rather of opinion,

---

[39] William Hakewill's oration, and the contribution that follows it, are undated, and Hearne's original manuscript source for his contribution has been lost. It is likely, however, that his work post-dates Spenser's (see *DNB*).

[40] Hakewill occasionally (and rather questionably) considers the manner in which laws reflect the condition of a people: the 'manner of sole inheritance', for example, 'is with great good reason still upheld rather in these North parts, than in the more Southern countries of the world; where by reason their women are not fruitful as here, the inheritance is not divided into so many small parts' (p. 7). In the main, however, the changes in law that he surveys are entirely the result of conquest. An exemplary instance of this antiquarian understanding of laws is to be found in William Lambarde's analysis of the overlaying of a series of legal codes in Kent; see *A Perambulation of Kent* (1576), 17.

[41] *Discourses*, i. 2. Hakewill's observation is comparable to Irenius's comment, appearing in only some of the *View* manuscripts, that the tale of Brutus's landing in Britain was but a false tale to glorify the nation (*View*, 86). The word 'motive' is indicative of the influence of Classical

that the laws of the Britaines were utterly extinct by the Romans; their laws again by the Saxons; and lastly, theirs by the Danes and Normans much altered' (i. 2–3). Depending on the extent of the conquest, each of the invasions of England, in Hakewill's assessment, brought with it a massive transformation in law (p. 4). Despite this, remnants of obsolete legal codes remain (even the ruins of an ancient Roman judgement hall may be identified), and it is through them that the antiquarian reconstructs the 'the Antiquity of the laws of England'.

This understanding of present-day laws as a record of past invasion is a fundamentally antiquarian one. Spenser shared that understanding and he allowed Irenius to articulate it. For Irenius, like Hakewill, is convinced that laws are the residue of conquest—a perspective that he again supplements with the notion that laws are to some degree matched to the condition of the people. The 'Comon Lawe', for example, is 'that which *William of Normandye* broughte in with his Conquest and laied upon the necke of Englande thoughe perhaps it fitted well with the state of Englande then beinge' (p. 46).[42] Eudoxus, in contrast, is at the start of the dialogue still naïvely confident that all laws are 'ordeyned for the good and safety of all' (p. 45). The mechanistic nature of Irenius's analysis strikes him as highly irreverent, and when Irenius questions the suitability of the English legal code for present-day Ireland, his interlocutor feels compelled to warn him that 'in findinge faulte with the Lawes I doubt me youe shall muche overshote your selfe and make me the more dislike your other dislikes of that government' (p. 46). This, especially for Eudoxus, is rough stuff.

Eudoxus's anger provides a window onto the political dangerousness

---

historiography. Hakewill's dismissal of Fortesque in the quotation above sets him apart from the English legal historians who continued to make claims for the 'immemorial' character of common law. As Pocock shows, the claims of antiquity made by Fortesque and his successors were maintained well beyond the 16th cent., not least by Englishmen wishing to enforce English common law in Ireland (*Ancient Constitution*, 32–3). Pocock's analysis of customary laws forms the basis for Baker's argument about the *View* (*Between Nations*, 66–123).

[42] This point, in particular, defines Irenius as an historiographical progressive. As Pocock's *Ancient Constitution* demonstrated, because of a lack of historical record it was possible for Englishmen 'to believe that, as far back as their history extended, the common law of the king's courts was the only system of law which had grown up and been of force within the realm' (p. 30). Significantly, '*Except for Ireland*, Celtic law was forgotten' (ibid., emphasis mine). Spenser's awareness of more ancient Irish laws helps to explain how he acquired an understanding of legal change analogous to that of progressive Continental and Scottish historians (described by Pocock, *Ancient Constitution*, 70–90) and not fully articulated in England until the 17th cent. (see ibid. 91–123). (For adjustments to and a defence of Pocock's original thesis see his 'Retrospect' to the 1987 edition, 255–387).

of the insights afforded by antiquarian enquiry. So fundamental was the reverence for the law in some quarters that Ciarán Brady believes Irenius's attack on it to be the real reason for the suppression of Spenser's text.[43] Whether or not the *View*'s publication was halted by the government, Brady is surely right when he says that 'even more disturbing' than the questioning of a revered institution was 'the implicit suggestion that the English law was not an organic entity that developed and expanded through the history of a community, but an artificial construct that could be imposed by power alone' (p. 43). This, as we have seen, was precisely the premise of antiquarian legal enquiry. As Hakewill says of the Romans 'who were the first, that conquered the ancient inhabitants of this island':

Considering, that it was their use alwayes to alter the laws of those nations which they subdued, as even this day may appear in France, Spain, Germany, and many other nations, and that in nothing more than this they placed the honor and safety of their conquests, it is very likely, that they also took the like course in this island, which they did in their other provinces; and indeed more reason had they so to do here, than perhaps any where else in the whole Empire, as being a province so farr remote, and a people even by nature disobedient. (i. 2–3)

For Hakewill, as for Irenius, there is no direct moral imperative governing legal change. Of course Hakewill is quite happy to acknowledge the divine sanction underlying England's laws, and Irenius too agrees with Eudoxus that laws are 'ordayned for the good of the Common weale' (p. 46). Within the framework they set themselves, however, Hakewill and Irenius alike are reluctant to stray into a discussion of these matters: such questions are best dealt with by a divine, or by what Renaissance

---

[43] Ciarán Brady, 'The Road to the *View*: On the Decline of Reform Thought in Tudor Ireland', *Spenser and Ireland: An Interdisciplinary Perspective*, ed. Patricia Coughlan (Cork: Cork University Press, 1989), 25–45 (41–2). David J. Baker, '"Some Quirk, Some Subtle Evasion": Legal Subversion in Spenser's *A View of the Present State of Ireland*', *Spenser Studies*, 6 (1986), 147–63, argues instead that it was Spenser's unwitting exposure of the Irish ability to abuse English Common Law that was unacceptable to the authorities. In an expanded version of this argument Baker contends that the *View*'s 'secret' is that English Common Law has 'its own ambiguous affinity with Gaelic law' in that both are rooted in custom rather than the transcendent authority of the monarch (*Between Nations*, 66–123 (91)). Whilst many English antiquaries did have faith in the ancient roots of Common Law, such a view—as Baker acknowledges— would run counter to Irenius's characterization of it as a system 'which *William of Normandye* broughte in with his Conquest and laied upon the necke of Englande' (*View*, 46). Baker's complex argument that in saying this 'Irenius proceeds to entangle his official readers in a contradictory but tactically evasive argument combining common law and royalist premises' (*Between Nations*, 110) is unnecessary if one recognizes the centrality of cultural change through conquest in Spenser's project.

England would have considered the separate discipline of 'history'.[44] In the role of antiquarian neither is prepared to treat the law as a monolithic or even organic entity. Recognizing, in Peter Burke's formulation of the modern historical mindset, 'that laws have to change because circumstances change, because (as we say) societies change', each is able to identify a set of distinct legal codes whose existence is the result of both societal factors and a history of migration and invasion.[45] Hence Irenius can construe the old Irish tanist system of landholding as the product of a longstanding necessity for 'the defence and maintenaunce of theire lande' against the English (p. 51), and the inadequately established Common Law as the legacy of an incomplete English conquest.

'Comparison of times likenes': English History and Ireland's 'Present State'

The _View_'s description of Ireland is indebted to a tradition of antiquarian thinking exemplified by the discourses of the Society of Antiquaries and carried over into printed texts such as Lambarde's _Perambulation_. Yet while retaining important connections with that tradition, Spenser's analysis also extends beyond it. For Irenius's investigations have a constructive role alongside their reconstructive one: the _present_ state of Ireland can certainly tell us much about its past; but for Irenius that _past_ also provides the key for the reform of its present. The likes of Hakewill, Camden, and Lambarde may or may not have concurred with this progression; it is certain, however, that they never explicitly make it in their work. If anything, their research translated itself into a conservative agenda whereby rights such as those of the Earl Marshall or Parliament were strengthened on the basis of ancient precedent.[46]

---

[44] On the moral, stylistic, structural, and other differences between histories and antiquarian works, see Woolf, _The Idea_, 21–2, and also 'Introduction', n. 47. Irenius's discussion of religion in the _View_ is itself demonstratively short and in large part limited to the physical state of Ireland's churches (a matter that clearly did fall within the antiquarian's competence).

[45] Peter Burke, _Renaissance Sense of the Past_, 34. In this awareness Irenius avoids what Pocock observes was a common intellectual blind spot amongst English common lawyers who, whilst supporting the notion that the English law was based on 'custom', held the paradoxical belief that it was also immemorial and unchanging (_Ancient Constitution_, 36–7).

[46] For an extensive account of this tendency, see Pocock, _Ancient Constitution_. As Pocock shows, the absence of evidence of other legal codes in England's historical record, combined with an emphasis on custom, facilitated a strong English tendency to 'read existing law into the remote past' (p. 31). In Ireland an older Celtic law survived (p. 30) making it possible for Spenser to see common law as a recent import. Furthermore, whereas Pocock's English lawyers were resisting an extension of power by the sovereign (_Ancient Constitution_, 42, 51, and _passim_) such an extension was precisely Spenser's objective.

For Irenius the relationship between the present and the reconstructed past is more dynamic, a point that his companion has once more failed to grasp. Laws, Irenius explains, 'oughte to be fashioned unto the manners and Condiction of the people to whom they are mente' (p. 54), and for him this has two implications. First, we can therefore be confident in concluding from those laws the state and origins of past societies. Second, by imposing a different set of laws we can change the people. The two systems of law—the old Irish, and the relatively newly imposed English—direct Irenius in opposite directions. The preservation of the first facilitates the reconstruction of the Irish past, the alteration of the second will enforce the transformation of Ireland into a newly civilized state.

Irenius's plan for the reformation of Ireland is based upon a radical realignment of historical epochs—a fact evinced by the backward-looking perspective of its projection into the future. The fulcrum of this argument is an analogy between today's Ireland and the England of many centuries before. If the current wild Irish are like the wild English of the past, Irenius reasons, then the ancient laws that reformed them will make the Irish of the future like the English of today.[47]

Although the comparison between the wild Irish and the barbarians whom the Romans encountered had been made before (for example in the far from antiquarian *Mirror for Magistrates*) this similarity had not previously been pursued at any length.[48] For Irenius the analogy is a central contention. As Stuart Piggott has observed, one of the greatest breakthroughs for the antiquarian movement was the development of a much more realistic image of the appearance and character of the ancient Britons. In his words: 'Camden seems to have been the first to make a direct comparison between native American body decoration and that recorded of the ancient Britons, and after Ralegh's Virginia expedition of 1585, and the subsequent publication of John White's drawings in De Bry's *America* of 1590, many people were able to make use of the parallel' (p. 74). Spenser's *View*, composed within a decade of this date, is certainly one of the texts that makes use of the newly strengthened parallel

---

[47] Although agreeing with Baker, *Between Nations*, 114, that Spenser prefers conquest over Common Law, this reading disputes his conclusion that Irenius proposes altogether to replace law with direct royal authority.

[48] In *Representing Ireland*, Brendan Bradshaw, Andrew Hadfield, and Willy Maley, as editors, also note that Sir Thomas Elyot had already made the observation that Caesar's histories of Gaul were worth reading because they provided an example of how to deal with such peoples as the Irish (p. 8).

between early societies and current primitive ones. Indeed, it may not even have been required of him to make the leap from American to Irish primitives. Piggott credits the Dutch artist Lucas de Heere, in drawings executed between 1573 and 1575, as perhaps the first to present the new view of the ancient Britons. As he says:

These de Heere Britons have usually been thought to reflect the influence of American Indian depictions (as with White), but in fact there seems no reason to look for any such connection. Body paint, long shields, swords and spears are all to be found in the classical texts relating to the Celts, while the rather melancholy shaggy heads come very close to de Heere's drawings of the 'Wilde Irish'.   (p. 75)

If we combine this with Ferguson's observation that the anthropological evidence linking ancient Britons with the native cultures encountered by sixteenth-century settlers came partly from 'the Irish experience of men like Edmund Spenser', it begins to become clear how fundamental the poet's antiquarian understanding was to his formulation of Ireland's problems and the supposed solutions to them (p. 110). In this respect the *View* differs significantly from the earlier Elizabethan proposals for Ireland's reformation with which it has so much else in common. For none of these make anything like the same in-depth use of antiquarian enquiry.[49]

In part, Spenser takes his material from a long-established tradition. English works as far back as Gerald of Wales's *History and Topography of Ireland* had characterized the Irish as a barbarous people—indeed Gerald's comments on the wearing of mantles, pride in horsemanship, and dependence on pastoral living made their way through Campion and Stanyhurst into Spenser's text.[50] Stanyhurst's 'Description' is full of such details on the 'mere' Irish as their wild outcries and respect for bards.[51]

[49] On the degree to which the *View* conforms to longstanding norms governing English depictions of the wild Irish, beginning, in large part, with the work of Gerald of Wales, see Walter J. Ong, 'Spenser's *View* and the Tradition of the "Wild" Irish"', *Modern Language Quarterly*, 3 (1942), 561–71. There are several other ways in which Spenser's *View* follows in a tradition of Elizabethan writing on Ireland, amongst which the adoption of the dialogue form is not the least important (see e.g. Hadfield, 'Who is Speaking', 137). A useful overview of the range of Elizabethan writing on Ireland is provided by Hadfield, *Irish Experience*, 20–50.

[50] Giraldus Cambrensis, *The History and Topography of Ireland*, trans. and ed. John J. O'Meara, Dolmen Texts, 4 (Dundalk: Dundalgan Press, 1951; repr. Atlantic Highlands, NJ: Humanities Press, 1982), 100–3, or in Holinshed, *Chronicles* (1587), ii. For a discussion of this and other sources for Spenser's description, as well as another model for dialogue, see Patricia Coughlan, '"Some secret scourge which shall by her come unto England": Ireland and Incivility in Spenser', in *Spenser and Ireland*, 46–75 (45 and *passim*).

[51] Stanyhurst, 'Description', in Raphael Holinshed, *Chronicles* (1587), ii. 44–5.

Like Spenser he enumerates the English victories that establish a right of control, notes the limited enforcement of Henry II's conquest, and argues that 'a conquest draweth, or at the leastwise ought to draw to it three things, to wit, law, apparell, and language' (ii. 11). In general, however, the earlier tradition is much less concerned with the way a history of conquest has left its mark upon the Irish people. In Stanyhurst as in Gerald of Wales, for example, the story of a Scythian invasion is restricted to a quite different part of the text, treated as the act of an individual, and in no coherent sense tied to the development of an Irish character.[52] In this respect Spenser differs from his sources, a fact that turns out to be politically useful. From the antiquarian perspective voiced by Irenius, invasions leave delible marks of variable strength. It is thus that he is able to argue that the impression left by the English invasion under Henry II (already widely acknowledged as partial) has begun to degrade, and that some of the Old English (amongst whom Stanyhurst himself was numbered) have become 'allmoste meare Irishe' (p. 96).

Irenius is consistently determined to draw conclusions (or at least *seem* to draw them) on the basis of real evidence. In the first part of the *View* Irenius considers several systems of law and government, in particular the *currently* coexistent Irish Brehon and English Common law. In the second half of the tract, however, his system of control is most fundamentally grounded in a *return* to Roman and Saxon methods of governance which, he maintains, have a historical track record of success in transforming wild peoples into civilized ones. Paradoxically, this track record is that of England's transformation into a civilized state: the once-barbarous inhabitants of Britain who were the subject of cultural imperialism from other peoples must now, as a civilized nation, use precisely those methods so as to impose their acquired culture on the Irish.

In making this cross-cultural and transhistorical analogy, Irenius draws directly upon the antiquarian movement's discoveries about England's cultural development. While it cannot be regarded as a source, a discourse such as Hakewill's, which explores the Roman treatment of a people 'by nature disobedient' (i.e. the Britons), nevertheless provides a template for Irenius's favoured method for the subjection of a similar people (i.e. the Irish). Brady tells but half the story when he states

---

[52] On the story of the arrival in Ireland of 'Nemedus from Scythia with his four sons' see Cambrensis, *History* (Dundalk), 95–6. On Spenser's possible direct access to Irish sources on the Scythian invasion see Smith, 'Spenser, Holinshed, and the *Laebhar Gabhála*', 396–400.

that Spenser's disquisition upon the dominance of Scythian customs was 'fundamental to his entire argument' because 'it is through this that the incorrigibility of the natives is established and the resort to force justified' (p. 37). The exposure of the supposed Scythian roots of the Irish is not in itself used to denigrate the Irish as a people. Irenius is quite willing to accept the Scythians as a once mighty nation and to acknowledge that 'theare is no nacion now in Christendome nor muche farther but is mingled and Compounded with others' (p. 92). It is not the specific conclusion about the Scythian origins of the Irish but the entire antiquarian mindset that is fundamental. The justification for the 'resort to force' is not so much racial as cultural: it is because of Spenser's antiquarian conception of the Irish as a primitive people comparable to the early Britons themselves that Irenius proposes the grossly violent programme he does.[53]

The suggestion that the *View* (especially in its denigration of common law) marks a significant break with earlier reform literature on Ireland lends weight to the thesis that Irenius's project represents a shift in the English perspective on primitive societies. In particular Irenius's conjunction of legal and societal change heralds important developments originating in the new antiquarian thinking. Taking Hakewill's study as a jumping-off point once more, we find it tells us that the Romans 'trained up some of the British kings and many of their noblemen even in the city of Rome itself, which they did for no other purpose, than to instruct them in their laws and civilitie'. This strategy for imposing a set of cultural values may productively be compared to that forwarded by Irenius whereby 'all the sonnes of Lordes, gentlemen, and suche others as are able to bringe them up in learninge shoulde be trained up thearein from theire Childhoodes'.[54] While this particular measure is not explicitly linked by Irenius to Roman precedents, such linkage certainly does occur at other points. In support of his plan for directly rewarding and maintaining English soldiers by means of confiscated Irish land, for

---

[53] The argument that Spenser's work is 'racist' is made e.g. in Julia Reinhard Lupton's otherwise excellent essay 'Mapping Mutability: or Spenser's Irish Plot', in *Edmund Spenser*, ed. Andrew Hadfield (London: Longman, 1996), 211–31 (214). Ong, 'Spenser's *View*', 565–8, points out that already in Cambrensis, and certainly in Campion, it is not the 'nature' of the Irish but their lack of cultivation that is identified as the root of their 'enormities'. The move towards a racial basis for national identity is a gradual one, but in the assessment of Kidd it is not until the 19th cent. that it can be called 'racialist' (*British Identities*, 83). In his assessment constitutional ideas were always central, although it should be acknowledged that he finds ethnicity of 'central importance' (p. 146) in 17th-cent. Irish politics.

[54] Compare *Discourses*, i. 3, and *View*, 218.

example, Irenius notes with antiquarian precision that: 'this was the Course which the Romaines observed in the Conquest of Englande for they planted some of theire legions in all places Conveniente the which they Caused the Countrye to maynteine Cuttinge uppon everie porcion of lande a reasonable rente which they Called *Romescot*' (p. 180). In both Ware's text and that of the manuscript edition in the Bodleian Library, the practice of supporting soldiers from the rent of conquered territory continues throughout to be referred to as 'Romescot', even when it applies to English actions in Ireland—a feature that stresses the adoption of Roman policy in Ireland still more strongly.[55]

In the case of the Saxons, Hakewill's description of historical events squares still more strongly with Irenius's proposals for present-day policy in Ireland. It is, once more, necessary to quote at length. As Hakewill tells us:

The next, that succeeded the Romans in conquest, were the Saxons, by whom so absolute and victorious a conquest was made of this land, as the like (I believe) in any history is scarce read of. For they did not only expell or drive into corners of the land the ancient inhabitants, planting themselves in their seats, and that not by small colonies, but as it were by whole nations of people; a point even in great conquests rarely heard of: but they altered also the religion, they razed out the old names of cities, towns, rivers, and whole countries, imposing new of their own invention; nay, the language itself they not only altered, but utterly abolished; and for a perfect consummation of their conquest they did at last also change the name of the whole island itself: than which, if there were no other argument proving the same, this methinks might very much persuade, that those great conquerors altered also the old laws, and established their own; than which as nothing is more of conquerors desired, and more usually put in practise; so indeed is there nothing of more honor and security in ages to come, if once it may be thoroughly performed.   (i. 4)

The Saxon emphasis on 'religion', 'names', 'language', and in particular the erasure of old laws and institutions is very much Irenius's; and Hakewill's evident admiration for the thoroughness of the Saxon conquest is likewise reminiscent of Irenius's zeal for a complete cultural reformation.

[55] Of the four texts regularly collated in the footnotes of the Variorum, only one uses the phrase 'cuttinge of the paie of the Soldiour uppon the lande' instead of 'Romescott', and that appears to be afterwards 'added in space left blank'. Both Ware and Bodleian Library, MS Rawlinson B 478 use 'Romescott': See *View* (Baltimore), 181 and *View* (Dublin), 88. In his later comments upon the choice of leadership in Ireland, Irenius, via Machiavelli, also expresses the desire to adopt 'the manner of the Romaines governement in givinge absolute power to all theire Consulls and governours' (p. 229).

As was the case with Roman measures, in his proposal for the administrative subdivision of the island, Irenius's reliance on Saxon precedent is prominently advertised by a considerable body of antiquarian reconstruction. With the same eye for detail as he displayed in his description of Irish customs, Irenius describes King '*Alured* or *Alfred*''s division of his realm 'into shieres and the shieres into hundreds and the hundreds into Lathes or wapentackes and the wapentackes into tythings', taking care to identify the distinct role of the elder 'whom they Called the Tithingeman or borsholder' (p. 201). The methodology employed here is again very characteristic of that found in the discourses of the Society of Antiquaries. If we look at a paper on the antiquity of shires delivered in 1591 by Arthur Agard, for example, we find that he describes the post-conquest policies of 'King Alured' (i.e. Alfred) in exactly the same manner.[56]

Irenius of course is never prepared to leave things at the level of mere description. In his assessment, Alfred's distant division of a kingdom, because it responded to 'like evills', is clearly applicable to Ireland (p. 201). Eudoxus's knee-jerk objection—'this is Contrarie to that youe saide before for as I remember you saide theare was a great disproporcion betwene England and Irelande so as the lawes which weare fitting for thone would not fitt thother' (p. 202)—is easily answered and provides an opportunity for his companion to reiterate the antiquarian understanding of societal change. As Irenius explains, 'this Lawe was made not by the *Norman* Conquerour but by a Saxon kinge at what time Englande was verie like to Irelande as it now standes'.[57] Ireland, according to Irenius's logic, must revisit the England of the ninth century before it can progress to become like the England of the sixteenth.

Ultimately, circumstances, and the desire to promote the law of the colonizing nation that Hakewill identifies, force Irenius to be more cautious—the English are too used to their laws, and the Irish had best follow them: 'Therefore sithens we Cannot now applie Lawes fitt to the people as in the firste institucion of Comon wealthes . . . onelye suche defectes in the Comon lawe and inConveniences in the statutes as in the beginninge we noted and as men in deeper insighte, shall advise

---

[56] Agard, *Discourses*, i. 19–20; Agard and Irenius even make the same observation about the roots of this practice in 'the Counsell of *Jethro* to *Moses*' (See *View*, 202). Agard's is the first of several, broadly similar, contributions on the subject of the antiquity of shires.

[57] *View*, 202. As with the example of 'Romescot', the Saxon model continues to be used as a point of reference in the discussion that follows, with even Eudoxus contributing antiquarian insights into the matter (pp. 210–14).

maye be Changed' (p. 199). This pronouncement is undeniably at odds with the proposals for Ireland's reform that both precede and follow it; there are, however, reasons to regard Irenius's apparent retreat on the question of legal change with a degree of scepticism. As with Irenius's hasty qualification of the oft-cited phrase 'even by the sworde' (p. 148), the limitations that are here placed on the alteration of the Common Law smack of last-minute authorial nervousness about the response of the *View*'s intended readership. In practice the tail end of Irenius's apparently conciliatory statement leaves him plenty of room for manœuvre, and it is significant that, in the copy text of the Variorum edition, Irenius's modest list of laws that need reforming should conclude with a comma and be succeeded by blank space in which, presumably, additional suspect ordinances could be added. Certainly the proposals that follow this statement (including one for the establishment of martial law) show no signs of the same pragmatic conservatism. Irenius's desire for radical legal change is only momentarily held in check by the fear of alienating the kind of audience anticipated in the figure of Eudoxus. The complete implementation of English Common Law in Ireland remains an objective—for this would prove the completion of the English conquest—but in the transitional period other (earlier) laws must be used.

The *View*'s reasoning forms a kind of chiasmus: in its first part it takes a legal *present* and draws from this a cultural *past*; in its second it takes a cultural *past* and draws from this a new legal *present*. The scale of Irenius's project for the transformation of Ireland should not be underestimated: alongside the deployment of troops and the establishment of garrisons we should notice plans for the creation of market towns inhabited by skilled artisans, the transition from semi-nomadic shepherding to arable farms and from illiteracy to education, the replacing of fords by bridges, the construction of broad, safe roads, and much besides.[58] In this respect Spenser's text is a kind of *Britannia* in reverse: where Camden's painstaking enquiries gradually reveal the ordered network of roads and settlements that was Roman Britain, Spenser's lead him *forward* to a neo-imperial vision of what could be.[59] The development is not merely one of merciless English colonialism (though it is that), it is also an example of imposed and accelerated cultural evolution—a concept that is dependent on the understanding of societal change exemplified in the

---

[58] *View*, 183, 215, 226–7; 216–17; 218; 224.

[59] Deborah Shuger, 'Irishmen, Aristocrats, and Other Barbarians', *Renaissance Quarterly*, 50 (1997), 494–525, suggests the *Britannia* 'supplies the blueprint' for Spenser's project.

discourses of a generation of English antiquaries. In no other kind of writing are we so routinely and unambiguously confronted with the realities of innovation through conquest;[60] Irenius's project is unimaginable without the historiographic grounding of its exponent.

The Cantos of Mutability: Debating Conquest on Arlo Hill

The Histories by Hanmer and Campion that precede the *View* in Ware's 1633 edition foreground important aspects of Spenser's text, at once covering and uncovering the radicalism of its approach to Ireland. Like the 'learned histories' that precede the tract, the 'verses of Mr Edm. Spenser's' that follow it both obscure and reveal its politics. They offset the *View*'s stridency, presenting a gentle, intellectual Spenser more concerned with the distant past than the present. But the poetry also provides an additional insight into the *View* and the anxieties that lay behind it. Both the major passages that Ware selects are taken from *The Faerie Queene*—a poem that he claims was completed by Spenser only to be lost amid the chaos of Irish rebellion. The second extract (the passage on Ireland's Arlo Hill from the Mutability Cantos) is itself a remnant of that supposedly lost work.[61] The Cantos were almost certainly written within a few years of the *View*;[62] in more than one sense they illustrate the violent intrusion of present-day politics into Spenser's discourse on Ireland's past.

In the Cantos too we find a debate about imperial control and the rights of succession structured 'dialogue-wise', this time between Jove

[60] Another instance, though far from routine or unambiguous, is the conquest effected by Brutus over the British giants. As Canny observes, Spenser's 'Hobbesian exultation of violence in pursuit of civil goals' at *Faerie Queene*, II. x. 9 bears comparison with the political philosophy of the *View* (*Making Ireland*, 23). From a euhemeristic perspective (on which see Ch. 4) the conflict between Jove and the Titans discussed below provides an additional parallel.

[61] As argued in Ch. 2, the first of Ware's extracts (Book IV's description of the Irish rivers) also involves the relation of some uncomfortable history. For perceptive analysis, see Highley, *Shakespeare, Spenser*, 131–3. David Miller has used another of the pieces collected by Ware as the basis of an argument against a determinate political reading of the *View* (see 'The Earl of Cork's Lute', in Judith H. Anderson, Donald Cheney, and David A. Richardson (eds.), *Spenser's Life and the Subject of Biography* (Amherst: University of Massachusetts Press, 1996), 146–71).

[62] Most critics, with the exception of Alice Fox Blitch ('The Mutabilitie Cantos: "In Meet Order Ranged"', *English Language Notes*, 7 (1969–70), 179–86), believe the Cantos were a late composition. As Hadfield observes, it is highly unlikely that Spenser would have made reference to Arlo before 1586 (see *Irish Experience*, 185). The description of the Irish rivers is also likely to post-date Spenser's arrival in Ireland, although the origins the 'Marriage of Thames and Medway' as a whole may be traced to a much earlier composition, itself of antiquarian pedigree (see Harper, *Sources*, 187–90).

and Mutabilitie. The initial stages of the argument are principally concerned with rights of inheritance. As the child of her mother Earth and
father Saturn, Mutabilitie asserts her claim both as a literal autochthon
and as a direct descendent of the universe's rightful ruler. The traditions
of matrilineal descent and primogeniture invoked in the goddess's plea
are a subject that would undeniably command the interest of antiquarians: Lambarde's famous investigation of the tradition of inheritance by 'gavelkind', and Spenser's own concern with the details of
tanistry being but two prominent examples.[63] In particular, her case, as
Patricia Coughlan has shown, has much in common with the basis of
Old English suits for land rights in Ireland.[64]

Jove, however, is ultimately uninterested in the niceties of this kind of
argument. Like Irenius, who (dismissive of the agreements for the submission of the Irish made during the reign of Henry VIII) insists that 'all
is the Conquerours' (p. 52), Jove argues that his conquest effectively
obliterates the claims of whatever system of inheritance precedes it:[65]

> But wote thou this, thou hardy *Titanesse*,
>   That not the worth of any liuing wight
>   May challenge ought in Heauens interesse;
>   Much lesse the Title of old *Titans* Right:
>   For, we by Conquest of our soueraine might,
>   And by eternall doome of Fates decree,
>   Haue wonne the Empire of the Heauens bright.   (VII. vi. 33. 1–7)

Jove's daring reuse of the root 'Titan' confidently flaunts a disregard for
pre-existing claims on the succession. Jove in macrocosm, and Spenser
in microcosm, rely on a belief in the realities of conquest as the ultimate
determinant of control. Just as the poet was no doubt frustrated by the

---

[63] Mutabilitie's physical tussle with Cynthia (resembling the legal conflict of the Duessa/
Mercilla case in Book V) brings the position of England's monarch still closer to the forefront.
As previous studies have shown, the spiteful withdrawal of the virgin Cynthia/Diana from Arlo
which is related in the first Canto of Book VII also implies a great deal about the Queen's
absence from territory of Ireland (see e.g. Hadfield, *Irish Experience*, 195, and Norbrook, *Poetry
and Politics*, 151–6). 'Gavelkind' is a recurrent concern in Lambarde's *Perambulation*. For a discussion of the *Perambulation* that illustrates its dialogic character and the importance of law as an
inscriptor of history, see William Keith Hall, 'From Chronicle to Chorography: Truth,
Narrative, and the Antiquarian Enterprise in Renaissance England' (unpublished doctoral dissertation, University of North Carolina, 1995), 49–51.

[64] Patricia Coughlan, 'The Local Context of Mutabilitie's Plea', *Irish University Review*, 26
(1996), 320–41 (331–41).

[65] On claims of absolute conquest and their conflict with claims of absolute antiquity see
Pocock, *Ancient Constitution*, 52–3.

repeated legal battles with Old English landowners such as Roche who asserted prior claims, so Jove is exasperated by the recurrence of claims that he hoped he had extinguished by conquest (VII. vi. 29).[66]

On this question, in practice if not in theory, Jove's assessment is allowed to prevail. The justice or otherwise of Mutabilitie's claim to the succession from a legal perspective is never properly addressed in the Cantos; all parties, including the judge, Nature, seem to agree that such matters must be restricted to the opening stages of an argument, almost as an ornamental preamble. Jove's effective victory on this point, however, cuts both ways: having asserted his rights on the basis of conquest but then failed to back them up with force as threatened, his appeal for Mutabilitie to acknowledge him as her 'gratious Lord and Soueraigne' ends up sounding very hollow (VII. vi. 34. 5).[67]

Mutabilitie rejects Jove's suggestion, and after once more declaring him a usurper she engages with the ruler of the heavens on his own terms. For the heart of the case that Mutabilitie presents rests on actual control and not mythical history. Her argument about the universal power of mutability, in effect, amounts to a claim based on the extent to which she has, in turn, conquered the world and made it conform to her 'culture' (i.e. mutability). Just as an antiquarian such as Hakewill is able to judge the success of the Saxon invasion of England by measuring the degree to which laws, customs, etc. have been transformed, so the Titaness proceeds to catalogue the regions in which she claims to hold sway.

The question that dogs Jove's claim, then, concerns the extent of his conquest; and here, once again, the parallels with England's conquest of Ireland are disturbing. As we have noted, it was a commonplace observation among English writers on Ireland that Henry II's takeover of that land had been left uncompleted. Holinshed reached all the way back to Gerald of Wales in cataloguing 'The causes why England could not make the full and finall conquest of Ireland'.[68] In Spenser's view, of course, it was not just that England had failed fully to conquer Ireland,

---

[66] For a readily accessible outline of the legal conflict with Roche, see Willy Maley, *A Spenser Chronology* (Basingstoke: Macmillan, 1994).

[67] Hadfield has noted the often cynical way in which English writers, including Spenser, made claims about the justice of England's sovereignty over Ireland on the basis of dubious ancient history (see 'Briton and Scythian', and *Irish Experience*, 85–112). Hadfield has also discussed the linked conceptions of conquest in the *View* and the Mutability Cantos (*Irish Experience*, 185–202, and 'Spenser, Ireland, and Sixteenth-Century Political Theory', 1–18).

[68] 'Conquest of Ireland', *Chronicles* (1587), ii. 54.

but that the first wave of English invaders had, in a reversal of the hoped-for civilizing process, become 'allmoste meare Irishe' (p. 96). The final stage of Mutabilitie's address to the gods, claiming that 'euen yee | Your selues are likewise chang'd' (VII. vii. 49. 8–9) must come as a particular blow to Jove—certainly we hear no more from him thereafter.

Despite Nature's verdict in his favour, the course that the debate takes arouses serious questions about the wisdom of Jove's attendance at Arlo. In particular, his policy is vulnerable to the criticism that Irenius levels at an attempt by Henry VIII to gain control of Ireland by agreement, whereby the monarch's subjects:

Before beinge absolutelye bounde to his obedience are now tyed but with tenures whearas bothe theire lives theire Landes and their Libertis weare in his fre power to appointe what tenures and lawes, what Condicions he woulde over them, which weare all his, againste which theare coulde be no resistaunce, or if theare weare he mighte when he woulde establishe them with a stronger hande. (*View*, 52)

In this Irenius is opposing a policy that had been actively backed by the majority of the Old English for whom both the persistence of established English Common Law and the use of consensual parliaments were key policy objectives. Old English proposals along these lines appeared throughout the period of Tudor government, suggesting, as one anonymous pre-Elizabethan writer put it, that the crown communicate with all Ireland's inhabitants and: 'Let their heads with the rest of the lords of the realm be persuaded to assemble all in one place, to the intent that there in open parliament not only those statutes which heretofore divided them asunder may be abrogated, but also henceforth that both Irish and English may be joined in one [regiment?].'[69] For Irenius this policy is anathema: such conjoining of peoples is a threat to English identity, and neither the Common Law nor the use of parliaments or assemblies is to be countenanced given the 'present state' of Ireland.

For Mutabilitie, however, the assembly proves on more than one level

[69] Anon., 'A Treatise for the Reformation of Ireland 1554–5', ed. Brendan Bradshaw, *The Irish Jurist*, 16 (1981), 299–315 (310–11). As Bradshaw says, the pamphlet makes it clear that the aim of a united and peaceful Ireland 'may be achieved by only one means, the operation of the processes of constitutional government, parliament, the judiciary, the institutions of central and local government' (p. 302). For further detail on Irish parliaments see Ciarán Brady, 'Court, Castle, and Country: The Framework of Government in Tudor Ireland', in Ciarán Brady and Raymond Gillespie (eds.), *Natives and Newcomers: Essays on the Making of Irish Colonial Society 1534–1641* (Dublin: Irish Academic Press, 1986) 22–49.

to be a useful tool by which to promote her objectives. Looking again at the opening stages of her speech at Arlo (which gives way to a more philosophical discussion of 'change' hereafter), we find that its vocabulary gives some telling insights into the political basis of her approach. 'Mauger *Ioue*, and all his gods beside', she tells us:

> I doe possesse the worlds most regiment;
> As, if ye please it into parts diuide,
> And euery parts inholders to conuent,
> Shall to your eyes appeare incontinent.   (VII. vii. 17. 2–5)

Jove's use of the words 'soueraine' and 'Empire' (VII. vi. 33. 5, 7) already told us much about the basis of his case, and Mutabilitie's wish to take the world and 'it into parts diuide, | And euery parts inholders to conuent' is equally revealing. 'Inholders' means 'inhabitants' and 'conuent' means 'assemble'.[70] The Titaness's enthusiasm for assemblies clearly extends beyond the limits of the divine gathering on Arlo Hill, an enthusiasm that invites parallels with the kind of gatherings that Irenius observes in sixteenth-century Ireland.

The Cantos' simultaneous concern with the politics of conquest and assembly provide us with a significant insight into the full range of the texts that have come under consideration in this chapter. It is revealing here to refer again to the contributions in the *Curious Discourses* concerning 'the Antiquity of Shires in England' (i. 19–32). As has already been noted, the majority of recorded speeches trace the formal establishment of these administrative units to the time of Alfred, the first Saxon ruler who secured anything like an overall conquest of England. Before this time, a number of contributors deduce, the land was still divided into a collection of smaller parcels centred, interestingly enough, upon a series of informal assemblies that were the basis for their defence against invasion (i. 281–310). Such assemblies, we will not be surprised to learn, were proscribed once a single conqueror attempted to assert control over the entire nation.

Mutabilitie, like the early Britons and Saxons, seeks to resist the power of a monarch on the basis of compartmentalized assemblies. The Irish of Spenser's day—who bear comparison to early Britons and Saxons as

---

[70] *Faerie Queene*, ed. Hamilton, 727 n. The *OED*, giving this line as the only instance of this usage, has 'inholder' as 'a tennant'. Hamilton's interpretation of 'convent' squares with that of the *OED*. The use of the words 'tenants' and 'massacred' along with a stress on change in men at VII. vii. 19 is also notable.

well as to Mutabilitie herself—also assert their control over the island of Ireland in this way. This, indeed, is one of the chief evils that Irenius identifies. 'Theare is', he tells us:

A greate use amongst the Irishe to make greate assemblies togeather uppon a Rathe or hill theare to parlye (as they saie) aboute matters and wronges betwene Towneshipp and Towneshippe or one private persone and another. But well I wote and trewe it hathe bene often times aproved that in these metinges manye mischiefs have bene bothe practised and wroughte. (*View*, 128–9)

Eudoxus, who is beginning to catch on as far as antiquarian matters are concerned, identifies these hills as '*Folkmotes*', and perhaps aware of what Irenius (like the contributor to the *Discourses*) immediately notes is their Saxon origin, is convinced of their benefits. Irenius, as so many times before, steps in to qualify the opinions of his companion:

Ye saie verye Trewe *Eudox.* the firste makinge of these hye hills was at firste indede to verye good purpose for people to mete but howe ever the times when they weare firste made mighte well serve to good accacions as perhaps they did then in Englande yeat thinges beinge since alltered and now Irelande muche defferinge from that state of Englande the good use that then was of them is now turned to abuse. (*View*, 129)

Again, Irenius is insistent on the importance of societal change: England *then* was in a pre-monarchical stage (or perhaps at a stage during which monarchy was embraced willingly) and this evidently is not the case in sixteenth-century Ireland. In another virtuoso display of antiquarian knowledge, he identifies a range of ancient hill-structures, most prominently the more pacific Saxon '*Folkemotes*' and the more defensive Danish '*Deanerathes*', but he remains implacably opposed to their present-day Irish incarnation (p. 130). Knowing, like the antiquarians in London, of the existence of these structures and their associated gatherings in a non-unified England before King Alfred, Irenius is well aware that the defensive role they fulfilled in those times will now constitute an impediment to successful English rule.

Eudoxus, however, still sees merit in the hill meetings: especially 'if at those assemblies theare be anye officers as Constables or Bayliffes or suche like amongeste them theare cane be no perill nor doutt of suche badd practises' (p. 131). Once more, it is instructive to draw parallels with Spenser's fictive presentation of the hill meeting in the 'Mutability Cantos', where 'at the time that was before agreed, | The Gods assembled all on *Arlo* hill' (VII. vii. 3. 1–2):

And thither also came all other creatures,
  What-euer life or motion doe retaine,
  According to their sundry kinds of features;
  That *Arlo* scarsly could them all containe;
  So full they filled euery hill and Plaine:
  And had not *Natures* Sergeant (that is *Order*)
  Them well disposed by his busie paine,
  And raunged farre abroad in euery border,
They would haue caused much confusion and disorder.   (VII. vii. 4)

The assembly on Arlo Hill is a select company, and as well policed as Eudoxus could hope.[71] Yet, like Irenius, we may remain convinced that 'Neverthelesse daungerous are suche assemblies' (p. 131). Jove, certainly, was cajoled into accepting the arrangements not because of the sage council of his fellow gods (who merely fell into dissension when the question was raised), but because he was (in a striking parallel with that other imposer of law by conquest, Artegall) seduced by the beauty of a rebellious female (VII. vi. 31). Mutabilitie's armed entrance at that earlier assembly provides a warning of the disturbances she may cause— the threat she poses to the gods who were 'All quite vnarm'd, as then their manner was' (VII. vi. 24. 3) again parallels the danger for English attendants at the Irish assemblies: 'for', Irenius observes, 'the Irishe never come to those Rathes but armed wheather on horse or fote which the Englishe nothing suspectinge are then Comonlye taken at advantage like shepe in the pinfoulde' (p. 129).

The interlocutors of the *View*, in the light of Irenius's recent return from Ireland, appear to be safely situated in England (perhaps not too far from the Herald's Office in London). Nevertheless, even at this comfortable distance, the Irish assemblies hold a palpable horror for Irenius. The location in which the debate between the gods takes place is, however, far more vulnerable. In contrast to the unspecified backdrop to the encounter between Irenius and Eudoxus, the 'Mutability Cantos' are set not only in Ireland, but in a part of Ireland that Irenius himself describes as a place of assembly, not for sage counsellors, but for thieves (p. 194). As Patricia Coughlan's excellent article on 'The Local Context of Mutabilitie's Plea' has highlighted, Arlo should be seen not just as 'the beautiful and sacred site where Nature gives her judgement against

---

[71] The 'infernall Powers', it is worth noting, have been proscribed for 'feare' of both their looks and their 'vnruly fiends' (VII. vii. 3. 6–8). The political vocabulary of the above passage again invites parallels with Spenser's prose tract.

Mutabilitie; but also as Galtymore, the highest peak of a mountain range above a heavily wooded and enclosed valley—the Glen of Aherlow— which during all the sixteenth century wars of Ireland had been notorious as an inaccessible fastness and stronghold for successive rebel armies and bands'.[72] In the light of this connection, parallels between Arlo and the Irish 'folkmotes' become still more insistent. We know nothing of Mutabilitie's response to Nature's decision. Irenius, however, would surely caution that even if she were to accept the verdict, she would, like the Irish, be quite free to invoke the Brehon law, which would absolve her successors from making the like submission. Still worse, perhaps (like the sixteenth-century rebels on Galtymore and the Irish of Irenius's description) she has brought her weapons to the hilltop meeting ready to spring upon the naïvely unarmed gods who will be 'taken at advantage like shepe in the pinfoulde'.

Assemblies where debates are conducted—whether antiquarian, Irish, or divine—are always potentially threatening, and it is not surprising that the proceedings of all three gatherings (the Society of Antiquaries, Irenius and Eudoxus, and the gods at Arlo Hill) should have remained unpublished throughout Elizabeth's reign. While there is no direct evidence of the government's suppression of any of the three, there are indications that they were at least unappreciated by the Elizabethan establishment. The petition of Sir Robert Cotton to have the Society of Antiquaries established as an official national institution appears to have gone unanswered, and when after a period of inactivity Spelman and other members attempted to revive the Society under James it seems the king 'took a little Mislike' to its proceedings, preventing any further assemblies.[73] The debate about whether or not Spenser's *View* was ever actively suppressed by the government rumbles on. It is generally acknowledged, however, that the piece would have been unsuitable for wide-scale public circulation, and in all likelihood remained restricted to manuscript circulation as a result.[74] There is no evidence that the 'Mutability Cantos' were blocked or withheld from publication; yet it is notable that the only substantial piece of verse by the poet not to be printed during his lifetime should concern itself with the issues of sovereignty and conquest, take place in Ireland, and be structured in large part as a discourse or dialogue. The fact that the Cantos were

---

[72] 'Local Context', 325.
[73] Cited by Van Norden, 'College', 414 and 74.
[74] For an overview of the debate, see Hadfield, 'Was Spenser's'.

eventually published by the same Lownes who had placed the *View* in the Stationers' Register in 1598 may or may not be significant.

King James's apparent reluctance to extend his blessing to a reformed Society of Antiquaries, and his increasingly antagonistic relationship with those who had antiquarian interests, stemmed to a considerable degree from the interest of antiquarians in the antiquity of that most prominent of assemblies: Parliament. The Society's gradual move towards more controversial subject matter for investigation is exemplified by the series of papers on Parliament that as a rule made strong claims for the inviolable rights of that institution.[75] Camden was one of a broad and divergent group of speakers whose contributions on the subject were recorded by the Society of Antiquaries, and he had numerous supporters when he argued for the existence of early parliament-like groups not just amongst the Saxons but also amongst the pre-Roman Britons.[76] Dodderidge, another antiquarian to speak 'Of the Antiquity, Power, Order, State, Manner, Persons, and Proceedings of the High Court of Parliament in England', likewise believed that 'the like assemblies as parliaments' were to be found in the British '*Kyfrithin*' and Saxon '*Gereduytsis*'.[77] Dodderidge's contribution, insisting on the 'binding' nature of Parliament's decisions, on its rights to 'free council', and on the requirement of a presence of commons, has a still more polemical edge than Camden's. In his speech, as by implication in Mutabilitie's, parliaments stand in opposition to the dictatorship of monarchy, for 'before our Britaines learned the laws of their victours, they held their common counsels' (p. 283). Still more strikingly, Dodderidge's argument reaches back to the very beginnings of civil society, where those who know the 'Mutability Cantos' will find a very familiar lawmaker: Nature.[78] 'Before the time of soveraignty', he tells us:

Nature's law directed men to the love of society, and care to preserve it; and gained free consent even of lawless men, to admit of certain customs as laws, from hence framing matter of form for a commonwealth. But new springing mischiefs standing remediless by the elder customs, caused, for remedy thereof,

---

[75] The shift is noted by Van Norden, 'College', 376.

[76] *Discourses*, i. 303–4. Other contributors (more accurately) find no genuinely comparable parliaments before the Norman age (e.g. Anon., *Discourses*, i. 293). The majority of speakers, however, lay great stress on the antiquity of proto-parliaments.

[77] Dodderidge, *Discourses*, i. 281–2; on the requisite presence of the commons, see the additional material submitted by Dodderidge (i. 292).

[78] On the polemical claims of parliamentarians for the immemorial and customary status of Parliament see Pocock, *Ancient Constitution*, 47–9 and *passim*.

the calling of yearly councils, the original no doubt of our after parliaments. And it shall appear, that our kingdome, from as grounded authority as any other nation, can prove of old the practise of these great assemblies, then called Counsels, now Parliaments (i. 282–3).

The very different dialogues of the *View*, the meetings of the Society of Antiquaries, and Arlo Hill all invoke the distant past to make claims about the basis of monarchical power. In particular, all stress the importance of conquest. Assemblies, however, become not just places in which the complexities of conquest are discussed; they also, in themselves, constitute structures with the capacity to resist the encroachment of the sovereign. Even in the 1610 *Britannia*'s apparently modest desire to refer a matter of historical controversy 'to the Senate of Antiquarians' there may be detected the latent presence of a political vocabulary (p. 6). Dialogues on hilltops, in the Herald's office, or in Westminster, can become a threat to the conqueror, and in this sense the *View*'s structure ultimately undermines its avowed purposes: Irenius and Eudoxus were not to be allowed to meet again, not even to discourse upon 'the Antiquities of Ireland'.

CHAPTER 4

'With Fayned Colours Shading a True Case': Euhemerism and Universal History

Reading Universal History

Elizabethan antiquarianism covered significant new ground in its exploration of Norman, Saxon, Roman, and Briton culture. Back before the arrival of the first Roman invaders, however, the historical ground became rapidly less navigable, and across the seas too lay lands into which England's antiquarians had determined not to venture. The Early Modern reader who wished to travel further called on a form of history whose manner of traversing the historical landscape was altogether different. That form used sweeping narratives in which a providential design was always implicit. Beginning with the Creation itself, charting the evolution of civil society, and describing the rise and fall of empires, such works were truly universal histories.

The concept of 'prehistory' was simply not available to the Christian chronographer: Moses was the greatest of all historians and his narrative began from the very dawn of time. Yet although the biblical account of the earliest ages was authoritative it was also frustratingly partial. Genesis provided an outline, but especially after the division of the races following the fall of Babel it offered few clues about the wider course of political history. The story of the Jewish race could certainly be used as a time-line against which to plot events occurring beyond the Holy Land. Until one reached the secure ground charted by Greek and Roman historians, however, those events themselves remained shadowy. Writing their narrative required an exceptionally creative mode of reading.

After Spenser's death his friend and fellow poet Sir Walter Ralegh was to become England's most highly regarded universal historian. Ralegh viewed the remains on which he was to base his narrative with a mixture of regret and optimism. For although the 'length and dissolving Nature of Time' had 'worne out or changed the Names and Memory of the Worlds first planters after the floud' the footsteps of Antiquity were 'not quite worne out nor over-growne'.[1] While there were no straightforward accounts of the first peopling and civilizing of the world, other sources —given the right treatment—would nevertheless yield the secrets of history. Such accounts existed, but in a corrupted or encrypted state. As Ralegh put it:

the Greekes and other more ancient Nations, by fabulous inventions, and by breaking into parts the Story of the Creation, and by delivering it over in a mysticall sense, wrapping it up mixed with other their owne trumpery, have fought to obscure the truth thereof; and have hoped, that after-ages, being thereby brought into many doubts, might receive those inter-mixt discourses of God and Nature, for the inventions of Poets and Philosophers, and not as any thing borrowed or stolne out of the Bookes of God. But as a skilfull and learned Chymist can aswell by separation of visible elements draw helpefull medicines . . . so, contrary to the purposes and hopes of the Heathen, may those which seeke after God and Truth, find out every-where, and in all the ancient Poets and Philosophers, the Story of the first Age, with all the works and marvels thereof, amply and lively exprest.   (Ralegh, *History*, 71)

The truth about early history was locked into the fables of ancient poets and philosophers, but—by the 'skilfull and learned Chymist'—it could nevertheless be extracted and put to good use.

The chemistry by which Ralegh recovers 'the Story of the first Age' is today named 'Euhemerism' after its first practitioner, Euhemerus of Messene (*fl.* 311–298 BC).[2] Based on the supposition that behind the myths of pagan antiquity lay real and recoverable history, Euhemerism could make inroads into a portion of time that was otherwise considered 'indeterminate'.[3] Gods and monsters, by this reasoning, had once been genuine historical persons. Although over time the excesses of

---

[1] Ralegh, *History of the World* (1614), 151. Ralegh, in fact, completed only the first part of the *History*, taking it up to the beginning of the Roman state.

[2] A clear and detailed account is given by Jean Seznec, *The Survival of the Pagan Gods: The Mythological Tradition and Its Place in Renaissance Humanism and Art*, Bollingen Series, 38, trans. Barbara F. Sessions (New York: Pantheon Books, 1953), 11–28. See also 'Euhemerism: The Medieval Tradition' in Arthur Ferguson's *Utter Antiquity: Perceptions of Prehistory in Renaissance England* (Durham, NC: Duke University Press, 1993), 13–22.

[3] On the Roman historian Varro's tripartite division of the past into the 'historical', 'mythical', and 'indeterminate' see William Adler, *Time Immemorial: Archaic History and Its Sources in Christian Chronography from Julius Africanus to George Syncellus* (Washington, DC: Dumbarton Oaks Research Library, 1989), 16.

storytellers had inflated the account of their lives, it was possible to recover key names and incidents. Zeus, for example, must surely have been an early and powerful king who had in some way supplanted his father in sovereignty. Seen from this perspective even reports of hilltop debates between divine beings were in some sense historical.

The euhemeristic method influenced Greek and Roman historians, but it took on a much greater importance for their Christian successors. First because a teleologically driven theology demanded an account of history from the beginning, and second because belief in the Old Testament made such an account appear newly viable, Christian chronographers enthusiastically set about the grand project of recovering the pagan past.[4] Their approach to the earliest ages, combining biblical sources with pseudo-historical and mythical material from other traditions, gained enormous currency. Reworked by generations of universal historians, the account that these scholars patched together became an important part of the Christian world picture.

Ralegh was but one accomplished figure in an ongoing tradition.[5] If anything distinguished his approach it was the clarity with which he set out his method and vision. The first chapter of the *History of the World* considered the mixing of heathen authority with the truth of God (pp. 2–5) and its sixth concerned 'the Reliques of Truth touching these ancient times, obscurely appearing in Fables and old Legends' (p. 71). It was not merely gods who could be reread as kings—whole narratives could be telescoped, edited, or interpreted allegorically. Thus, 'the Fable of the dividing of the World betweene the three Brethren the Sonnes of Saturne' arose 'from the true Story of the dividing of the Earth betweene the three Brethren the Sonnes of Noah' and the 'Fiction of those Golden Apples kept by a Dragon' could be reconciled with the truth of 'the Serpent which tempted Evah'.[6] In part, Ralegh's approach follows the longstanding pragmatism of chroniclers by which the least-bad source, however weak, is always worth recording. Yet it also reflects a deeply entrenched respect for 'the old stories'. Like so many commentators, stretching from the very beginning of written culture, Ralegh invests ancient texts with a wealth of intentionally and unintentionally

---

[4] For a comprehensive overview of the writing of universal history see Adler, *Time Immemorial.*

[5] Ferguson, *Utter Antiquity*, 23–45, describes Ralegh as accepting euhemerism 'without question' (p. 28), although he also notes Renaissance 'ambivalence' (p. 27) about the process.

[6] Ralegh, *History*, 73.

hidden knowledge.[7] Looking back at a medieval chronographer such as Ranulph Higden we find the same conviction. In his *Polychronicon* myth is read not just as bearing disguised historical narrative, but also as containing hidden moral instruction. Generations of readers built upon the Classics in this way (even Higden's English translator felt free to add his own readings when so inspired).[8] In the eyes of the chronographer, ancient myth became a kind of unintended allegory—a historical 'darke conceit'.

The euhemeristic decoding of myth was exceptionally common in sixteenth-century England. Numerous vernacular universal histories followed the great European chronographers in using this method to read the past. Still more widely distributed was the *De Inventoribus Rerum* of Polydore Vergil. Running to over a hundred editions, this work sifted classical myths alongside biblical sources in order to determine the originators of numerous apparently 'immemorial' innovations, ranging from wine, agriculture, and shipping to poetry and law.[9] Perhaps most importantly, euhemerism was also extremely common in Classical dictionaries and mythological compendia.[10] Renaissance reference books such as the *Mythologiae* of Natale Conti are replete with such explanations, and in this they reflected and enforced assumptions that had prevailed in Western Europe for over a thousand years.[11]

Spenser would undoubtedly have been familiar with euhemerism. On

[7] This broad cultural assumption lies at the heart of Seznec's seminal work *The Survival of the Pagan Gods* (esp. 84–121) and finds graphic expression in the anonymous Medieval *Ovide moralisé*. For proof that some of the earliest readings of literature were allegorical see Robert Parker, 'Early Orphism', in A. Powell (ed.), *The Greek World* (London: Routledge, 1995), 488, and Adre Lax and G. W. Most, *Studies in the Derveni Papyrus* (Oxford: Oxford University Press, 1997).

[8] Richard Arthur Seeger, 'The English Polychronicon: A Text of John Trevisa's Translation of Higden's *Polychronicon*', based on Huntingdon MS 28561 (Unpublished doctoral dissertation, University of Washington, 1974), 48 and *passim*, shows the chronographer interpreting aspects of myth in both historical and moral ways, with the translator adding his own readings.

[9] For the text and an account of the popularity of Vergil's *Inventoribus* see Beno Weiss and Louis C. Pérez, *Polydore Vergil's De Inventoribus Rerum: An Unabridged Translation and Edition with Introduction, Notes and Glossary*, Bibliotheca Humanistica & Reformatorica, 56 (Nieuwkoop: De Graaf, 1997), 8.

[10] See Seznec, *Survival of the Pagan Gods*, esp. 185–312, and also DeWitt T. Starnes and Ernest William Talbert, *Classical Myth and Legend in Renaissance Dictionaries: A Study of Renaissance Dictionaries in Their Relation to the Classical Learning of Contemporary English Writers* (Chapel Hill: University of North Carolina Press, 1955).

[11] On the way in which these manuals for the most part represented Classical and Medieval thinking, see Seznec, *Survival of the Pagan Gods*, 219–56. On Spenser's use of Conti, also referred to as Comes, see Henry Gibbons Lotspeich, *Classical Mythology in the Poetry of Edmund Spenser*, Princeton Studies in English, 9 (Princeton: Princeton University Press, 1932), 18 and *passim*.

an incidental level it was all but ubiquitous in the culture that surrounded him. Indeed, for an allegorist and Poet Historical there could scarcely be a more intriguing form of history. As he read the commentaries attached to Classical works, or consulted manuals in the composition of his own poetry, this way of reading and (implicitly) of writing would have been a constant presence. Because Spenser composed his poetry on the model of the ancients there were areas where this mode might slip into his verse almost unseen. There were others, however, at which it might become more conspicuous. Whilst no accounts of the past were exclusively euhemeristic, there were areas where the dependence on that system of interpretation was especially strong. Above all, for the development of early statehood there were no adequate biblical accounts. In Genesis the development from patriarchy to monarchy was nebulous, and here especially a number of pagan stories seemed to offer a useful supplement. For here, unlike the Bible, one found what looked like a record of the first foundation of cities, and the invention of the arts and crafts that contributed to civil life. To turn again to Ralegh, it is here that he most skilfully combines the two traditions at his disposal:

For all that the Egyptians write of their ancient Kings, and date of times, cannot be fained. And though other Nations after them had by imitation their Jupiters also, their Saturnes, Vulcans and Mercuries, with the rest, . . . Yet was Cain the sonne of Adam (as some very learned men conceive) called and reputed for the first ancient Jupiter; and Adam the first Saturne: for the first Citie of the world was built by Cain, which he called Enoch . . . Now as Cain was the first Jupiter, and from whom also the Ethnicks had the invention of Sacrifice: so were Jubal, Tubal, and Tubalcain (inventors of Pastorage, Smiths-craft, and Musicke) the same which were called by the ancient and prophane writers, Mercurius, Vulcan, and Apollo.   (*History*, 73)

Here and in the pages that follow Ralegh begins to tell the stories of Greek, Roman, and sometimes Egyptian mythology as if they were the stories of the world's first kings. Spenser too would have found such accounts in contemporary chronicles. When the poet began to consider those earliest historical moments, therefore, it was all the more likely that he should come to contemplate the processes through which this narrative had been composed. Once more, it is instructive to turn to the encounter with the past that Spenser presents in the chamber of Eumnestes.

The Antiquity of Fairyland: Spenser's Universal History

In Book II, Canto x, after Arthur has finished reading the '*Briton moni-ments*', the narrator's attention turns to the '*Antiquitie* of *Faerie* lond'. For this text, read by Guyon, 'Ne yet has ended' (II. x. 70. 2). Unlike the British Chronicle, which has come to a sudden stop, the work held by Arthur's companion appears to extend indefinitely. Certainly the Antiquity is far too massive a work to absorb into Spenser's poem:

> it was a great
> And ample volume, that doth far exceed
> My leasure, so long leaues here to repeat:
> It told, how first *Prometheus* did create
> A man, of many partes from beasts deriued,
> And then stole fire from heauen, to animate
> His worke, for which he was by *Ioue* depriued
> Of life him selfe, and hart-strings of an Ægle riued.   (II. x. 70. 2–9)

In part for numerological reasons, in part because of the sequential arrangement of the two chronicles, Guyon's history has sometimes been regarded as a kind of idealistic abstract of Arthur's.[12] Because it ends with images of Henry VIII and Elizabeth, the Fairy Chronicle can indeed be read as an inspired vision of historical progress. Yet any blunt distinction between the Antiquity as 'fiction' and the Monuments as 'fact' is—as has already been suggested—inadequate. In the world of Renaissance historiography definitions are rarely so rigid. The figure of Prometheus, who opens the history, is a case in point: as one of the Titans his name appeared frequently in Renaissance accounts of early civilization as one who 'made men' in a metaphorical sense by leading them from uncouthness to civility.[13]

It was well over half a century ago that Isabel Rathborne first made the connection between the Antiquity of Fairyland and universal history.[14] Despite the author's subsequent retraction of several parts of

---

[12] McCabe (*Pillars*, 91–103) provides a thorough overview of the theories that critics have forwarded about the nature of the distinction between fairies and British or Saxon knights. Fichter (*Poets Historical*, 183) claimed 'the two chronicles are fact and fiction juxtaposed,' and Berger (*Allegorical Temper*, 104–5) suggested that 'the point about the two chronicles is the very clear contrast between them: they present two different worlds, two utterly irreconcilable views of life'. On the contrasts between the 'allegorical' fairy history and the 'real' Briton one, see Erickson, *Mapping*, 93.   [13] On this view of Prometheus see Adler, *Time Immemorial*, 108.
[14] Isabel E. Rathborne, *The Meaning of Spenser's Fairyland*, Columbia University Studies in English and Comparative Literature, 131 (New York: Columbia University Press, 1937).

her argument, as an overall judgement on the nature of the history it remains very worthwhile. For the Elfin chronicle goes back to Adam and Eve as grand chroniclers do, with the first stanza of Spenser's narration shadowing the discussion on the creation of Man that formed the first chapter of the universal histories. Looking at the early elfin emperors, Rathborne presented some convincing candidates for their identity. Elfin, the 'first and greatest', is, for example, to be placed in the tradition that traces an ancestry from Ham, a son of Noah, to Osyris, the just ruler whose empire divided the world with the Babylonian (p. 79).

The Antiquity's relation to what was believed to be genuine history need not conflict with its status as an idealistic contrast to the fortunes of the Briton kings. In writing world history the existence of an over-arching scheme of providence was as much a prerequisite as an eventual discovery.[15] This drive was far stronger than that which occasionally surfaces in the more irregular national chronicles. It gave the universal histories their aim and structure. Ralegh's *History* was to lay continual stress on the workings of the divine plan in world history (so much so that the *History of the World*'s imposing frontispiece, featuring the eye of providence, is in part responsible for the overemphasis on the place of this thinking in earlier national histories).[16]

If the narrative gestured at by Guyon's history would be familiar to the Elizabethan reader, the Antiquity's conjunction with the roll of British kings would make it even more so. Although the Briton history was but a sub-strand of the universal, the treatment of the two as parallel narratives was well established in English printed chronicles. A graphic image of such pairing is to be found on the frontispiece of Richard Grafton's *Chronicle at Large* (1569), in the margins of which a party of ancient British leaders faces a Jewish one. Such popular Tudor compilations as Cooper's Chronicle use the same twin structure, and even Holinshed's work would have included a universal element had not the bulk of British material restricted it to its eventual (far from modest) proportions.[17] Given the fact that Arthur and Guyon read their histories concurrently, the match with the practice of popular chronicle histories

---

[15] See Adler, *Time Immemorial*, 2.

[16] For a description and analysis of the frontispiece see Sir Walter Ralegh, *The History of the World*, ed. C. A. Patrides (Philadelphia: Temple University Press, 1971), p. xv, in which see also 'Introduction'. On the difference between Ralegh and earlier chroniclers in this regard see Kelly, *Divine Providence*, 301.

[17] On the development of Holinshed's work see Vernon Snow's introduction to *Holinshed's Chronicles*, ed. Henry Ellis (London: J. Johnson, 1807; repr. New York: AMS Press, 1979), i. p. i.

is a close one. Even the peculiar shift in the last two stanzas of the Fairy Chronicle from mythical emperors to a set of analogues for Tudor monarchs (Henry VII, Henry VIII, and Elizabeth) is reminiscent of Grafton's practice. In the *Chronicle at Large* the emphasis on the English strand increases as one progresses further into the work until the reigns of the Tudor monarchs (three of whom we would recognize as the fairies '*Elficleos*', '*Oberon*', and '*Tanaquill*') take up the last third leaving virtually no room for rival narratives.[18] Like the Briton and Fairy Chronicles, national and universal histories come together at their points of closure. The frontispiece of Grafton's work illustrates this point perfectly: for, at its foot, the separate lines of Judaic and Briton kings meet at the figure of Elizabeth Regent.

To those well versed in the practices of Elizabethan history writing, the double narration of Canto x must have been reasonably familiar. The fact that Guyon's narrative in large part concerns goblins and fairies would have complicated matters, but not to an impossible degree. The suggestiveness of the chronicle's opening on Prometheus followed by the garden-dwelling Elfe and Fay must have strengthened the sense that Fairyland was in some ways a land of types: a place in which figures from the everyday world, including those from history, found their equivalent.[19] Perhaps time moved more slowly there and some of the dross of everyday life was missing.[20] In essence, however, this was a shadowy version of the world around us. To give that world its own early history was a provocative twist. For it makes the Fairy Chronicle a nebulous version of history that was itself already very cloudy.

As with the Briton Chronicle, Spenser is here concerned with the interlaced demands of poetry and history. Elfin, the Fairy monarch who ruled India and America (II. x. 72. 4–6), corresponds in some way to the ancient King Osyris. The great ruler of those territories always made an appearance near the beginning of Renaissance universal histories, and he

---

[18] See Grafton, *Chronicle at Large*, 853–1369. Cooper's coverage, whilst remaining even-handed for longer, also concludes with a strong emphasis on English history.

[19] McCabe (*Pillars*, 91–103) provides an overview of opinion on the nature of Spenser's Fairyland and offers the conclusion that Fairyland is a 'land of "types"' (p. 100). See also Michael J. Murrin's entry in A. C. Hamilton (ed.), *The Spenser Encyclopedia* (Toronto: University of Toronto Press, 1990), 296–8.

[20] A typical example of a tale employing this double time-scheme is *The Romance and Prophecies of Thomas of Erceldoune*, ed. James A. H. Murray (London: Early Modern Text Society, 1875). The notion is clearly of relevance to much of *The Faerie Queene*, including Redcrosse's encounter with early history in the Eden Lands of Book I.

cuts a very similar figure in the 'rolles of Elfin Emperours'.[21] Yet Elfin is clearly also a literary fiction. Spenser had thus taken a king supposedly recovered from 'poets fables', only to mytholgize him once more as a Fairy emperor. If the Canto was composed with half an eye on the historiographically literate audience of the Leicester House circle, then Spenser's obscure games with the obscurities of history would not have gone unappreciated.

As with all pagan histories, the beginning and the end of the Fairy Chronicle is easy enough to decode as accepted history. The opening of Hesiod's *Theogony* or Ovid's *Metamorphoses* offered comforting echoes of the creation account in Genesis.[22] Similarly, Elfe and Fay as authors of all man- and womankind, are undeniably parallels for Adam and Eve, and Tanaquill (who reigns 'this howre') must stand for Elizabeth. The middle portion is, however, characteristically difficult and partial. Whilst suggestive correspondences exist, they are never entirely comforting. Many of Spenser's Fairy emperors seem to be deliberately insoluble puzzles. It is hard, for example, to imagine any of Spenser's contemporaries finding an undisputed candidate for the identity of Elfinor. This emperor, we are told, 'was in Magick skild' and 'built by art vpon the glassy See | A bridge of bras, whose sound heauens thunder seem'd to bee' (II. x. 73. 7–9). Read allegorically the bridge across the sea, in combination with the 'three sonnes' also mentioned (II. x. 74. 1), might suggest Brutus, who crossed the ocean to found his empire in Britain. Rathborne did indeed make this suggestion, but it is difficult to make this logic stick in detail, and Yates (to Rathborne's satisfaction) subsequently changed this identification to Constantine II.[23] That king too had three sons and—in Yates's view—the 'bridge of bras' should consequently be understood as an idealized (and allegorical) London Bridge symbolizing the King's defence against paganism. Through an extended series of

---

[21] Rathborne (*Meaning*, 108–11), Frances A. Yates, 'The Elfin Chronicle', *Times Literary Supplement*, 3 July 1948, 373, T. D. Kendrick, 'The Elfin Chronicle', *Times Literary Supplement*, 7 February 1948, 79, and Hamilton (*Faerie Queene*, 271n.) all suggest Osyris, or a composite of Osyris and Hercules or Bacchus; the point stands regardless of the specific identification.

[22] The *Metamorphoses*, in its description of the division of the elements, its suggestion that a divine creature may have created man from earth, and its account of a golden age provided a rich source for euhemeristic reading. The *Theogony*'s older account was a great deal more violent, but with the right kind of filtration was still used as a source for such readings. Apollodurus's *The Library* offered a later synthesis of these and other sources.

[23] Rathborne, *Meaning*, 119; Yates, 'Elfin Chronicle', 373. For a response see Isabell E. Rathborne, 'The Elfin Chronicle', *The Times Literary Supplement*, 24 April 1948, 233.

hypotheses and adjustments, similar historical candidates have been found for all Spenser's Fairy monarchs.

In a process remarkably similar to that which created the universal chronicle in the first place, commentators have turned Spenser's abstruse poetical imaginings into a neat chronology of ancient kings. The poet, one suspects, would have been pleased with these interpretative endeavours. Without acknowledging it, Yates and Rathborne themselves made full use of the armoury of euhemerism. Indeed, their faith in the underlying coherence of the chronicle was remarkably similar to that of the universal historians in relation to *their* primary texts. Determined in their belief that the Fairy Chronicle must shadow another, both were willing to overlook gaps in the chronology or explain away inconvenient detail. Such thinking had always played a central role in the creation of universal histories, a process that involved filtering out irrelevant material, matching similar names, dates, places, or stories, as well as the use of allegorical interpretation.[24] It is above all to this last mode that the commentators on the Fairy Chronicle have recourse: so that (in the case of Elfar) a triumph over a two-headed giant can stand for victories against Maxentius and Licinius, and the defeat of a three-headed giant equate to the destruction of pagan religion.[25]

The Fairy Chronicle both invites and exposes such reading strategies. For in the seven cantos of fairy history the poet produced a narrative so brilliantly obscure yet suggestive that it appears designed to set earnest chronographers scrambling for their time charts. In the *History of the World* Ralegh was to speak with genuine ire about the fables of the poets. Spenser as 'Poet historical' is less absolute about the role assigned to him. In Eumnestes's chamber he both erects and dismantles such fables. With a new generation of scholars radically shifting the ground of the old universal history, such an approach must have been especially appealing.[26] Spenser's riddling Fairy Chronicle gives shape to a providential vision of history while at the same time foregrounding the inter-

[24] See Adler, *Time Immemorial*, 4.

[25] Rathborne, 'Elfin Chronicle', 233.

[26] From their first publication in 1498 the forgeries and euhemeristic commentaries of Joannes Annius Viterbensis had been the subject of scepticism. Walter Stephens, in *Giants in Those Days: Folklore, Ancient History, and Nationalism* (Lincoln, Nebr.: University of Nebraska Press, 1989), 100–38, provides a useful summary of the pseudo-Berossus. In 1583 Scaliger had published *De Emendatione Temporum*—a revolutionary critique that demanded a major reassessment of received ideas about ancient chronology. For a detailed study see Antony Grafton, *Joseph Scaliger: A Study in the History of Classical Scholarship*, ii. *Historical Chronology*, 2 vols. (Oxford: Clarendon Press, 1983–93); and also Adler, *Time Immemorial*, 4–6; 23; 234.

pretative process that allows it to emerge. In such circumstances the writing and reading of allegory begin to overlap.

Revealing Fables in The Faerie Queene, Book V

In Eumnestes's chamber we find the Briton Chronicle running in parallel with events in Fairyland that dimly shadow the grand narrative put forward by the universal historian. That narrative was one of ongoing struggle against incivility and of great heroes battling against lawlessness. The same pattern is also to be found in Book V of Spenser's poem. In the second half of the Legend of Justice we find episodes that allude to British conquests as well as to an older, more nebulous, world history. Set against the exigencies of national politics we have the unceasing drive of the forces of order. Specifically, we find the achievements of English foreign policy set in tandem with those of the greatest hero of universal history: Hercules. The respective virtues of Books II and V (Temperance and Justice) go some way towards explaining this analogy.[27] Both Temperance and Justice counter what might be called 'natural' tendencies towards unruliness: those within the body, and those within the body politic. These tendencies are articulated especially strongly at the formation of civic society. Perhaps as a consequence, both books have proems that focus on the analogy between present and antique history. In the seventh canto of each, moreover, we find a complex allegorical episode involving a deity (Mammon of wealth, Isis of equity) again concerning the nature of the earliest times.[28] Temperance (it is clear from the cave of Mammon) is an antique virtue threatened by the material 'progress' of civilization. Justice (as is clear from the initial description of Isis Church) is similarly ancient, and again threatened by the decay of time. While in one sense history seemed to record an ongoing struggle against the wild and the lawless, on the other it could appear to be a process of ceaseless decline. Those twin perspectives were evident in Classical accounts (Ovid had written mournfully of mining that delved 'into the very bowels of the earth') and also found their way into Christian universal chronicles such as

---

[27] On this and other patterns of correspondence between the books see James Nohrnberg, *The Analogy of The Faerie Queene* (Princeton: Princeton University Press, 1976), pp. xi and 261–81.

[28] On Mammon as an antique figure marking a break with the Golden Age, see Cynthia Collins, 'The Golden Age and the Iron Age of Gold: The Inversion of Paradise in the Cave of Mammon', *Comitatus*, 20 (1989), 43–58.

Ralegh's.[29] In the legends of temperance and justice we feel their presence strongly.

The universal narrative gestured at in Guyon's chronicle looms large in Book V of Spenser's epic. At its start we hear of Saturn's ancient reign (V. Proem. 9), the departure of Astraea (V. i. 11), the war between Jove and the Titans (V. i. 9), and the conquests of Bacchus and Hercules (V. i. 2). All these had a place in the euhemeristic account of early world history, and all were linked specifically to the establishment of justice. Ralegh relates how Adam came to be called Saturn (*History*, 73) and how his time in paradise was one before the need of law. The departure of Astraea (on which Ralegh quotes Ovid) allegorically figured the disappearance of justice as 'a vertue abstract' (p. 73).[30] The Titan's assault on heaven (again related by means of verse quotation) corresponds to the Tower of Babel, by which man 'would have given the Law to Heaven it selfe' (p. 74).[31] Finally, in the ensuing triumphs of Bacchus and Hercules, Ralegh sees the defeat of a number of earthly tyrannies and the establishment of just princely rule (p. 77).[32] In these readings Ralegh was following in a tradition that had run throughout the sixteenth century and indeed many centuries before. Such figures appear at the beginning of Book V not simply as Classical exempla—they are there as joining points between moral and political allegory.

For the intersection between history and allegory functioned in a double sense by way of euhemerism. First, mythical figures could be read as direct moral allegory—their actions or characters being inter-

[29] See Ovid, *Metamorphoses*, ed. and trans. Frank Justus Miller, 3rd edn., rev. G. Goold, in *Ovid*, 6 vols., Loeb Classical Library (Cambridge, Mass.: Harvard University Press, 1977; repr. 1999), iii. 12, l. 138. This passage records the invention of all kinds of modern technology—such as sailing—as a marker of decline. A similar perspective is found in Hesiod, *The Works and Days*, in *The Homeric Hymns and Homerica*, trans. Hugh G. Evelyn-White, Loeb Classical Library (Cambridge, Mass.: Harvard University Press, 1914; repr. 1982), 12–16, ll. 140–78. Both accounts are important for the universal scope of Book V as discussed below. Such accounts could easily be matched, for example, with declines in life-span and stature recorded in Genesis.

[30] On the departure of Astraea as a watershed dividing existence *ante legem* and *sub lege* see Donald Cheney, *Spenser's Image of Nature: Wild Man and Shepherd in 'The Faerie Queene'* (New Haven: Yale University Press, 1966), 160.

[31] Ralegh, like Spenser and many other Renaissance writers, is not consistent about the distinction between 'Titans' and 'giants' which, in Classical mythology, belong to different generations. On the general lack of clarity in using these words see Starnes and Talbert, *Classical Myth*, 74.

[32] For Ralegh and Spenser alike the establishment of law and monarchy are strongly linked. The connection is set out in *Faerie Queene* V. Proem. 10. It is reinforced as Spenser tells us that under Bacchus 'Iustice first her *princely* rule begonne' and that through Hercules 'Iustice dread, with *kingly* powre endewed' (V. i. 2. 5 and V. i. 2. 9, emphasis mine).

preted as abstract qualities. When Spenser consulted Renaissance classical dictionaries on the matter he would have found such associations set out with clarity. Second, the legends could be decoded as allegory in a different sense: veiling the actions of men who were once true enforcers of justice—traversing continents, putting down tyrannies, and establishing just rule. This too was an element set out in the scholarly manuals. The fact that these two kinds of allegory sit happily alongside one another in the commentaries reflects the accretive disorder of these collections, but it also says something about their vision of universal coherence. In a process that has something in common with the four-fold interpretation of scripture, secular history could bear a complex, if rickety, system of analogies.[33] An active engagement with that system allows the reader of Book V to transform what is sometimes considered a rather flat narrative into a text that is three- or even four-dimensional.

Spenser's interest in the allegories that history writes comes to the surface at a number of points in the Legend of Justice. To begin with, in Canto vii we hear of Osyris, the figure to whom Spenser alluded in the Fairy Chronicle under the name of Elfin. He appears here as the husband of Isis (whose temple is visited by Britomart). Osyris is typical in his twinned significance. In moral readings he was commonly seen as a figure for justice, and in historical ones he was read as the father of Hercules (in Cooper's Chronicle, for example, it is the murder of King Osyris that drives Hercules to begin his conquests).[34] There could scarcely be a more exemplary figure for the operation of euhemerism: Polidore Vergil's *De Inventoribus* had fixed specifically on Osyris in its opening disquisition on the process of decoding early history.[35] Before describing events at Isis Church, Spenser himself reflects upon this process of creating allegory. 'Nought is', he tells us, 'on earth more

---

[33] On the fourfold interpretation of scripture see Bruce M. Metzger and Michael D. Coogan, *The Oxford Companion to the Bible* (Oxford: Oxford University Press, 1993), 305–24. Other studies, notably Darryl J. Gless's *Interpretation and Theology in Spenser* (Cambridge: Cambridge University Press, 1994) have shown the complex interaction between scripture, biblical prophecy, and secular history in Book I of *The Faerie Queene*. For a study of the relationship between the political allegory of Book V and the divine allegory of Revelation, see Kenneth Borris, *Spenser's Poetics of Prophecy in The Faerie Queene V*, ELS Monograph Series, 52 (Victoria, BC: University of Victoria Press, 1990).

[34] Thomas Cooper, *An Epitome of Chronicles* (1559), fols. 21ᵇ–22ᵃ.

[35] *De Inventoribus*, 29. In addition to the moral and historical, there was also a tradition of reading Classical myth in terms of physical phenomena. Spenser is equally attuned to the physical significance of Osyris as a figure for the sun, mentioning it at V. vii. 4. 8. Plutarch ('Of Isis and Osiris', 23) had rejected the euhemeristic decoding of these deities (see McCabe, *Pillars*, 113).

sacred or diuine . . . Then this same vertue, that doth right define' (V. vii.
1. 1–3):

> Well therefore did the antique world inuent,
>   That Iustice was a God of soueraine grace,
>   And altars vnto him, and temples lent,
>   And heauenly honours in the highest place;
>   Calling him great *Osyris*, of the race
>   Of th'old Ægyptial Kings, that whylome were;
>   With fayned colours shading a true case:
>   For that *Osyris*, whilest he liued here,
> The iustest man aliue, and truest did appeare.　(V. vii. 2)

Spenser discovers both moral and historical allegory in the story of the
poet—beginning his stanza with an ethical abstraction and ending it with
an actual monarch. (The ancient world invented a god to figure justice;
but it also shaded a real historical figure in the shape of that god.) With
nicely balanced half-seriousness, Spenser ascribes to time itself a kind of
poetic sensibility. Antiquity shades 'cunningly' with 'fayned colours', just
as the poet of the present age depicts justice by what some consider a
'painted forgery' (II. Proem. 1. 4).

Isis Church is an exemplary site for the action of allegory. Not only
does it illustrate the ways in which the antique world has come down to
the Elizabethan reader in the form of a 'double allegory', it also allows
Spenser himself to shape a dark conceit (constituting both a moral allegory about the nature of justice, and a historical one about the Briton
dynasty).[36] In a manner characteristic of the whole of *The Faerie Queene*,
fictions and histories intertwine to the point where they become almost
inseparable. To cap the point, at the end of the canto we find that
Britomart, having received instruction at the Temple, herself becomes
both a practitioner and a deity of justice. The slippage from adored
monarch to imagined god that underlies euhemerism is here played out
in Spenser's fiction. After defeating Radigund, Britomart temporarily
takes over the Amazon kingdom 'During which space she there as
Princess rained' (V. vii. 42. 3). In repealing the liberty of women 'and

---

[36] For representative readings of the temple's moral and historical allegory see Frank
Kermode, *Shakespeare, Spenser, Donne* (London: Routledge & Kegan Paul, 1971), 55–6, and
Angus Fletcher, *The Prophetic Moment: An Essay on Spenser* (Chicago: University of Chicago Press,
1971), 277, respectively. On the practice of 'double allegory' see Rosemond Tuve, *Allegorical
Imagery: Some Mediaeval Books and their Posterity* (Princeton: Princeton University Press, 1966),
106–7.

them restoring | To mens subiection' Spenser declares she 'did true Iustice deale':

> That all they as a Goddesse her adoring,
> Her wisedome did admire, and hearkned to her loring.   (V. vii. 42. 8–9)

In a line that includes a typical Spenserian pun we move from law to folklore and from justice to divinity.[37] In the Proem to the fifth book, too, we have had that progression. For having considered the 'soueraine powre' (V. Proem. 10. 3) of justice Spenser turns to address his own queen as a 'Dread Souerayne Goddesse' (V. Proem. 11. 1). The poet is speaking metaphorically—this, however, is a metaphor with a history.

In the action that follows we find Spenser repeatedly concerned with such overlapping allegories: those that the present poet writes, and those that we can read from the old stories. Hercules in particular is an insistent presence throughout the legend of justice. Many of the actions of Book V's central protagonists (Artegall and Arthur) have a Herculean parallel.[38] In this Spenser made an apt choice, as for generations the trials of Hercules had been read allegorically as the triumphs of virtue.[39] In the *Mythologiae* of Natale Conti (a book the poet certainly used) the story of the demigod's deeds is approached as a kind of collective poetic enterprise. 'To show that wisdom is the gift of God', Conti tells us, the ancients 'imagined that the son of Jove was Hercules, who represents fortitude, probity and a greatness of spirit conquering over all vices'.[40] Conti interprets a series of violent encounters in this way as victories against 'those gravest of monsters pride, wrath, arrogance and fury of mind' (p. 371).

As with other Classical myths, however, the notion that the Herculean narrative encoded abstract moral lessons sat alongside the idea that it also hid one-time physical realities. In Cooper's Chronicle we find that

---

[37] Spenser's pun cannot be on 'folklore' itself (a word that did not appear until the 19th cent.) but instead connects 'law' as statute and 'lore' as instruction.

[38] For an extensive examination of the place of Hercules in Book V see T. K. Dunseath, *Spenser's Allegory of Justice in the 'Faerie Queene' V* (Princeton: Princeton University Press, 1968) and also Jane Aptekar, *Icons of Justice: Iconography and Thematic Imagery in Book V of 'The Faerie Queene'* (New York: Columbia University Press, 1969).

[39] Allegorical interpretations of Hercules's labours can be traced back to pre-Christian times. For a survey, see G. Karl Galinsky, *The Herakles Theme: The Adaptations of the Hero in Literature from Homer to the Twentieth Century* (Oxford: Basil Blackwell, 1972), esp. 206–11, on Spenser. On the poet's 'Herculean displacements' see also Patrick J. Cook, *Milton, Spenser, and the Epic Tradition* (Aldershot: Scholar, 1996).

[40] Natale Conti, *Mythologies*, trans. Anthony Dimatteo (London: Garland, 1994), 371.

the story of the labours is read allegorically to reveal not moral but historical truths. Here, as in other Early Modern chronicles, the actions of what is distinguished as the Libyan Hercules are recounted as those of a successful martial hero who conquers various recalcitrant peoples. Thus:

> Herculus Lybius, the sonne of Osyris, and moste valiant capitain of his warres, for to be revenged of his fathers deth, toke his armour, and slue bothe the Typhons, one in Aegipt, the other in Phrigia, and also distroied Busyris in Phenicia, Antheus in Lybia, Milinus in Candie, Lestrigones in Italye, the Geryones in Spayne. After whiche victories he substituted Hispalus kynge of Spayne . . . Finally, after many notable actes by hym done, he deceased veraie aged amonge the Spaniardes, nigh to the Gades, where he was buried in a temple dedicated to him with divine honoures.
>
> (Thomas Cooper, *An Epitome of Chronicles* (1559), fols. 21^v–22^r)

Cooper's progression from hero to emperor and on to divine being neatly illustrates the logic of euhemerism. Geryon, the giant from whom Hercules took the red kine, has become a Spanish tyrant supplanted in order to form a new just government. This approach is entirely characteristic of the other Tudor world histories: so much so that this passage, which was originally composed by Lanquet, was to be absorbed wholesale into Grafton's *Chronicle at Large*. The story of the anti-tyrannical conquests of the Libyan Hercules spanned the whole of Europe. Even features of the landscape bore his name.[41] As Spenser wrote of what he considered England's anti-tyrannical wars on the same European territory the historical overlap could not have failed to register either with the poet or his audience.

In a number of incidents in Book V we find Spenser appealing directly to this Herculean paradigm. In Canto x, for example, Arthur encounters the dreadful three-bodied giant Geryoneo who has taken advantage of the defenceless lady Belge and her seventeen sons:

> But this fell Tyrant, through his tortious powre,
>   Had left her now but fiue of all that brood:
>   For twelue of them he did by times deuoure,
>   And to his Idols sacrifice their blood,
>   Whylest he of none was stopped, nor withstood.
>   For soothly he was one of matchlesse might,

---

[41] See e.g. Daniel Woolf, 'Of Danes and Giants: Popular Beliefs about the Past in Early Modern England', *Dalhousie Review*, 71 (1991), 166–209 (183).

Of horrible aspect, and dreadfull mood,
    And had three bodies in one wast empight,
And th'armes and legs of three, to succour him in fight.

And sooth they say, that he was borne and bred
    Of Gyants race, the sonne of *Geryon*,
    He that whylome in Spaine so sore was dred,
    For his huge powre and great oppression,
    Which brought that land to his subiection,
    Through his three bodies powre, in one combynd;
    And eke all strangers in that region
    Arryuing, to his kyne for food assynd;
The fayrest kyne aliue, but of the fiercest kynd.

For they were all, they say, of purple hew,
    Kept by a cowheard, hight *Eurytion*,
    A cruell carle, the which all strangers slew,
    Ne day nor night did sleepe, t'attend them on,
    But walkt about them euer and anone,
    With his two headed dogge, that *Orthrus* hight;
    Orthrus begotten by great *Typhaon*,
    And foule *Echidna*, in the house of night;
But *Hercules* them all did ouercome in fight.

His sonne was this, *Geryoneo* hight,
    Who after that his monstrous father fell
    Vnder *Alcides* club, streight tooke his flight
    From that sad land, where he his syre did quell,
    And came to this, where *Belge* then did dwell,
    And flourish in all wealth and happinesse,
    Being then new made widow (as befell)
    After her Noble husbands late decesse;
Which gaue beginning to her woe and wretchednesse.   (V. x. 8–11)

Spenser here does a fascinating thing: wrapping his own myth around an older one and in the process revealing the kinds of writing and reading that make up his text. In these four stanzas the poet creates a personal syncretism in which the ancient tale of Hercules is grafted to a contemporary political allegory. The stories that he gives us interpenetrate in a curious two-way movement: the one gives us Spenser's new myth of a monstrous tyrant of Spain (the hated King Philip); the other gives us an ancient myth that hides a similar story. In the light of the historical and moral reading of Hercules, these narratives open one another up. On the one hand—when coloured by the Geryon episode—Spenser's allegory of Philip II gains a new mythic splendour: a monstrous triple three-bodied creature that subtly combines tyranny with theological absurdity. On the other—when placed alongside the realities of Continental politics—the Geryon myth can itself be decoded in the opposite direction. Set beside Spenser's new allegory this giant body with monstrous arms can now be seen as a transformation of history—a once true story, played out on the same terrain, which time and poets have changed 'with fayned colours painting a true case'.

As Spenser's reader progresses through these four stanzas he or she is confronted with a series of alternative allegories: moral and historical, past and present. Stanzas 9 and 10 offer a literalized version of Geryoneo's literary genealogy. In doing so they present not just an old story but also an old double allegory. Spenser's fiction thus forges connections between ancient times and present ones, between moral quandaries and political realities. Like the Briton and Fairy Chronicles, the English and universal aspects of Spenser's allegory strive towards synthesis. The ancient struggle is like today's; the moral struggle is like the political one. As the reader progresses through Book V and finds that the events depicted shadow both recent history and ancient myth, he or she is invited to find in Philip II a kind of Geryon and in Geryon a kind of Philip II.

Giants, Real and Allegorical

That Geryoneo is a complex allegorical creation is clear. From where that creation ultimately stems is altogether more nebulous. In one sense, of course, the giant is merely Spenser's fiction: a representation of what the poet understands as the tyranny of Spanish rule in the Low Countries. As we have seen, that representation had its roots in ancient myths, and, at least according to the logic of euhemerism, those myths themselves shadowed a more prosaic history. The ancients had corrupted the truth about the past to the point it had become monstrous, and the story of Geryon was literally one of those tall tales. All the same, even this did not prove that the physical bulk of Hercules's enemy was necessarily the creation of over-enthusiastic poets. If Geryon had in reality been a tyrant, this did not preclude his having been a giant as well. The two propositions might sit rather well together. Arguably, the giant's bulk was allegorical only as a physical reality that was authored by a moral God.

Certainly, Sir Walter Ralegh, who vehemently insisted on the record 'without all allegorical construction' of giants in early history, felt that there was a logical connection between literal giantism and tyranny.[42] Dismissing the 'superlative strayning of words' of those who held ancient giants to be mere allegories, he argued that historians 'might with better reason call them Oppressors, because they were Giants; and therefore had ability to oppresse, then say, That they were called Giants only, because Oppressors' (*History*, 70). The author of *The History of the World* was far from being alone in this opinion. In Spenser's lifetime the majority of historians took the one-time existence of giants seriously. The well-known 'Description of Britain' that opened Holinshed's *Chronicles* of 1587, for example, included a chapter examining 'Whether it be likelie that any giants were, and whether they inhabited in this Ile or not' which pronounced firmly in favour of both propositions.[43] Belief in the one-time existence of genuinely massive giants continued throughout the sixteenth, seventeenth, and even eighteenth centuries.[44] Far from being an unexamined hangover that belief was often the result of reasoned scholarly enquiry. Surprisingly, the Renaissance antiquarian movement in some ways strengthened the case for their existence. The examination of supposed remains, the medical description of giantism in the present-day generation, and the rationalistic unpicking of Classical legend all went to raise their intellectual (if not physical) stature. *A View of the Present State of Ireland*'s dismissal of stories concerning 'olde Geauntes Trivetes' does not in itself imply disbelief in the accounts of ancient giants.[45] Even at the very end of the seventeenth century antiquarians who refuted popular opinion about the origins of Ireland's 'Giants Causeway' could nevertheless accept supposed palaeontological evidence for their existence.[46]

---

[42] Ralegh, *History*, 82.

[43] Holinshed, *Chronicles*, i. 8. Harrison's essay therein is largely directed against the *Gigantomachia* of Goropius (1512–78), which had questioned the existence of giants. Jean de Chassanion's *De Gigantibus* (Basle, 1580) was probably the most significant treatise supporting the genuine existence of giants written in Spenser's lifetime, and a likely influence on Harrison as well as Ralegh.

[44] See Jean Céard, 'La Querelle des géants et la jeunesse du monde', *The Journal of Medieval and Renaissance Studies*, 8 (1978), 37–76; Antoine Schnapper, 'Persistance des géants', *Annales ESC* 41 (1986), 177–200; Ferguson, 'A Digression on Giants', *Utter Antiquity*, 106–13, and Walter Stephens, *Giants in Those Days: Folklore, Ancient History, and Nationalism* (Lincoln, Nebr.: University of Nebraska Press, 1989). As the last of these notes, even at the end of the 19th cent., the *Encyclopaedia Britannica* (1887) examined the debate from both sides and declined to give an absolute verdict.

[45] *View*, 131. McCabe, *Pillars*, 43, feels that in this passage giants are dismissed as 'ymaginacions'.

[46] See Thomas Molyneux, 'Some Notes upon the Foregoing Account of the Giants

The subjects of these accounts were not the creatures of pageantry and folktales—vast monsters who had supposedly thrown mountains or made gashes still to be seen in the landscape.[47] At around three times average human height, the giants in whom men like Harrison and Ralegh believed could function within society.[48] Indeed this role within the body politic made them all the more significant from a historical point of view. Most persuasive of all, in this as in other respects, was the biblical evidence. The antediluvian account in Genesis reported that 'there were giants in the earth in those days; and also after that, when the sons of God came in unto the daughters of men, and they bare children to them, the same became mighty men which were of old, men of renown'.[49] Crucially this passage was often liked to the ensuing report of Nimrod the founder of Babel. In this reading the first founder of tyranny could be seen as a giant.[50] In Ralegh's work and elsewhere giants (especially Nimrod) are seen as key players in the overthrow of patriarchy and perhaps even the establishment of kingship.[51] Especially in the light of more literal Protestant interpretation of scripture the giant remained a solid presence in accounts of early history.

This prosaic insistence on the reality of giants in the Early Modern historical imagination greatly extends the scope of Spenser's Legend of Justice.[52] Giants today stand almost as metonymy for fiction. The

Causway', *Philosophical Transactions*, 18 (1694), 175–82 (176), and 'An Essay concerning Giants,' *Philosophical Transactions*, 22 (1700), 487–508. The latter, after examining a fragment of skull, confirms that 'it appears there have been truly Gigantick Bodies, twice or more surpassing the usual size of Men . . . confirming the truth of several Passages in Holy Writ, where there is mention made of Giants' (p. 488).

[47] On this popular tradition see Suzan Stewart, *On Longing: Narratives of the Miniature, the Gigantic, the Souvenir, the Collection* (Baltimore: Johns Hopkins University Press, 1984), 70–103, and also F. W. Fairholt, *Gog and Magog: The Giants in Guildhall* (London: John Camden Hotten, 1859), which gives an extensive description of the festive role of giants in Spenser's day.

[48] Harrison's description of giants in Holinshed's *Chronicles*, i. 8–12, calculates most giants at between 12 and 18 feet.

[49] Genesis 6: 4. Postdiluvian giants are mentioned at Numbers 13: 28–34, Deuteronomy 3: 11, 1 Samuel 17: 4, and 2 Samuel 21: 16–20.

[50] Nimrod's status as giant is not clear-cut in the biblical account, but universal historians (who tended to see him as the first monarch) generally agreed that this is what he had been.

[51] See Ralegh, *History*, esp. 74, 159–63, and 185. On the link between giants, monarchy, and tyranny see also, Adler, *Time Immemorial*, 114–29. Ralegh wisely does not commit himself on the relation between giantism and kingship, but (writing in prison under sentence of death from King James) the connections that others had drawn may have occurred to him.

[52] This argument has been forwarded in Roger O. Iredale's excellent essay 'Giants and Tyrants in Book Five of *The Faerie Queene*', *Review of English Studies*, NS 17 (1966), 373–81. This piece looks at all Book V's giants and draws to the fore a proportion of the material examined in the following paragraphs.

position in the sixteenth and seventeenth centuries was different but not diametrically opposite. Giants did not necessarily signify the fabulous, but nor did their physical reality preclude a fictional or symbolic significance. In the assessment of Saint Augustine, the Old Testament Giants were created as a kind of living allegory—alike in their physical and moral enormities.[53] They provided a prime example of the way in which a divinely authored history inscribed moral lessons. These great figures had fallen through their overweening pride and lust. As a result, they set a telling precedent for all would-be tyrants.

If giants provided lively parallels for the current age, they also served to highlight the distance between theirs and the present time. For Augustine and Ralegh alike, the evidence that giants were abundant in the first age and less so by the third and fourth provided additional proof for the teleology that lay at the heart of their great projects: the world had seen the excesses of superabundant youth just as it might now be suffering the extremities of a decrepit old age.[54] This idea was most spectacularly adopted in Simon Forman's manuscript 'Booke of Giantes and Huge and Monstrouse Formes' which described a rapid decline from Adam's daughters (at an astounding 1,020 feet) to Cham (at 900), Gogmagog (at 200), and Sir Lancelot (at a mere 14 feet).[55] Though this thesis stood on the lunatic fringe of giantology, it was built upon mainstream assumptions about changes in the nature of time. Here again there were reassuring parallels in ancient mythology, in which the notion of a golden age sat alongside stories of the vast monstrous creations of the earliest days.[56] Biblical giants symbolized the vitality of the first age whilst at the same time their strength and primitive desires seem to have been important factors in its deterioration. In them was encapsulated one of the key paradoxes that concerned Spenser over the course of *The Faerie Queene*: the fact that 'progress' towards civility was at the same time

---

[53] Augustine, *De Civitate Dei* 15. 23, cited in Stephens, *Giants*, 75. For an excellent examination of this divine and historical allegory in the case of Orgoglio see S. K. Heninger, Jr., 'The Orgoglio Episode in *The Faerie Queene*', *ELH*, 26 (1959), 171–87.

[54] The decline in height and longevity from the first age is forwarded by Augustine, *De Civ. Dei* 15. 8.

[55] For details see Bodleian MS Ashmole. 244, fols. 192–9, and also Bodleian MS Ashmole 802.

[56] The complex conjunction of Christian Millennialist thought with Classical golden age mythology is examined by Harry Levin, *The Golden Age and the Renaissance*, in Carroll Camden (ed.), *Literary Views: Critical and Historical Essays*, Rice University Semicentennial Publications (Chicago: University of Chicago Press, 1964), Levin, *The Myth of the Golden Age in the Renaissance* (Bloomington: Indiana University Press, 1969), and Frances A. Yates, *Astraea: The Imperial Theme in the Sixteenth Century* (London: Routledge & Kegan Paul, 1975), 29–87.

'degeneration' from an ideal state.[57] The figure of Astraea offers this double perspective very effectively. She is the embodiment of a golden age justice who finds a type in Elizabeth. Yet in her abandonment of the earth Astraea is also an emblem of earthly decline. The Proem to Book V subtly holds these two possibilities in suspension. Hercules thus provides an ennobling model for Spenser's questing knights, but in contrast to the Geryon conflict Elizabethan skirmishes on Belgian soil can also feel Lilliputian.

All these associations are pertinent to the understanding of Book V's giants. From the height of Canto ii's egalitarian giant there is even a kind of internal degeneration in the legend. The last of Book V's giants is also the smallest and most transparently contemporary of these figures. In Grantorto the political, allegorical, and even racial aspects of the giant are all in evidence. Artegall's final adversary strongly recalls the native Irish in his dress and weaponry, but he is equally reminiscent of the tyrants that Hercules faces in the universal chronicles.[58] Grantorto is:

> All armed in cote of yron plate,
> Of great defence to ward the deadly feare,
> And on his head a steele cap he did weare
> Of colour rustie browne, but sure and strong;
> And in his hand an huge Polaxe did beare,
> Whose steale was yron studded, but not long,
> With which he wont to fight, to iustifie his wrong.

> Of stature huge and hideous he was,
>   Like to a Giant for his monstrous hight,
>   And did in strength most sorts of men surpas,
>   Ne euer any found his match in might;
>   Thereto he had great skill in single fight:
>   His face was vngly, and his countenance sterne,
>   That could have frayd one with his very sight,
>   And gaped like a gulfe, when he did gerne,
> That whether man or monster one could scarse discerne.

> (V. xii. 14. 3–15. 9)

One can 'scarse' find the human in Grantorto, but it is ultimately

---

[57] The debate is held e.g. between Guyon and Mamon at *Faerie Queene* II. vii as well as in the Proem to Book V.

[58] For evidence of—less canonical—legends that Hercules had also faced Irish giants, see H. J. Massingham, *Fee, Fi, Fo, Fum; or The Giants in England*, Psyche Miniatures, 5 (London: Kegan Paul, Trench, Trubner, 1926), 67.

there. He is 'huge' but not too huge—he could not weigh the world in a balance as the giant with scales in Canto ii threatens, and he is without the multiple limbs of his immediate predecessor Geryoneo. Like the biblical giants after the flood he dominates most men, but is also a part of their society. As Artegall lands on Grantorto's territory he encounters for the first time 'Great hostes of men in order martiall' (V. xii. 4. 8). The giant calls on 'scouts' (V. xii. 6. 8), makes use of a 'Herauld' (V. xii. 8. 5), and issues commands to the local population (V. xii. 10. 3). He has sometimes been seen as a limp climax—matching neither the stature nor the complexity of a giant like Book I's Orgoglio.[59] From a historical point of view, however, the economy of Spenser's description has its own rewards. Had the poet wished to depict a genuine ancient giant he could hardly have done so more convincingly. Unlike Orgoglio his stature does not seem 'to threat the skye' (I. vii. 8. 5), nor does he use a primitive 'snaggy Oke' (I. vii. 10. 7) for a weapon. Instead he more closely resembles the biblical Goliath in dress and proportions. This giant wore 'an helmet of brass upon his head, and he was armed with a coat of mail . . . the staff of his spear was like a weaver's beam; and his spear's head weighed six hundred shekels of iron'.[60] Like Grantorto, and like the rest of the Old Testament giants, he stands as part of an oppressive army. As Spenser brings his allegory closer to the surface-detail of sixteenth-century conflicts he simultaneously narrows the gap between them and these ancient but, to him, analogous battles. The rust on Grantorto's armour, too, neatly connects the ugliness of contemporary Irish warfare with an older Iron Age. If the end of Book V lacks allegorical colour and presents too 'real' a picture of the situation in Ireland it might also be uncomfortably close to an earlier 'real' conflict between giants and their slayers. For Spenser that affinity had a deep-seated appeal. In his eyes the ancient giants and current Irish represented the same sort of enemy. The overthrow of giants or Titans by a new order had a complex allegorical resonance.[61] Giants had been associated with

---

[59] Certainly it is difficult to find in Grantorto the same intense congregation of reference we find in Redcrosse's captor. Paul J. Alpers's influential work *The Poetry of 'The Faerie Queene'* (Princeton: Princeton University Press, 1967), 137–48, uses the encounter with Orgoglio to exemplify complex surface meaning in Spenser's poetry. The moral and physiological resonance of the episode has also been set out by Vern Torczon, 'Spenser's Orgoglio and Despaire', *Texas Studies in Literature and Language*, 3 (1961), 123–8, and John W. Shroeder, 'Spenser's Erotic Drama: The Orgoglio Episode', *English Literary History*, 29 (1962), 140–59. As Spenser becomes ever more historical it is perhaps a strain for him to maintain his role as poetical allegorist.

[60] 1 Samuel 17: 5–7.

[61] For a powerful reading of the Titan overthrow see Gordon Teskey's 'Mutability,

tyranny, pride, rebellion, and lust, but, above all, the 'giants in the earth' of Genesis 6: 4 could be read as indigenous savages whose 'unjust' possession of the land preceded a violent conquest.[62] Their defeat, consequently, was of key significance in the establishment of civility, a quality that according to *A View of the Present State of Ireland* lay most directly in the enforcement of justice.

This opposition had racial as well as cultural underpinnings. In Cooper's chronicle the post-diluvian giants are traced from Nimrod (equated with the Titans) to a variety of recalcitrant peoples including the Scythians, whom the chronicle describes from much the same perspective as Spenser in the *View*.[63] Admired aristocrats, on the other hand, were often provided with ancestries that went back to the deified ancient heroes. Just as it was common to associate the Scythians with fierceness and nomadic cattle-grazing, it was usual to link Osyris both with law and agriculture.[64] In the conflict that Cooper depicts between the unruly, cow-herding Scythians and the law-abiding, earth-tilling followers of Osyris Spenser would have found an attractive genealogy. The 'mere Irish' strength on their own soil, their ancient claims, their supposed pride and agricultural unproductiveness could all be associated with the giant race. The fact that giants were often seen as the first inhabitants of the land (as figurative or even literal autochthons) must have made stories of their eviction especially valuable to the colonist.[65] Giants, like the 'Old' English and 'mere' Irish of Spenser's day, had

Genealogy, and the Authority of Forms', *Representations*, 41 (1993), 104–22, and its revised version in *Allegory and Violence* (Ithaca: Cornell University Press, 1996), 168–88.

[62] For the link see Martin Luther, *The Creation: a Commentary on the First Five Chapters of the Book of Genesis* (from the 1544 Wittenberg edn.), trans. H. Cole (London, 1858), 42. See also Heninger, 'The Orgoglio Episode', 171–87 (183).

[63] Compare Cooper, *Epitome*, fols. 12ᵃ–13ᵇ with Spenser, *View*, 82–110. As noted in Ch. 3, however, the racial dimension of Spenser's polemic should not be overstated. In Kidd's subtle formulation 'the orthodox scholarly elites of the early modern British world did not think in essentialist terms of innate ethnic *difference*, but historically in terms of processes of *differentiation* from a common stock' (*British Identities*, 290).

[64] As noted above, Osyris was seen as a founder of law and his wife Isis as the inventor of agriculture. This euhemeristic reading was exceptionally common and appears in Cooper, *Epitome*, fol. 17ᵃ.

[65] Theories that giants had been earth-born rested on Classical sources (see e.g. Hesiod, *Theogony*, in *The Homeric Hymns and Homerica*, trans. Evelyn-White, l. 180) and were also helped by the ambiguous reference to 'earth' at Genesis 6: 4. The giant Alcyoneus, another of Hercules's foes, was immortal on his own land; similarly, Antaeus revived upon contact with the earth. Autocthonous giants are also amongst Britain's first inhabitants in Geoffrey's *Historia*. As a result giants have strong dynastic claims: the Bible associates them with the earliest ages and in pagan accounts the Titans have a stronger genealogy than the Olympians.

strong genealogical claims on the land they inhabited. Yet the narrative of universal history, as well as that of Geoffrey's *Historia*, erased such legitimacy by means of 'just' conflict. 'Antique' claims were recast as evidence of a savage redundancy and turned against those who possessed them. It is with dismissive reference to such genealogy that Spenser observes of the slain Grantorto that 'falling on his mother earth he fed' (V. xii. 23. 7).

In other ways, too, ancient claims could be made to tell against established powers. Annius of Viberbo's pseudo-Berossus (which, though discredited, was still a presence in historical debate) had tried to redefine giants as the great founders of modern dynasties.[66] Instead of villains, Annius had cast the giants as superhuman founders of civility. Noah, he claimed, had been a giant, and had reigned in Rome as a direct forerunner of the modern Pope.[67] In the wake of the theory's early success numerous royal dynasties in Europe had their family trees connected up to these great founder-giants. Catholic monarchs or Popes—Book V implies—are indeed the descendants of giants, but instead of civilizing heroes they are the ancient enemies of Hercules. Both groups are wicked tyrants, and just as those earlier examples were defeated by the ancient champion of justice, so his modern Elizabethan counterpart will re-enact the same conquest.

The distinction between Osyris (the deified just prince) and the Titans (the inflated images of evil tyrants) provides historical endorsement for Spenser's ideal of monarchy.[68] For him it seems monarchy lies not so much in popular acclaim, or even in dynastic legitimacy, as in the maintenance of law.[69] In spite of his high praise for Elizabeth's 'great auncestry', for the lowly-born poet amongst a community of new planters, genealogy was not always a strong suit.[70] Spenser might even

---

[66] For a clear survey of the pseudo-Berossus, and responses to it, see Stephens, *Giants*, 99–138. Elements of this alternative narrative of civilizing giants originating in the pseudo-Berossus survive in numerous English chronicles. The pseudo-Berossus also gave new historical specificity to Hercules, something that may indirectly have affected Spenser's representation (see Robert E. Hallowell, 'Ronsard and the Gallic Hercules Myth', *Studies in the Renaissance*, 9 (1962), 242–55 (244)).

[67] See Stephens, *Giants*, 134.

[68] The defeat of the Titans, which was wrapped up with the victories of Hercules, is a recurrent concern in Book V. Beyond being flagged up at V. i. 9 it is inserted, for example, in the middle of the Isis episode at V. vii. 10–11.

[69] This perspective on the function of monarchy is very evident in *A View* and is reflected in the Mutability Cantos (see Ch. 3).

[70] Of course the poet did not neglect to call on ancestral claims when they fitted his purposes, for example in praise of his sovereign (e.g. II. Proem. 4. 9) or in the claim of connection

have entertained some doubts about the pedigree of his aristocratic patrons, or that of the Tudor monarchy itself. Certainly, new imperial conquests won out over established interests when they accorded with Spenser's beliefs. This is one of the ideological constants of Book V and something articulated especially in the slaying of giants.

Earlier in his career Spenser had encountered this same paradigm in the *Ruines of Rome* by Du Bellay. Here the triumph of imperial rule is repeatedly associated with the repression of giants. In the fourth sonnet of the sequence we find Rome founded on the slain bodies of the 'old Giants' (l. 48) and in Sonnets 11 and 12 the unruly Goths who rise against her are characterized as the 'new Giant brood' (l. 149) and as 'the children of the earth' (l. 155). The victory of barbarism in Sonnet 17 is also seen as a reversal of the old battle between gods and giants. In the still earlier *Theatre for Worldlings* Spenser's translation of one of Du Bellay's visions had been used to cast yet another enemy as giant. For here the sonnet on 'great Typhæus sister' had been positioned so as to become an attack on papal tyranny.[71] Add to this the association of giants with the earthquakes foretold in the Book of Revelation and we begin to see the way in which these incidents find a place in the universal trajectory of time.[72]

Historically and metaphorically the giant gives shape to Spenser's imperial vision. In these figures euhemeristic commentaries found their richest source. Sacred and profane allegory, ancient and recent history, could all be interpreted to point to the same conclusions. Placing Spenser alongside the world histories of his age shows allegory to be a more complex process than is sometimes assumed. With the giant and for universal chronicles more generally, history and allegory are inextricably intertwined. Looking back on ancient myths while at the same time composing new fictions, the Poet Historical placed himself at a complex intellectual juncture. Spenser was imitating stories that had, over the centuries, been the subject of numerous allegorical readings. Moreover,

---

with the Spencers of Althorp (e.g. Dedication, *Prosopopoia*). Neither his own family history, that of the Earl of Leicester, nor that of the Queen herself, however, had great weight in comparison with the old Catholic families of Ireland, England, or the European mainland.

[71] See *Theatre for Worldlings*, Sonnet 11, which precedes van der Noot's versification of Revelation 13 interpreted allegorically as a vision of the Papacy. Such connections are very much drawn upon in *Faerie Queene* Book I, where Spenser again runs recent political allegory alongside ancient history.

[72] On the association of giants with the earthquakes at the end of the world, see Heninger, 'The Orgoglio Episode', 175–83.

he was writing a 'dark conceit' that was itself to be read again and again in the search for new significance.[73] From this perspective giants manage to be history and poetry at the same time. In their depiction we find both Spenser and the ancients 'With fayned colours shading a true case' (V. vii. 2. 7).

[73] On these processes see e.g. Isabell G. MacCaffrey's *Spenser's Allegory: The Anatomy of Imagination* (Princeton: Princeton University Press, 1976) or Kenneth Borris, *Allegory and Epic in English Renaissance Literature: Heroic Form in Sidney, Spenser, and Milton* (Cambridge: Cambridge University Press, 2001).

CHAPTER 5

'Antique Praises vnto Present Persons Fit': Analogy and History in the Public Sphere

Queen Elizabeth and Historical Praise

In his adoption of both euhemerism and antiquarian discourse, Spenser made polemical use of supposed parallels between past ages and the present. His sources for those forms of history were themselves often much more reluctant to make such analogies. Not all forms, however, fought shy of this overtly political logic. In the courts of princes there were modes of address whose effect depended entirely on past comparison. When courtiers consulted chronicles or other worthy collections they often scanned them only as phrasebooks for this other language of history. For it was through 'mirrors' drawing analogies from past ages that one sought to influence a prince.

The oration that John Hales made on Queen Elizabeth's accession (itself to become one of the 'monuments' included in Foxe's work) is a typical example.[1] From the start the address makes use of explicit historical framing. It praises a queen who will take the kingdom and not 'destroy it as did *Cæsar*, but make it as did Romulus' and compares the monarch to the greatest of the ancient Judaic princes (*Actes*, 2118). Certainly, the speech is one of enthusiastic welcome. But the fact that it praises a queen who has, as yet, performed almost no actions also makes apparent the extent to which this was an act of historical persuasion. For Hales's appeal highlights what Patrick Collinson has called a visionary religious republicanism 'not yet incompatible with monarchy'—a stra-

---

[1] *Actes and Monuments* (1583), 2116. Subsequent references in the text, unless otherwise specified, are to this edition. Given that Hales was a zealous Protestant later imprisoned for writing a work on the succession in favour of the claims of Lady Catherine Grey, Foxe's selection was a provocative one.

tegic misprision that attempted to align sixteenth-century England with earlier desired states.[2] The orator's distinction between Romulus and Caesar reveals the radicalism of a religious belief concerned not with reformation but with return to ultimate beginnings.

The inclusion of Hales's speech at the close of the *Actes and Monuments* was itself a pointedly political act. While the bulk of these first accession day celebrations were in fact concerned with Tudor stability and reconciliation, Foxe's account anticipates the apocalyptic mixture of return and renewal that was to characterize their future more radically Protestant incarnations.[3] From the moment of the Queen's coronation, and with increasing complexity over the years ahead, she was the subject of this polemical, highly flexible, mode of historical address. Her ascent to the throne was presented as a beginning that was also a return. The early editions of the Book of Martyrs praised Elizabeth as a second Constantine; in line with the new reformation historiography hammered out by Bale and the other exiles in Basle, her accession 'at once' transported the imaginations of Protestants 'from the conditions of apostolic Christianity to the godly Commonwealth of Israel'.[4] For them it was through past comparison, and only through past comparison, that the reign of Elizabeth could be celebrated. In the words of F. J. Levy, 'Bale's view of the past saw perfection only in the beginning: corruption began in the age immediately following that of the Apostles'.[5] In the new faith championed by Elizabeth, Foxe was determined to find the old religion of the 'florishyng time of the Church' (*Actes*, sig. A1ᵃ); a church that 'was, when this church of theirs was not yet hatched' (sigs. A1ᵇ–A2ᵃ). From the perspective of radical Protestantism, and increasingly in a more widespread popular representation, Elizabeth stood not just at an end-

---

[2] Patrick Collinson, *Elizabethan Essays* (London: Hambledon Press, 1994), 17. An accessible overview of debate on the religious culture of the period is provided by Margo Todd (ed.), *Reformation to Revolution: Politics and Religion in Early Modern England* (London: Routledge, 1995).

[3] For contemporary accounts of these first celebrations see J. Osborne (ed.), *The Quenes Maiesties passage through the citie of London to Westminster the day before her coronacion* (1558; repr. New Haven: Yale University Press, 1960) and Holinshed, *Chronicles* (1587), iii. 1172–9.

[4] See Patrick Collinson, *The Elizabethan Puritan Movement* (London: Jonathan Cape, 1967), 25. More recent studies tend to interpret Foxe's descriptions of his sovereign more as persuasive strategies than as absolute convictions. For the relationship between Foxe and Bale see King, *English Reformation*, 407–43. On the flexibility of the Protestant apocalyptic reading of the place of the Elizabethan state in history see Jane E. A. Dawson, 'The Apocalyptic Thinking of the Marian Exiles', in Michael Wilks (ed.), *Prophecy and Eschatology*, Studies in Church History, 10 (Oxford: Blackwell, 1994), 75–92.

[5] F. J. Levy, *Tudor Historical Thought* (San Marino: The Huntington Library, 1967), 84.

point of chronicle history, but also at a point outside it as a stressed analogy to its most glorious figures.[6]

It was not only the religious left that found itself transported in time by the moment of accession: the new nationalism that was so closely allied to it also developed a trans historical language in which to encompass the monarch. The 1592 edition of William Warner's verse history of Britain, *Albions England*, which in fact shows very little in the way of an overt religious agenda, likewise stumbles at the threshold of Elizabeth's reign.[7] For Warner as for Foxe, Elizabeth's accession saves the nation from 'tyranny' and marks a point of closure beyond which narrative is unsustainable.[8] As with the *Actes and Monuments* a chronological approach is abandoned in favour of laudatory address. In place of narrative history we are presented with ideologically charged parallels for Elizabeth's reign as Warner lists again the greatest of the kings who have made up his account (p. 185). Of the current queen he cannot speak: 'The *Muses* Check my sawsie Pen, | for enterprising her, | In duly praising whome | even *Artes* themselves, might err' (p. 189).

While there is more than a little strategic self-deprecation in the poet's declaration of his incapacity (Warner was to extend the history with little difficulty in a posthumous edition leading up to the reign of King James) the difficulties in 'enterprising' the monarch within her own time were nevertheless genuine, and the problem of closure is once more graphically evident on the verso page of the poet's closing address. Here the superficially misplaced 'Addition in Proese to the second Book of Albions England' presents us not with a continued history of Elizabeth, but with 'a Breviate of the true Historie of Aneas', the very first of the Queen's legendary ancestors.[9] Warner thus ends with a more nationalistically charged stand-in for Hales's Romulus. Aeneas provides an illustrious parallel for Elizabeth. As a forefather of Brutus, the supposed Trojan conqueror of Albion, he also represents the ultimate starting point for a line of British kings culminating in her reign. As Warner asserts: 'Misapplyed hee is not for Matter precedent, howsoever the

---

[6] From the perspective of the Tudor historian, of course, it made no sense to ask what would have happened had Elizabeth not ascended to the throne—as Woolf, *The Idea*, 9, observes, given the assumption that God himself was the writer of history such a position would have been absurd.

[7] William Warner, *Albions England* (1592). Subsequent references to this edition appear in the text. Harper (*Sources*, 177) actually cites the first edition of *Albions England* as a possible source for parts of Spenser's chronicle material.

[8] *Albions England*, 185 (misprinted as '158').

[9] Ibid., sig. 2A3[b] (no page number).

penning or misplacing may like or mislike for the English or Order' (sig.
2A3ᵇ). Like Foxe, Warner can find conclusion only in beginnings;
Aeneas, even more than Romulus, marks Elizabeth's accession as a
point of simultaneous departure and return.

In 1602, only a year before the Queen's death, Warner published an
updated and considerably expanded edition of his poem. Yet his claim to
have produced a 'Continued Historie' covering events 'unto, and in the
happie Raigne of our now most gracious Soveraigne', is a questionable
one.[10] The uneasiness over a narrative of Elizabeth's reign persists: her
accession is again displaced by a 'Catalogue' of famous and valiant
British and English kings (*Albions England* (1602), 205) and Aeneas is
once more placed at the endpoint of the story (though this time followed
by 'An Epitome of the whole historie of *England*' (p. 351)). Where
Warner does attempt to cover the 'Alterations and Accidents' (sig. A1ᵃ)
of Elizabeth's time, his text is testimony to the pressures exerted by
the period's analogically charged culture. Warner represents only the
glorious high-points of his sovereign's government: the defeat of the
Armada (p. 225), the trial and execution of Mary Queen of Scots (p. 243),
the French wars (p. 250), and the intervention in the Low Countries (p.
263). Even these choice historical moments, however, are embedded in
a mass of other historical, bibilical, and mythological material. Warner's
coyness about the details of that history remains. He reluctantly tells us,
for example, that he is unable to relate the deeds of Elizabeth's knights
on their expedition to the Netherlands: 'I cannot but devine | Their
chivalrie to be reserv'd for higher Muse than mine'.[11] The 'Epitome
of the whole history of *England*' (p. 351), which concludes the work,
mirrors the *Actes and Monuments* by ending at the point of Elizabeth's
accession, a point again marking the perfection of true religion (p. 398).
That the Queen has reigned for forty-four years is nowhere apparent;
that the reign could soon end seems utterly unthinkable. For Warner
there can be no narrative of the recent past that does not violate the
image of the present queen; her reign is approachable only in terms of a
set of static 'Accidents' that stand on a par with the biblical, mythological, and folkloric episodes that surround them. Elizabeth can be represented only by means of glorious ancient parallels.

[10] William Warner, *Albions England* (1602), title-page. Subsequent references to this edition
appear in the text.
[11] *Albions England* (1602), 265. Perhaps significantly, all that Warner *is* able to report are
rumours of less than heroic behaviour.

Foxe and Warner exemplify the congruent historical perspectives of a new religion and a new nationalism. If we add to this polemical anachronism a growing intellectual climate that envisioned the return of aspects of Classical civilization it becomes apparent just how multi-faceted the language of analogy could be.[12] An almost obsessive awareness of parallels haunted the writers and readers of history alike: not only did the 'example' of the past justify the practice of history, alleged allusions to the present could also be its downfall. Notably in treatments of the life of Richard II, it seems the Queen herself sought out the subversive implications behind such apparent linkage.[13]

The importance of such parallels was more than simply comparative; for many they provided the key to discovering the vast harmonious superstructure of God's divine plan. As Richard McCabe has put it, 'the adoption of a providential outlook made possible the extension of typological interpretations from the written word to the living word', so that even the Reformation itself could be justified as the 'antitype of Israel's escape from Babylon'.[14] By tracing historical patterns it was believed possible to confirm the predestined design of history. The pervasive influence of omens, numerology, and the like on men such as Jean Bodin thus greatly complicates any image of a more 'modern' or sceptical Tudor historiography.[15] Warner stoutly denies superstition in finding 'H. the letter still | Might be observed ominous to *Englands* good or ill' (*Albions England* (1592), 187). Holinshed equally made great play of the significance of 'fatal numbers' connecting Noah, Hercules, and Brutus, 'where I would ad the time of restoring the gospell by Queene Elizabeth, were it not that it wanteth one full yeare of 2'.[16] It was not merely the

---

[12] For a discussion of the period's understanding of this 'return', see Sukanta Chaudhuri, 'The Rebirth of Time: Tradition, History and the Renaissance Mind', in Sukanta Chaudhuri (ed.), *Renaissance Essays for Kitty Scoular Datta* (Calcutta: Oxford University Press, 1995), 26–51 (26–31).

[13] This doubling was most famously discovered by the Queen in Sir John Hayward's *The First Part of the life and Raigne of Henry IIII* (1599) which, despite its apparently innocuous contents, resulted in its author's imprisonment for the rest of the reign (see *DNB*).

[14] McCabe, *Pillars*, 119. As McCabe cautions, 'in order to be strictly typological such interpretations had to involve appropriate biblical reference . . . to identify, say, Mary Queen of Scots with the Whore of Babylon or the papacy with the Beast from the Sea was not, strictly speaking, to engage in typological interpretation' (p. 120). The most authoritative account of the nature of 'figura' remains Erich Auerbach's essay of that name in *Scenes from the Drama of European Literature* (New York: Meridean, 1959), 11–76.

[15] On this influence, see Levy, *Tudor Historical*, 4–5.

[16] Holinshed, *Chronicles*, (1587), iii. 29. Subsequent references are to vol. iii and appear in the text. As set out below, this work was heavily cut by order of the Privy Council. Reference here is made to a copy in the Cambridge University Library (Sel 2.34–5) that appears to have eluded

144 Analogy and History in the Public Sphere

ancient and Renaissance art of numerology that bolstered such beliefs. Cyclical ideas of time—whose intellectual influence was very great throughout this period—likewise implied a set of powerful affinities between moments in history.[17] The twin concepts of an eternal 'nature' and an endlessly repeated 'history', as Achsah Guibbory points out, inevitably implied that 'events and people find their parallels in different ages'.[18] In a multitude of ways history could thus be justified as a blueprint for the design of church or nation, both now and in the future.

Although inevitably the language of analogy came to be set down in the written accounts of professional historians, this was not its only, or even its primary medium. Instead, analogical representations of Queen Elizabeth functioned through a complex conjunction of pageantry, orations, portraiture, and print. Sir Roy Strong's survey of Tudor media shows this language of analogy to be an identifiable tradition that took shape in the first months of the Queen's reign.[19] Through the years of Elizabeth's rule that tradition was maintained and adapted in the light of political developments. Biblical analogies with Old Testament figures such as Judith, Esther, and Deborah (each a protector of Israel in times of desperation) were largely a feature of the early years of Elizabeth's reign.[20] In 1579, Strong tells us, 'there appears the first of a long series of portraits of Elizabeth which introduce a heavy overlay of imperial pretensions stemming from maritime power and from a reassertion of dominion based on the descent of the House of Tudor from the imperial stock of Troy and on the conquests of King Arthur' (p. 11). In the years that followed, and especially in the wake of the naval triumph against the Armada, these develop a growing tendency to depict Elizabeth's

---

the censor (see *Early Printed Books in the University Library Cambridge*, ed. C. E. Sayle, 5 vols. (Cambridge: Cambridge University Press, 1900), i. 219).

[17] On the 'almost total domination' of the theory, see Robert Nisbet, *History of the Idea of Progress* (London: Heineman, 1980), 103. G. W. Trompf, *The Idea of Historical Recurrence in Western Thought: From Antiquity to the Reformation* (Berkeley: University of California Press, 1979), traces in Christian history up to the Renaissance 'the withering away of a linear-cyclical, or better still, a linear-recurrence dichotomy' (p. 309).

[18] Achsah Guibbory, *The Map of Time: Seventeenth-Century English Literature and Ideas of Pattern in History* (Urbana: University of Illinois Press, 1986), 8–9.

[19] See Sir Roy Strong, *The Tudor and Stuart Monarchy: Pageantry, Painting, Iconography*, 3 vols. (Woodbridge: Boydell Press, 1995–8), ii, and also Yates, *Astraea*. For a more hagiographic depiction of Elizabeth's popular representation see Elkin Calhoun Wilson, *England's Eliza*, Harvard Studies in English, 20 (Cambridge, Mass.: Harvard University Press, 1939; repr. New York: Octagon Books, 1966), 61–5.

[20] See Jean Wilson, *Entertainments for Elizabeth I*, Studies in Elizabethan Culture, 2 (Woodbridge: Brewer, 1980), 2–7.

London as 'New Troy' and the monarch herself as Astraea, Aeneas, Romulus, Brutus, or Arthur.[21] Even as antiquarians and chronographers exposed the weakness of its intellectual foundations, this form of history retained and even expanded its rhetorical scope.

The Faerie Queene *(1590): 'In this faire mirrhour maist behold thy face'*

Spenser influenced, and was influenced by, this tradition of analogy. *The Faerie Queene* presented England's monarch with a series of historical mirrors. The time of Eden, the reign of Astraea, the foundation of Troynovant, and the age of Arthur were all used by Spenser as epochs to set against the reign of this current queen. Through Fairyland Spenser established a palimpsest of historical moments, and in a series of prefatory Proems to his books he attempted to engage his monarch directly in the task of connecting them with her own time. In the central Proem of the first instalment the poet glories in the hall of mirrors he has created, inviting the Queen to do likewise:

> And thou, O fairest Princesse vnder sky,
> In this faire mirrhour maist behold thy face,
> And thine owne realmes in lond of Faery,
> And in this antique Image thy great auncestry.   (II. Proem. 4. 6–9)

This 'mirror' occurs in each of the first instalment's Proems, and on each occasion Spenser relates it to an 'antique' image. Through a variety of historical analogies, from the pure Christian church of Saint George's legend to the imperial glory of Arthur's reign, the monarch is brought to reflect upon her own condition. As with Hales's address to Elizabeth on her accession, the message is certainly one of praise but it also one of forceful persuasion.

Spenser was profoundly self-conscious about the interactive dynamic that sustained his fiction. Historical collections such as the Tudor *Mirror for Magistrates* were 'mirrors' precisely because the message they bore changed in relation to their reader.[22] That this is true of Spenser's poem as well is especially apparent in one of the last episodes of *The Faerie*

---

[21] Yates, *Astraea*, and Strong, 12, 26, 131, 139, and *passim*.

[22] For an overview of the mirror tradition see Herbert Grabes, *The Mutable Glass: Mirror-imagery in Titles and Texts of the Middle Ages and English Renaissance*, trans. Gordon Collier (Cambridge: Cambridge University Press, 1982). The *Mirror* appeared in several editions over the years of Tudor rule; for a scholarly text see *Mirror for Magistrates*, ed. Lily B. Campbell (Cambridge: Cambridge University Press, 1938).

Queene's first instalment. For, like George in Book I, and Arthur in Book II, in the closing stages of her book Britomart too is afforded a moment to gaze upon her nation's place in history.[23] Britomart as a female knight has some affinities with Elizabeth, and as a result the episode looks with particular focus at the complexities of analogy.

At Malbecco's castle Britomart shares a meal with Paridell (III. ix. 25–53). That knight, it turns out, is a very distant relative. For when Paridell proudly proclaims his lineage from the bastard child of the Trojan Paris, his misguided boasting inspires in the lady knight a more elevated piece of historical reminiscence. As Merlin has confirmed at an earlier stage in the Legend of Chastity, Britomart also stems from 'the auncient *Troian* blood' (III. iii. 22. 6), and in the stanzas that follow she and Paridell begin to piece together the scattered Trojans' history. Heather Dubrow has written perceptively about this encounter with the Briton past—a point where 'two competing historians, Britomart and Paridell, direct their telescopes on the distant, receding coastline of Troy and on Troynovant'.[24] As they do so, she notes, they participate in, and comment upon the complex debates about history and historiography that occurred both in England and on the Continent during the Renaissance. Dubrow finds in the stories told by Britomart and Paridell not only a juxtaposition of conflicting modes of historical discourse (this time the Romance and the Epic), but also an admission of Spenser's own partiality in his rendition of the past. For, 'if Paridell tells the story of Troy to woo Hellenore, so too Spenser tells it to woo Elizabeth' (p. 325).

Looking back at Hales's address and Warner's 'Addition', it is appropriate that the 1590 *Faerie Queene*'s final segment of history brings us back once more to beginnings. From the mouth of Paridell we hear of the fall of Troy and the removal of its 'reliques' to build a new town called Nausicle (a parodic type of Troy just as he is a parodic type of Paris). It

---

[23] Each of these three encounters pairs an element of national history with a fairy one. Like that of Arthur and Guyon at II. x, George's vision at the conclusion of I. x is a complex conjunction of British and fairy elements. George is told by Contemplation that he will do good service for the virgin Queen of Fairyland, but is also informed of his origins in the 'ancient race | Of *Saxon* kings, that haue with mightie hand | And many bloudie battailes fought in place | High reard their royall throne in *Britane* land' (I. x. 65. 1–4). Paridell, as we shall see, likewise provides a fairy narrative that interlaces with Britomart's British story.

[24] Heather Dubrow, 'The Arraignment of Paridell: Tudor Historiography in *The Faerie Queene*, III, ix', *SP* 87 (1990), 312–27 (312). See also Berger, *Revisionary Play*, 113, and Galbraith, *Architectonics*, 52–74. Galbraith builds productively on the work of Berger and Dubrow, especially on the reasons why the legend of chastity should be 'a major site for the exploration of the relationship between poetry and history' (p. 65).

is with that illegitimate line that Paridell proudly proclaims his connection. The newly inspired Britomart, however, interrupts his tale to tell us of the other types of Troy that have made their mark upon history. First she asks of Aeneas's journey and Romulus's foundation of a city (III. ix. 38–43), but this too is to be but a stepping stone towards greater glories. Talk of Rome prompts Britomart once more to interrupt Sir Paridell. This time it is to proclaim that:

> a third kingdome yet is to arise,
> Out of the *Troians* scattered of-spring,
> That in all glory and great enterprise,
> Both first and second *Troy* shall dare to equalise.   (III. ix. 44. 6–9)

'*Troynouant*' here appears to lie ahead at the endpoint of the mythic journey of the Trojan race. Yet in each of the following stanzas the tense of the narration changes. In Stanza 45 Britomart speaks of a present-day town 'which standes so hy, | That it a wonder of the world is song' (III. ix. 45. 6–7), and by Stanza 47 Paridell remembers what seem like old reports of the new Troy. 'Whilome', he tells her, 'I heard tell | From aged *Mnemon*':

> That of the antique *Troian* stocke, there grew
> Another plant, that raught to wondrous hight,
> And far abroad his mighty branches threw,
> Into the vtmost Angle of the world he knew.   (III. ix. 47. 6–9)

Translatio imperii here functions by means of a productively ambiguous time-frame, allowing Britomart's first exclamation to anticipate the glory of Brutus, Arthur, and Elizabeth equally. Paridell, it transpires, is here speaking of the first of those three great national imperial moments. The double meaning of 'Angle', however, already encompasses other identities, and as Paridell completes the foundation legend of Brutus's capital the time at which Troynovant exists is once more thrown into doubt. This city (together with Lincoln) is Brutus's great work:

> That who from East to West will endlong seeke,
> Cannot two fairer Cities find this day,
> Except *Cleopolis*: so heard I say
> Old *Mnemon*.   (III. ix. 51. 3–6)

The phrase 'this day' seems to mark the city as a current wonder—either for Britomart or for the Elizabethan reader. The concluding half-line of Paridell's speech, however, once more draws us back to the long-remembered account of 'Old *Mnemon*'. The imperial projects remembered, witnessed, and anticipated here link the times of Brutus, Arthur, and Elizabeth. As 'new' Troy metamorphoses from a city of the future to one of the present and past these three monarchs are thrown into conjunction. In one sense the 'types' that Britomart and Paridell assemble are mutually supportive, but in another the manner in which these signifiers slip into one another exposes a disconcerting insubstantiality. Given the questionable status of Paridell's praise of his own city—built from the transported '*Troian* reliques sau'd from flame' (III. ix. 36. 8)—we can begin to doubt the foundations of Britomart's vaunted city 'built of old *Troyes* ashes cold' (III. ix. 38. 9). By a strange logic its stability seems to depend upon the new empires that may be built upon it.

The 'antique' mirrors of the Queen and her capital city thus change their aspect in response to the monarch's own achievements. Elizabeth could fashion her kingdom in the image of the past, but that process could also be inverted. In the work of John Dee in particular we see the extraordinary pressure that the Elizabethan perception of the future exerted on a past through which it saw itself. As the voyages of Drake and others discovered new lands upon which English rule could be established so Dee made 'discoveries' of a parallel ancient empire covering North America and the Arctic. The 1577 publication *General and Rare Memorials Pertayning to the Perfect Arte of Navigation* exemplifies this two-way dynamic of Elizabethan archaism. It was a work of which Elizabeth approved and which in one form or another was certainly known to Spenser.[25] Dee's argument is for restoring a British Empire which, we learn, includes England, Ireland, and Scotland, and the Orkneys.[26] As Elizabethan imperial ambitions grew, so too did the scope of this past dominion. Thus, when included as part of Richard Hakluyt's *Principall Navigations* of 1589, such claims covered Iceland, Denmark, and Norway as well as many more distant territories.[27] The 1602 edition of *Albions England* was clearly influenced by such ideas, and it consequently incor-

[25] On their respective knowledge see Charles Bowie Millican, *Spenser and 'The Table Round': A Study in the Contemporaneous Background for Spenser's Use of the Arthurian Legend*, Harvard Studies in Comparative Literature, 8 (Cambridge, Mass.: Harvard University Press, 1932), 42 and 45.

[26] See Josephine Waters Bennett, *The Evolution of 'The Faerie Queene'* (Chicago: University of Chicago Press, 1942), 70.

[27] See Richard Hakluyt, *The Principall Navigations, Voyages, Traffiques, and Discoveries of the English Nation* (London: George Bishop & Ralph Newberie, 1589) in which Elizabethan exploration is overlaid with that of kings including Edgar, Malgo, and Arthur. These ancient British or English journeys, like their modern counterparts, seem to cover all the known world.

porated a new verse chapter 'Of the Seventeene Kindomes in Tymes by-passed, whereof her majestie is now sole Monarch' (p. 298).

Dee's historic discoveries, like Paridell's, translate directly into prophecies, so that for them past and future work to construct what Fletcher calls 'an overloaded present'.[28] Fixing on a specific sentence in the treatise describing the British Empire as it 'hath bene: yeah, as it, yet, is: or rather, as it may, and (of right) ought to be', William Sherman has observed how Dee 'struggles with the appropriate *tense* of the imperial outlook', reminding us that 'it was as much retrospective as prospective'.[29] Just so the multiple 'presents' of the Paridell episode work to underpin one another's validity. If national greatness was to be founded on a glorious past then the process of glorification needed to work both ways. The complex relationship between analogical praise and persuasion that operates throughout the first instalment of *The Faerie Queene* was one means of facilitating such a double transformation. Whether it be a return to the purity of a true church or the glory of a great empire, the praise offered through analogy was always prospective. As an unfinished poem whose fairy monarch had yet to appear *The Faerie Queene* offered Elizabeth a mirror whose perfection, like hers, was still incomplete.

The Faerie Queene *(1596): The 'state of present time'*

The moment of triumph envisaged by Foxe at the conclusion of the *Actes and Monuments* was a fragile one. Over the years that followed the work's first publication the disjunctions in time surrounding England's monarch increased. The Queen's own lukewarm support for the Protestant project of reformation, the possibility of a foreign and Catholic husband, the serious threat of foreign invasion and (for a while) the increasing likelihood of a Catholic succession all worked to change the implications of the closure at the end of the Book of Martyrs—an alteration that the author himself acknowledged by demoting Elizabeth from England's Constantine to a second Deborah.[30] The significance of the hundreds of individual stories that made up Foxe's volume still

---

[28] Fletcher, *Prophetic Moment*, 5.
[29] *General and Rare Memorials*, sig. A2ᵃ, and William H. Sherman, *John Dee: The Politics of Reading and Writing in the English Renaissance* (Amherst: University of Massachusetts Press, 1995), 151.
[30] The change famously created problems for Foxe's parsimonious printers, who, reluctant to lose the investment they had put into the opening capital 'C' for Constantine, thriftily altered the first word of the work's preface to 'Christ'.

depended on a narrative drive towards glorious fulfilment, but, as he reluctantly admitted, that moment might prove to be as uncertain as the earlier glimpse of the Godly kingdom afforded by the reign of Edward. Before the Queen's enthronement the Protestant faithful focused their millennial expectations on Queen Elizabeth, whose accession seemed to offer a return to the halcyon climate of Edward VI's reign.[31] Yet that was an analogy with a profoundly tragic bent. The panegyrical dedication of Bale's *Image of Both Churches* published during Elizabeth's reign was an exact parallel to the earlier praise of Edward—a fatal symmetry that cast an unavoidable shadow of doom on even the most luminescent praise for the new queen. While the 'cesure' at the end of Foxe's history could always anticipate the 'secret pleasure' at the close of Arthur's chronicle (II. x. 68. 8), it might also have posited the darker vision afforded by the conclusion of Merlin's prophecy to Britomart (III. iii. 50. 1). The nebulous doubts that conclude Merlin's prophecy echo those of Foxe's last pages. For, however much he may celebrate the 'happy reign' of Elizabeth, Foxe is forced to conclude that the older the world grows 'the more Sathan rageth: geving still new matter of writing bookes and volumes' (*Actes*, 2154). Despite the emphasis on closure and return, there are still 'volumes' of potential narrative in the future.[32] At the same time as returning us to religious beginnings, Foxe's biblical framework also throws us forward to the fulfilment of the last prophecies of the book of Revelation. While Foxe was no millenarian there is still a profound sense of finality to his history.[33] The time-scheme at the opening of the *Actes and Monuments* (p. 1) had placed the 'reformation' in the last of five great eras of history; while Elizabeth's reign was not *the* end it constituted a significant precursor.

If the central Proem of the 1590 *Faerie Queene* looks back in time to mirror a point of national arrival, the poet who inhabits the same textual space in the 1596 instalment seems much less convinced that the age of Elizabeth is the fairest of them all:

---

[31] For this assessment and its potential negative associations, see King, *English Reformation*, 425.

[32] Trompf identifies this dual perspective in other Protestant interpretations of history. Of Luther in particular he observes that 'at points the Reformation meant for him the dawning of a new Age', at times referred to as 'golden', but at the same time 'Luther could envisage the whole of history as a scene of degeneration' (p. 297).

[33] On Foxe's approach see Florence Sandler, 'The Faerie Queene: An Elizabethan Apocalypse', in C. A. Patrides and Joseph Wittreich (eds.), *The Apocalypse in English Renaissance Thought and Literature: Patterns, Antecendents and Repercussions* (Manchester: Manchester University Press, 1984), 148–74 (160 and 148).

So oft as I with state of present time,
  The image of the antique world compare,
  When as mans age was in his freshest prime,
  And the first blossome of faire vertue bare,
  Such oddes I finde twixt those, and these which are,
  As that, through long continuance of his course,
  Me seemes the world is runne quite out of square,
  From the first point of his appointed sourse,
And being once amisse growes daily wourse and wourse. (V. Proem. 1)

In place of the optimistic reflections offered in the first books of *The Faerie Queene*, the opening of the most contemporary book instead forwards the concept of universal decay. The stock of this notion was itself on the wane by the time Spenser was writing.[34] Indeed, so offensive was the notion that decay was to be found in the time of Gloriana that Gabriel Harvey was to admonish Spenser: 'you suppose the first age was the golden age. It is nothing soe. Bodin defendith the goulde age to flourishe nowe'.[35] While the Proem does mark the decline of Spenser's faith in the Elizabethan establishment, however, its negative contrast with ancient times (like the positive one in the Proem to Book II) is also a strategic use of analogy. Spenser was well aware of the historical innovations of Bodin and other Continental historians, and in part his mournful observations on the decline of the outmoded cosmology described by 'learned *Ptolomæe*' (V. Proem. 7. 6) are themselves an ironic piece of archaism.[36] Throughout the Proem the poet anatomizes the 'state of present time' in a way that significantly complicates Harvey's conception of 'nowe'. On the one hand the line implies a 'state' (in the sense of 'condition') for time itself—a decline from the 'golden age' (V. Proem. 2. 1) manifested in the physical deterioration of the heavenly markers of time. Yet the first recorded use of the phrase in 1594 conveys current political actuality: 'a juncture or posture of affairs' to which a distinct response is merited.[37] It is a 'now' subtly different from the 'now' of Elizabeth's glorious reign—one reflective of the political actualities of

---

[34] See Guibbory, *Map of Time*, 5. For a useful survey of this and other Classical and Renaissance theories on time, see C. A. Patrides (ed.), *Aspects of Time* (Manchester: University of Manchester Press, 1976).

[35] *The Works of Gabriel Harvey*, ed. Alexander B. Grosart, 3 vols. (London: Hazell, Watson, & Viney, 1884–5), i. 146. Bodin's *Method* included a chapter offering a 'refutation of those who postulate four monarchies and the gold age'.

[36] Mills, for example, finds evidence of Spenser's familiarity with Bodin in the poet's adoption of numerological patterns in his verse. See 'Spenser and the Numbers', 282.

[37] *OED*, s.v. 'State' n. 5c.

the state's foreign and domestic policies. For while the first stanza of the Proem is pessimistic about both a declining world and a troublesome present, its last—addressing the 'Dread Souerayne Goddesse, that doest highest sit | In seate of iudgement, in th'Almighties stead' (V. Proem. 11. 1–2)—returns to the transcendent analogies of the first instalment. As noted in the preceding chapter, the Queen had been addressed as a sovereign 'Goddesse' in the Proem to Book I, and here a euhemeristic reading of the past once more allows Elizabeth to be seen as a kind of Astraea. Her reign remains glorious despite or perhaps even because of both universal and particular faults that surround her.

So too in the *Actes and Monuments* there is room for a declining age alongside the new golden one. Foxe had doubts both about the present-day practices of the half-reformed English church and about its ultimate prospects. Like Spenser, however, he is nevertheless determined in his assertion that 'it cannot sufficiently be expressed what felicitie and blessed happines this Realme hath received in receiving her at the Lordes almighty and gracious hand' (*Actes*, 2115). Significantly, it is time that for Foxe is the supreme arbiter of Elizabeth's achievement:

In speaking whereof I take not upon me the part here of the morall or of the devine Philosopher, to judge of thinges done but onely keep me within the compasse of an historiographer, declaring what hath bene before, and comparying thinges done, with thinges now present, the like whereof as I sayde, is not to be found lightly in Chronicles before. And this as I speak truely, so I would to be taken without flattery, to be left to our posteritie.   (ibid. 2115)

It is both in the light of past 'Chronicles' and a future 'posterity' that the present must be judged. While the eyes 'of the moral or of the devine Philosopher' may trace ongoing decay from the moment of man's fall, that vision stands outside the remit of the church historian. In assessing Elizabeth as sovereign it is not primarily to the Bible that Foxe turns, but to chronicle history. Of all the 'reformations' of Europe the English was, in terms of its justification, the most historical.[38] It was not just that Foxe had found in the Reformation a return to the ancient form of the church, but also that the unique Erastian nature of England's church could be defended only in terms of historical contingency. Whitgift's debate with Cartwright had been concluded in the former's favour on the combined principles of historical parallel and difference; in MacCaffrey's summary 'a Church struggling under Neronic persecution was a world away from

[38] See Levy, *Tudor Historical*, 78.

one nursed by such a Christian princess as England's Deborah'.[39] In Whitgift's conception parallel allowed difference as well as similarity, and, while the extent to which he pushed his conclusions was disputed by many on the puritan wing of the church, his method could not be significantly undermined.[40]

These ambiguous negotiations between past, present, and future are very much apparent in Book V's search for justice. Just as in the discussion between Britomart and Paridell, the glorious moment that Spenser presents as an analogy to the present state is difficult to determine. At the beginning of the Proem Spenser tells us he has abandoned his own age as an unrewarding source for the Legend of Justice;

> Let none then blame me, if in discipline
>   Of vertue and of ciuill vses lore,
>   I doe not forme them to the common line
>   Of present dayes, which are corrupted sore,
>   But to the antique vse, which was of yore,
>   When good was onely for it selfe desyred,
>   And all men sought their owne, and none no more;
>   When Iustice was not for most meed outhyred,
> But simple Truth did rayne, and was of all admyred.   (V. Proem. 3)

This 'golden age' at first suggests a return to the pastoralism of a Saturnine world, the loss of which Spenser bemoans in the ninth stanza of the Proem. The fifth book itself, however, returns to the Arthurian setting of the rest of the work and, in the last stanza of the poem, that Saturnine world is itself transported to the person of Spenser's Queen. Addressing her at the close of the Proem, Spenser begs to be able to write of present glory:

> Pardon the boldnesse of thy basest thrall,
>   That dare discourse of so diuine a read,
>   As thy great iustice praysed ouer all:
> The instrument whereof loe here thy *Artegall.*   (V. Proem. 11. 6–9)

It is with an emphatic gesture of present ownership—'loe here thy *Artegall*'—that we are presented with the book's hero. Artegall, however, remains a figure from the Arthurian past, and, in so far as he represents Lord Grey and the Earl of Leicester, it is also of the past glories of

---

[39] Wallace T. MacCaffrey, *Queen Elizabeth and the Making of Policy: 1572–1588* (Princeton: Princeton University Press, 1981), 97–118 (101).

[40] See Collinson, *Elizabethan Puritan*, 123–4, and also Helgerson, *Forms*, 271.

Elizabeth's reign that Spenser is to write. The moments of Astraea's and Arthur's reigns provide changeful mirrors to the age of Elizabeth. Their alteration does not even require the intervention of the author. A childless King Arthur can be seen as the culmination—but also the apocalyptic endpoint—of a dynasty.

Book V's overlapping Arthurian and golden age analogies speak directly to the culture of late Elizabethan England. Over the course of the Queen's reign the parallels that Foxe and Warner drew were to prove increasingly attractive to the society that surrounded her.[41] The second edition of Holinshed's *Chronicles*, published some ten years after the first, in one sense maintained its precursor's resolutely unteleological perspective. In contrast to such explicitly end-structured works as Halle's *Union of the Two Noble Families of Lancaster and York* (whose conclusion appeared in the very title), the *Chronicles* aspired to what Patterson calls 'up-to-the-minute topicality' and concluded, as had the first, with a demonstratively low-key report: this time with a proclamation for the preservation of corn and starch.[42] Yet, at the same time, the work shows a remarkable increase in concern with the veneer of ancient history that was applied to very recent events. In their 'augmenting' of Holinshed's original text the editors of the 1587 work greatly increased the emphasis on courtly displays: the description of the Queen's accession (*Chronicles* (1587), iii. 1170–80), for example, was expanded to cover ten folio pages, and as such provided an original for the annual accession day celebrations that went on to punctuate the work. The removal of the woodcuts of the 1577 edition, generally attributed to a lack of space, also facilitated the expression of a new historical perspective. The very format of the earlier Holinshed had implied a flat, unchanging field of history by means of the constant repetition of the same engravings of monarchs, battles, and burials. History remained the same and if this implied parallels they were not in any sense 'dynamic'. The plate that illustrated Queen Mary's funeral, for example, had been used almost a thousand pages earlier for Edward III.[43] In the second edition, in contrast, analogies are intentional and pointed. Splendid descriptions such as those of the death of Essex (iii. 1264) or the royal tournament (iii. 1316) expressly

---

[41] See e.g. Wilson, *England's Eliza*, or Strong, *Tudor and Stuart*. Studies on the political subtext of these pageants include Susan Frye, *Elizabeth I: The Competition for Representation* (Oxford: Oxford University Press, 1993) and Woudhuysen, 'Leicester's Literary Patronage', 305–46.

[42] *Reading Holinshed's*, 12; *Chronicles* (1587), iii. 1589.

[43] Holinshed, *Chronicles* (1577), 1785 and 915.

establish links between the contemporary aristocracy and their fore-
bears. The editors, always eager to explain the significance of the 'shews'
they describe, on several occasions drive home the affinity between
England and ancient Israel (e.g. iii. 1177 and 1270). At the Norwich
pageants in which, as so often, she was depicted as a new Deborah or
Judith (iii. 1290), the Queen forcefully expressed her satisfaction at such
analogies.

Yet it was exactly these conjunctions of the ancient and modern that
were to prove the most politically sensitive additions to the 1587 text.
The second edition fell notoriously foul of the censors, and the letter of
the Privy Council ordering the Archbishop of Canterbury to halt its dis-
tribution finds particular fault with its 'augmentation'. It is the 'matters
of later yeeres' that are of most concern to the council: being of importance to the affairs of state they are 'not therefore meete to be published
in such sorte as they are delyvered'.⁴⁴ The qualification 'in such sort as
they are delyvered' is significant. For, as Patterson says, under super-
vision the offending material 'was not just deleted but carefully
condensed'.⁴⁵ Condensed, that is, in such a way as to remove the conspicuous overlaying of the past and the present. In the case of the
section on Leicester, it was not just a laudatory family history, but
dangerous historical parallels that caused offence. In them we see how
the language of analogy could be a useful and dangerous political tool
not just in relation to the Queen but also for her courtiers.

The great bulk of the (censored) report of Leicester's expedition concerns itself with public feasting and pageantry. Following his campaign's
disastrous outcome Leicester himself is said to have objected to the
Holinshed reports, as they seemed to confirm Elizabeth's accusations
about his wasteful administration. Yet the council are also likely to have
been worried by the ways in which the shows and ceremonies reflected
the Earl's political ambition. Reading the reports it is not difficult to see
why. Entering the Dutch city of the Hague, Leicester is presented with a
series of 'shews' that not only represent 'Arthur of Britaine, whome they

---

⁴⁴ For the Privy Council's judgement see *Acts of the Privy Council: 1586–87*, ed. J. R. Dasent
(London, 1890–1907), 311–12, quoted in Patterson, *Reading Holinshed's*, 238.

⁴⁵ Patterson, *Reading Holinshed's*, 234. For some of the details of the censorship see Keith I.
Maslen, in 'Three Eighteenth-Century Reprints of the Castrated Sheets in Holinshed's
Chronicles', *The Library*, 13 (1958), 120–4, Steven Booth, *The Book Called Holinshed's Chronicles:
An Account of its Inception, Purpose, Contributors, Contents, Publication, Revision, and Influence on William
Shakespeare* (San Francisco: Book Club of California, 1968), and also Elizabeth Story Donno,
'Some Aspects of Shakespeare's Holinshed', *Huntington Library Quarterly*, 50 (1987), 229–48.

compared to the earle' (iii. 1426) but also anticipate further conquests envisioned by the ambitious Protestant faction. The sixth 'shew' presented 'a conceived battell fought betweene the English soldiors and the Spaniards, the English men still prevailing' (iii. 1426) which had yet to happen. The last, 'running as it were at tilt in botes' (iii. 1426), provides a curious analogue both to the events in the English Channel some four years later and to their representation in *The Faerie Queene*.

The expurgated report of the Earl of Leicester's expedition to the Netherlands is presented to us as an actuality overlaid by both the future and the past. It is a perspective that finds a textual equivalent in Foxe's 'Kalender' (*Actes*, sig. π2ᵃ) which, by means of a system of colour-coding, places the names of the Marian 'martyrs' alongside those of the victims of the early Roman persecutions. Foxe's method insists upon the temporal distancing and spiritual conjoining of the 'old' and the current church; the inevitable implication of the Arthurian pageantry surrounding Leicester was just such a connection. Just as Spenser would have found the historical Pope already moulded to the image of 'antichrist' by Foxe, in Holinshed (both editions of which Harper has shown him to have used),[46] or with his own eyes at court or in Leicester's service, he would have found a present that self-consciously represented itself in terms of the past.

The events of Book V did not simply constitute a distant analogue for Elizabethan policy; they confronted their readers with a literary landscape imbued with present-day realities. It was a depiction of recent history with rather more in common with the reports encountered by Spenser's contemporaries than is generally recognized. For, in the language of public pageantry recent history was frequently already to be found in 'pre-allegorized' form: the embattled Dutch Protestants appealing for English assistance, for example, had already fashioned 'a damsell named Antwerpe' and a 'cunning devise of a giant' in a public show.[47] There is a particularly clear link to be made here with Spenser's depiction of Belge. She does not 'represent' the low countries in the way that Una could earlier have been said to have represented the 'true church' and nor do her 'seuenteene goodly sonnes' (V. x. 7. 4) stand directly for the Dutch provinces. When Arthur comes to Belge's aid,

⁴⁶ See Harper, *Sources*, 11–12.
⁴⁷ Holinshed, *Chronicles* (1587), iii. 1339. In an analogous case Anne Lake Prescott, 'Foreign Policy in Fairyland: Henri IV and Spenser's Burbon', *Spenser Studies*, 14 (2000), 189–214, shows that Spenser would have encountered an already mythologized French monarch.

instead of confronting a damsel entrapped by a dragon, he finds a 'Ladie sad' complaining of a very sixteenth-century situation:

> Ay me (sayd she) and whether shall I goe?
>   Are not all places full of forraine powres?
>   My pallaces possessed of my foe,
>   My cities sackt, and their sky-threating towres
>   Raced, and made smooth fields now full of flowres?
> Onely these marishes, and myrie bogs,
>   In which the fearefull ewftes do build their bowres,
>   Yeeld me an hostry mongst the croking frogs,
> And harbour here in safety from those rauenous dogs.   (V. x. 23)

The stanza is one that exploits the intrusion of modernity into the mythical Arthurian past. In that magical setting we expect 'myrie bogs' to contain something 'fearefull' in the more common sense of 'inspiring terror'; when Spenser reveals that it is instead 'frightened' or 'timid' newts that are the cause of Belge's distress he brings us down to a very Belgian earth with a bump.[48] In a sudden moment of deflation the 'bowres' and 'hostry' of the romance plot are swamped by 'croking' amphibians. On a more serious level the language of 'cities' and 'forraine powres' and the physical details of exile in 'marishes, and myrie bogs' also corresponds to the conditions of the Continental wars. In tandem with the two-way dynamic of euhemerism, Spenser here also exploits the supposed proximity of Arthurian and Elizabethan history. For the story of Book V is still also the story of the last Britons. 'British' characters in the poem were hypothetically historical beings who had existed at a specific period in time: that is to say during the reign of Uther Pendragon, shortly before Arthur succeeded to his father's throne. There were serious doubts about their historicity, but as with Hercules (and in a way that was not the case with pre-Roman British history) there was a shadow of truth in at least some of their conflicts. Many English historiographers believed there had indeed been twelve battles (for this report was to be found in Nennius, independently of Monmouth), and Spenser (perhaps allowing his desires to get the better of him) seems to have believed that Arthur conquered Ireland.[49] Whether or not he believed in

---

[48] *OED*, s.v. 'fearful' n. 1 versus n. 3.

[49] On Arthur's appearance in Nennius see Tatlock, *Legendary History*, 180. On the King's conquest of the Island see *View*, 95. The extent to which Spenser himself believed there was 'good recorde' of Arthurian conquest remains open to question (see Hadfield, *Irish Experience*, esp. 87–8, 98–9, 110, 112).

this or other Arthurian exploits, they constituted a useful pre-cast narrative in the minds of his readership. The Arthur of that narrative was not solely, or even mainly, a knight errant, he was a famous king, famous especially for his foreign conquests. Warner's treatment of the reign confirms doubts about the evidence for Arthur as he appeared in the *Historia*, yet it is precisely this high-minded discrimination between aspects of the legend that enforces the credibility of its most important aspects:

> Yeat blazing *Arthur* as have some, I might have over-seene:
> He was victorious, making one amonst the worthies neéne.
> But (with his pardon) if I vouch his world of kingdomes wonne
> I am no Poet, and for lacke of pardon were undone.
> His *Scottish, Irish, Almaine, French,* and *Saxone* Batteles got,
> Yield fame sufficient: these seeme true, the rest I credite not.
>
> (*Albions England* (1592), 80, or (1602), 90)

Spenser represents Arthur before those '*Scottish, Irish, Almaine, French,* and *Saxone* Batteles' are won—as a prince with the certainty of glory before him—and in doing so he presents a tempting analogy for Elizabeth. For in the eyes of some Elizabeth too was within reach of such greatness, should she choose to grasp it. She was a picture of a queen 'before she was an empress' in the same way that Arthur is a prince 'before he was king'.[50] Arthur (like Hercules in the universal history) performs his deeds on familiar ground. If Arthur roved the Continent aiding those in distress as a prelude to the establishment of his empire, then for Elizabeth, who in her own propaganda professed to be doing the same, this provided an analogue implying a specific onward trajectory.[51]

Just such historiographical strategies governed public pageantry in Early Modern England—sometimes to the distaste of the sovereign herself. If 'Arthur' functioned as a analogue bearing an onward narrative, so too 'the Arthurian' could be used to express a distinct political vision. For the Tudors the age of Arthur had worked to represent a unified Britain under an 'original' native monarchy, but it was also to carry other associations. Not only could it be used in support of an expansionist foreign policy about which the Queen herself had the gravest doubts, it

---

[50] Letter to Ralegh, *Faerie Queene*, 737. On the Arthurian 'moment' of Spenser's historical fiction see McCabe, *Pillars*, 80–4.

[51] See 'A Declaration of the causes moving the queene of England to give aid to the defence of . . . the Lowe Countries', summarized in MacCaffrey, *Making of Policy*, 340–2.

could also imply the particular means by which empire was to be achieved.[52] As Helgerson has observed, the depiction of the Arthurian court allowed no place for the representation of a powerfully centralized and absolutist governmental order.[53] It was exactly by means of the archaic bravado of knight errantry that Elizabethan aristocrats expressed their frustration with such central control.[54] The tilts, feasting, and Arthurian iconography of Leicester's expedition to the Netherlands consequently implied not just political ambitions in terms of Continental empire, but also provided a means for the Earl to assert his individual autonomy through the image of the questing knight. In the end such attempts by Leicester, and later Essex, proved futile. Leicester ultimately had to settle for 'sheer appearances', while Essex was to push the implicit violence in such 'warlike shews' to breaking point when he confronted Elizabeth in open rebellion. Both men, however, had first turned to what McCoy has called 'the rites of knighthood' as a way of asserting their own rights and ambitions.

In the interaction between Arthur and Mercilla over the Belge episode we are thus presented with an analogy that is also a pointed reminder of difference. Throughout, the Prince is the active party. He steps forward 'with courage bold and great, | Admyr'd of all' to request that the Queen 'graunt him that aduenture' (V. x. 15. 6–9)—something that she immediately and 'gladly' does in the line that follows. Unusually, Spenser goes into some detail about Arthur's departure: telling us, for example, that he 'all his armours readie dight that day, | That nought the morrow next mote stay his fare' (V. x. 16. 3–4). The two stanzas devoted to his preparation work to confirm his self-reliance and independence. From the moment the adventure is granted Mercilla effectively disappears: we hear that she has given Arthur 'roiall giftes and riches rare, | As tokens of her thankefull mind beseene' (V. x. 17. 2–3), but for the rest she is

---

[52] On Elizabeth's doubts about such foreign policy objectives see e.g. MacCaffrey, *Shaping of the Elizabethan Regime: Elizabethan Politics, 1558–1572* (Princeton: Princeton University Press, 1968), 90, and Collinson, *Elizabethan Puritan*, 166–7. As Tatlock's *Legendary History* observes, 'no interest stands out in the *Historia* more prominently than imperialism' (p. 305).

[53] *Forms of Nationhood*, 48.

[54] See e.g. Mervyn James, 'English Politics and the Concept of Honour, 1485–1642', in *Society, Politics and Culture: Studies in Early Modern England* (Cambridge: Cambridge University Press, 1986), 308–415 (first publ. as *Past and Present*, Supplement 3 (1978), and Richard C. McCoy, *The Rites of Knighthood: The Literature and Politics of Elizabethan Chivalry*, The New Historicism, 7 (Berkeley: University of California Press, 1989). Whilst the *View* shows Spenser to be an advocate of imperial governance it also unequivocally supports a high level of autonomy for local governors.

unmentioned even at the moment when the Prince completes Belge's liberation. Leicester too had entreated Elizabeth to grant him 'aduenture' in the Low Countries. Her agreement, however, had been a good deal less swift, and, more importantly, it had not been followed by a similar politic disappearance. In a desperate parody of Arthurian autonomy Leicester had equipped his own expedition and bankrupted himself in the process.[55] When he, like Arthur, attempted to act as an independent agent in accepting the governorship of the Low Countries he had been humiliated by his sovereign's wrath.[56]

Especially in the second instalment, the new realities of the Tudor state intrude upon the world of fairy. The order that recalls Artegall from Ireland 'ere he could reforme it thoroughly' (V. xii. 27. 1) comes not only from the physically distant court of Glorian ruling 'this howre', but also from the historically distant time of Elizabeth's England. It is just such a moment that comes at the end of Book VI, where, in McCabe's vivid description, 'the Blatant Beast comes rampaging down the centuries and finds Spenser himself in his path'.[57] At such points the complexities that colour Spenser's 'state of present time' come momentarily to the surface. It is very much to such disparities between the treatment of present and former questing knights that Spenser refers when, in the Proem to Book V, he complains of the 'oddes I finde twixt those, and these which are' (V. Proem. 1. 5).

'Mirrours more then one'

Throughout *The Faerie Queene*, Spenser sets up historical mirrors for Elizabeth and her court, and (in line with humanist didactic theory) these are always intended to imply distance as well as aspiration towards a projected ideal. There is, however, a shift between the material of 1590 and that of 1596. In place of earlier moments of arrival the later work (like Foxe in his move from Constantine to England's Deborah) allowed its analogy to slip from hopeful religious return to a more combative and contingent political state. This 'contemporary' quality of Spenser's later verse in fact worked brilliantly to illustrate the genuinely cyclical nature

---

[55] MacCaffrey, *Making of Policy*, 352–3.

[56] Ibid. 357. In the light of this reading, Fichter's belief that in Mercilla Spenser portrays Elizabeth as 'the embodiment of the perfect virtue of justice' (p. 201) evidently requires some adjustment.

[57] McCabe, *Pillars*, 79.

of Elizabethan politics. Books IV–VI were entered in the Stationer's
Register on 20 January 1596, a pocket in history that gives a unique view
on the significance of Book V.[58] In one sense the allegory evidently
looked back to the events of the Elizabethan past: 1580 had seen Lord
Grey sent to Ireland, 1586 Leicester in action on the Continent, 1587 the
execution of Mary Queen of Scots, 1588 the scattering of the Spanish
Armada, and 1589 another in a whole series of turnabouts on matters
of religion in France. Yet the events of the past were also those of the
present and future. The successful delivery of Belge related more closely
to Norris's very recent victories on the Continent, and many expected
his current expedition to Ireland to follow in the tracks of Grey's more
than a decade earlier. There was, at the same time, news of an armada
reportedly greater than that of 1588, whose sailing was planned for June
or July of 1596.[59] Leicester, Grey, Norris, Essex, and others found themselves confronted in turn with the perennial problems of England's
'crisis management' foreign policy. Arthur and Artegall consequently
acted as signifiers with a bewildering series of signifieds.

This was not a play of analogy that Spenser attempted to delimit;
instead his text expertly promoted it. There are a good many points at
which Spenser implies a Leicester–Arthur parallel, though not so many
as to prevent plausible deniability. Not only do the pageants at Kenil-
worth and The Hague provide evidence of Leicester's use of Arthurian
iconography, but at several points in the text the detail of Spenser's
description invites specific analogies.[60] The actions of the Souldan
(Philip II of Spain) against Mercilla's knights, whom 'He either spoiles, if
they against him stand, | Or to his part allures, and bribeth vnder hand'
(V. viii. 18. 8–9), for example, seems to suggest the Duke of Parma's
highly successful policy of demanding the abject surrender of Dutch
cities and his notorious bribery of the Queen's officers, Stanley and
Yorke.[61] Likewise, the Souldan's wife's treatment of Mercilla's peace
envoy—'Me like a dog she out of dores did thrust' (V. viii. 22. 7)—is a
potential allusion to Spain's refusal to admit English ambassadors in the
run-up to the Armada crisis.[62] Yet the Leicester parallel is by no means

[58] Arber (ed.), *Transcript of the Registers*, iii. 7.
[59] On these reports see MacCaffrey, *Elizabeth I: War and Politics 1588–1603* (Princeton:
Princeton University Press, 1992), 110.
[60] On Leicester's pageantry see e.g. John Nichols, *The Progresses and Public Processions of Queen
Elizabeth* (Edinburgh: privately published, 1788), sig. 17B1ᵃ.
[61] See MacCaffrey, *Making of Policy*, 376.
[62] See ibid., e.g. 328 and 341.

an exclusive one. References to Sir John Norris are at least as convincing, and certainly the Bourbon episode could apply directly to no other English general. The allusion to Lord Grey in the Blatant Beast episode speaks for itself, and the depiction of an Ireland left 'ere he could reforme it thoroughly' (V. xii. 27. 1) provides an obvious analogy with Spenser's own experiences in the Lord's service.[63] Finally, associations with Essex, who after Cadiz became the model of English knighthood, were inevitable, whether Spenser promoted them or not.

To the late sixteenth-century reader, the historical allegory would have presented a patchwork of contemporary politics whose interchangeability itself drove home a political message. If, as Josephine Bennett long ago suggested, Spenser reworked Book V's allegory 'at a white heat' to include the latest political references, then that incorporation deliberately facilitated the recognition of internal analogies.[64] In this way Norris became not just a new Arthur or Hercules but also a new Leicester or Grey. So too Spenser invited parallels between Mary Tudor and Mary Queen of Scots (whose actions are shadowed by Duessa in Books I and V of the poem).[65] The receptivity of Spenser's readership to such more recent linkage is proved by early manuscript annotations. In 1597 John Dixon was certainly quite comfortable with the idea that Duessa could be first the Queen of England and then the Queen of Scots.[66] For others it was not even required that the action move on for additional parallels to accumulate: in another copy of the poem Arthur's request for the commission to rescue Belge is accompanied by the autograph addition of the names of Leicester and Essex alike.[67] As these

---

[63] Catherine G. Canino, 'Reconstructing Lord Grey's Reputation: A New View of the *View*', *Sixteenth Century Journal*, 29 (1998), 3–18, argues that in large part Spenser created rather than responded to the notion that Grey had suffered a loss of reputation.

[64] Bennett, *The Evolution*, 204. For criticisms of the theory see W. J. B. Owen, 'The Structure of *The Faerie Queene*', *PMLA* 68 (1953), 1079–1100, and Woudhuysen, 'Leicester's Literary Patronage', 214–22. Owen's own conclusions (usefully summarized in n. 47 on 1098) differ little from Bennett's as far as Book V is concerned.

[65] On the way in which Spenser transfers his analogy see Richard A. McCabe, 'The Masks of Duessa: Spenser, Mary Queen of Scots, and James VI', *ELR* 17 (1987), 224–42.

[66] Hough (ed.), *First Commentary*, 8–10.

[67] See Alastair Fowler, 'Oxford and London Marginalia to "The Faerie Queene"', *N&Q* 206 (1961), 416–19 (417) and also John Manning, 'Notes and Marginalia in Bishop Percy's Copy of Spenser's *Works* (1611)', *N&Q* 229 (1984), 225–7. Another near-contemporary set of annotations (appearing in the Cambridge University Library copy of *The Faerie Queene*) blithely assign to Arthur and Artegall at the court of Mercilla the roles of '[Fr]ench and Scotch [amba]ssadors'—the author evidently being unconcerned about the fact that this reading could not possibly be sustained for any of the knights' other actions. For details see Anon., 'MS Notes to Spenser's "Faerie Queene"', *N&Q*, 202 (1957), 509–15 (512).

annotations testify, by bringing his distant analogies closer to the present age Spenser had made them still more sensitive mirrors of current concerns. By offering both a distant parallel with Arthur and a recent one with Grey or Leicester, the poet's depiction of foreign policy contained a potentially critical combination of similarity and difference.

It is not surprising that Spenser should have expressed such caution about circulating the now lost work *Stemmata Dudleiana*. As he tells Harvey in the *Letters*: 'especially of the sundry Apostrophes therein, addressed you knowe to whome, muste more advisement be had, than so lightly to sende them abroade'.[68] Historical 'apostrophes' to Elizabeth (and certainly to Lord Leicester) could be dangerous things. In a culture attuned to historical analogies the implications of connection between past and present were far-reaching. During the years of the monarch's reign the complexity of analogy increased. The implications of the most favoured parallels (Astraea and Arthur) were productively double-edged, and their reuse over the decades also built up a more recent pattern of correspondence. *The Faerie Queene* takes a central place in these developments: it was marked by the influence of a wider culture, but also helped to determine the 'antique' images through which the age saw itself. Not only did the 1596 material record an alteration of the monarch's image, time also changed the implications of parallels set up in the 1590 text. Above all, fears or aspirations regarding a reformed church and empire took on a different aspect as the years went by. The historical mirrors in Spenser's text proved highly changeable. As the final chapter of this study sets out, under certain circumstances they might even seem to project beyond history to prophecy.

---

[68] *Three Proper and Wittie Familiar Letters* (1580), in *Spenser: Complete Poetical Works*, ed. J. C. Smith and E. de Selincourt (Oxford: Oxford University Press, 1912; repr. 1970), 612. Further references appear in the text and are to this edition.

CHAPTER 6

'By Cyphers, or by Magicke Might':
Prophecy and History

In Merlin's Cave and King Ryence's Closet

Spenser and his contemporaries used historical analogy in a way that inevitably implied future developments, offering either encouragement or warning to those of the present age. The interpretation of history in this form required a forward as much as a backward projection on the part of the reader. Looking into a historical mirror allowed one to envisage the road ahead. History, in this sense, might prove prophetic—a basic assumption that stood at the heart of all its claims to offer practical instruction. It was possible, however, to turn history to prophecy in a more direct manner. By imagining some ancient source and attributing to it a vision of action that had, in reality, already come and gone, past events could also be envisaged as a certain future. All that was required was a change of tense.

It is in this form that the *The Faerie Queene* gives an account of events from the time of Arthur to the Elizabethan present. Through the figure of Merlin in the third canto of Book III, the history of Britain begun in Alma's castle is completed in the guise of a prophetic vision. To the writer of epic romance this mode of historical narrative had a well-established pedigree. Both Virgil and Ariosto had represented their patron's forerunners in this way. But Spenser was as much an adapter as a follower of generic traditions. His Merlin, unlike Virgil and Ariosto's prophets, is displaced in neither spirit nor body: he is a man who emerges from his own time and space. Merlin's Maridunum ('now by chaunge | Of name *Cayr-Merdin* cald' (III. iii. 7. 3–4)), is, as we have seen, a place that Spenser renders with an unusual degree of historical and geographical exactitude. Maridunum is also surrounded by wars, plots, and secret councils. It is worth recalling the events that lead us to this location.

At the end of the first canto of Book III of *The Faerie Queene*, the knights of holiness and chastity decide that they will travel together on the next stage of their journey. By way of small-talk, Redcrosse asks Britomart about the origins of her quest. This well-intentioned question, however, sets off an extraordinary attack of panic. Horror-stricken, and shaking 'with hart-thrilling throbs and bitter stowre, | As if she had a feuer fit' (III. ii. 5. 3–4), the lady knight at last attempts to extract herself from the situation by means of some outrageous lying. Falsely claiming to have been brought up 'in warlike stowre' from infancy, she proceeds to level wild and slanderous accusations at the knight of Justice— Artegall.[1] Claiming to know nothing of that knight's appearance, she cajoles the hapless Redcrosse into providing her with a description:

> Yet him in euery part before she knew,
> How euer list her now her knowledge faine,
> Sith him whilome in *Britaine* she did vew,
> To her reuealed in a mirrhour plaine.   (III. ii. 17. 1–4)

This earlier encounter, which Britomart is at such pains to hide from her companion, provides the trigger for the events described in Cantos ii and iii. Britomart, it transpires, was afforded a vision of Artegall well before she became a 'maid martial', while looking into a kind of crystal ball kept in her father's castle in Deheubarth (III. ii. 18. 4). This 'mirrhour plaine' turns out to be the work of Merlin—the prophet, who, in the following canto, is himself to step in to interpret Britomart's vision. Artegall and she, he tells her, are destined to produce a child who will establish a great royal dynasty. The story of that dynasty, concluding with the reign of Elizabeth herself, is to be the subject of Merlin's prophecy.

In structure the prophecy is much like the chronicle of Book II for which it provides a continuation. Partly as a result, those looking at the narration of national history in the first instalment of *The Faerie Queene* have tended to view it as a complex, but ideologically orthodox, expression of providential history.[2] While the abruptness of Merlin's conclu-

---

[1] *Faerie Queene*, III. ii. 6–9. The falsity of Britomart's claims about the 'foule dishonour' done to her be Artegall is self-evident. Britomart's description of her martial upbringing is not always seen as false. It is implicitly credited, for example, by Hamilton (ed.), *Faerie Queen*, 318 n. (a reading improved in the more recent A. C. Hamilton (ed.), *The Faerie Queene*, 2nd edn. (London: Longman, 2001), 303 n.). As is clear from III. iii. 51–7, it is only as a grown woman, after hearing Merlin's prophecy, that Britomart takes on the role of warrior.

[2] See e.g. McCabe, *Pillars*, 184–93; O'Connell, 82–3; Darryl J. Gless, *Interpretation and Theology in Spenser* (Cambridge: Cambridge University Press, 1994), 195; and Berger, 'Structure of

sion—with its implied fears about the Queen's childlessness—has been noted, the models of dynastic prophecy provided by Virgil and Ariosto have allayed any worries about the probity of the act of prognostication itself.[3] Merlin's status as prophet has been ameliorated by reference to a context of Christian conceptions of time: in particular by the depiction of prophecy as the revelation of a pre-ordained and intricately patterned divine plan.[4] So much so, in fact, that the 'prophetic' element of Spenser's poem has been routinely depicted as the structural opposite of the political and historical allegory.[5]

Merlin's Chronicle'. Even Howard Dobin's perceptive analysis of the episode, in *Merlin's Disciples: Prophecy, Poetry, and Power in Renaissance England* (Stanford, Calif.: Stanford University Press, 1990), sees Spenser's intention as entirely adulatory—the only dissident element he discovers in the episode being the unintended result of the textual instability inherent in all prophecy. Fichter's argument that Britomart's encounter with Merlin is a moral lesson teaching the heroine that she must subjugate her desire for martial triumph in favour of the still greater glory of love does not hold water, as it ignores the fact that Britomart, at this point, has as yet no aspiration to knightly valour (*Poets Historical*, 156–81). Kathleen Williams's reading of Merlin's lesson about love, *Spenser's 'Faerie Queen': The World of Glass* (London: Routledge & Kegan Paul, 1966), 93–4, is probably closer to the mark. Patrick Gerard Cheney, '"Secret Powre Unseene": Good Magic in Spenser's Legend of Britomart', *Studies in Philology*, 85 (1988), 1–28, sets out the allegorical function of good magic in the presentation of Book III's vision of providence. Theresa M. Krier, *Gazing on Secret Sights: Spenser, Classical Imitation, and the Decorums of Vision* (Ithaca, NY: Cornell University Press, 1990), 166–76, examines the traditions that influence the development from Britomart's original vision in the mirror to her eventual providential encounter with Merlin.

[3] See e.g. Bulger, *Historical Changes*, 96; Pope, *National History*, 42–68; Rodgers, *Time in the Narrative*, 59–100; and Katherine A. Hoffman, 'Reading History in the *Orlando Furioso* and *The Faerie Queene*' (unpublished doctoral dissertation, Northwestern University, 1991). For a succinct overview of the traditions of dynastic epic, and a commentary on Spenser's narration of national history, see Colin Burrow, *Edmund Spenser* (Plymouth: Northcote House, 1996), 27–42. As well as following Ariosto, Spenser, when describing the interchange between Glauce and Britomart (III. ii. 30–51), translates and adapts from the pseudo-Virgilian epyllion *Ciris*.

[4] The concept is set out with lucidity in R. W. Southern's influential lecture 'Aspects of the European Tradition of Historical Writing: 3. History as Prophecy', *Transactions of the Royal Historical Society*, NS 22 (1972), 159–81 (172). Clearly the idea was integral to the Protestant understanding of Old Testament prophecy and history (for some recent views see Wilks (ed.), *Prophecy and Eschatology*). Non-biblical Prophecy was also read in this context: the most influential work of political prophecy—Geoffrey of Monmouth's *Vita Merlini*—originally formed part of what claimed to be the national history. Histories and prophecies continued to coexist, with manuscript prophecies frequently bound up with various histories (for examples, see H. L. D. Ward, *Catalogue of Romances in the Department of Manuscripts in the British Museum*, 3 vols. (London: Longmans, 1883), i. 278–338).

[5] The contrast is especially strong in Fletcher's *Prophetic Moment* and O'Connell's *Mirror and Veil* (notably pp. 126 and 156). William Blackburn, in 'Spenser's Merlin', *Renaissance and Reform*, 4 (1980), 179–98, in line with Fletcher's perspective, argues for Merlin as a figure for the poet. On this overlap see also Lawrence F. Rhu, 'After the Middle Ages: Prophetic Authority and Human Fallibility in Renaissance Epic', in James L. Kugel (ed.), *Poetry and Prophecy: The Beginnings of a Literary Tradition* (Ithaca: Cornell University Press, 1990), 163–84. Highley has argued that Merlin allows Spenser 'imaginatively [to] reconstruct his own position on the margins of the Elizabethan state in Ireland into a priviledged site of vision and power' (*Shakespeare, Spenser*, 17).

There can be no doubt that the concept of divine providence *is* an important aspect of what the poet is exploring in the chronicle sections. Yet Britomart's terror about revealing her prophetic knowledge cannot be entirely written off as maidenly modesty—especially as her 'bitter stowre' echoes the 'half extatick stoure' which, we learn, overcame Merlin when he looked too far into the political future. The Britomart who gazes at the 'glassie globe that *Merlin* made' (III. ii. 21. 1) is still a princess at a royal court rather than a maid martial in Fairyland. Again, it is worth taking note of this location: the scene at King Ryence's court in South Wales marking one of a number of significant instances in the poem where Spenser refers to a world outside Fairyland—a place of more prosaic political concerns—and the King's use of the mirror to anticipate treason and invasion (III. ii. 21) reflects this fact.[6] Parallels with the world of Elizabeth's court are inviting, and Howard Dobin has pointed to an intriguing connection between the events in Book III and Elizabeth's visit (in 1575) to the unofficial court historian and astrologer John Dee.[7]

Dobin is surely right to link Britomart's exploits with Elizabeth's own dabbling in prophecy. He is right also when he goes on to note the way in which Britomart's mirror reflects those that appeared earlier in the book's Proem. For, Spenser's use of the words 'mirrhour fayre' (III. ii. 22. 5) to describe what is a 'glassie globe' (III. ii. 21. 1) 'round and hollow shaped . . . Like to the world it selfe' (III. ii. 19. 8–9) is one of the clearest examples of deliberate verbal linkage in *The Faerie Queene*. Three cantos before, the poet, referring to Ralegh's work and his own, has recommended to the Queen 'In mirrours more then one her selfe to see' (III. Proem. 5. 6), and—as observed in the previous chapter—in the Proem to Book II the poet tells her:

> In this faire mirrhour maist behold thy face,
> And thine owne realmes in lond of Faery,
> And in this antique Image thy great auncestry.   (II. Proem. 4. 7–9)

In Book II Elizabeth finds her 'antique Image', Prince Arthur, reading chronicle history. Like that passage, Merlin's prophecy in Book III has long been read as a (fleeting) vision of a universal order in which the

---

[6] It is also noteworthy that Britomart and Glauce, the instant they return from visiting the prophet's cave, 'in secret counsell close conspird, . . . And diuerse plots did frame, to maske in strange disguise' (III. iii. 51. 5–9).

[7] Dobin, *Merlin's Disciples*, 5.

Queen is invited to take her rightful place. Here too, moreover, Elizabeth will find an 'antique Image' of her own act of interpretation. For Britomart and Elizabeth—as they look into their respective mirrors —stand at opposite ends of the narrative laid out by Merlin: for the one it is prophecy, for the other, history. At both ends, however, Merlin's time-line extends beyond its recipient. In the case of Britomart, Merlin begins with history, placing her in the context of the famous lineage that she is later to set out proudly for Paridell. 'For from thy wombe', Merlin tells her:

> a famous Progenie
> Shall spring, out of the auncient *Troian* blood,
> Which shall reuiue the sleeping memorie
> Of those same antique Peres, the heauens brood,
> Which *Greeke* and *Asian* riuers stained with their blood.   (III. iii. 22. 5–9)

At the moment of its annunciation, Merlin's address to Britomart points two ways, and in so doing puts a heavy burden on its recipient. At the other end of the time-line, however, the pressure is perhaps still greater: the concluding stanzas of Merlin's prophecy which herald 'a royal virgin' overshoot the reign of Elizabeth in a way that is suddenly disquieting:

> But yet the end is not. There *Merlin* stayd,
> As ouercomen of the spirites powre,
> Or other ghastly spectacle dismayd,
> That secretly he saw, yet note discoure:
> Which suddein fit, and halfe extatick stoure
> When the two fearefull women saw, they grew
> Greatly confused in behauioure.   (III. iii. 50. 1–7)

Merlin himself immediately laughs off this momentary loss of composure, and critics of the episode have likewise tended to make light of it.

Yet some of the assumptions about Spenser's orthodox intentions— what Dobin calls 'the allegorical design of the poem' (*Merlin's Disciples*, 5)—need to be questioned. The match between Britomart and Elizabeth is not nearly so comforting as critics have made out. Indeed, in the shift from the 'faire mirrhour' found in the Proem to Book II and the 'mirrhour fayre' encountered here we find reversal as well as reflection. In making his mirror 'round and hollow shaped' Spenser may again be drawing our attention to inversions: Elizabeth's mirror, which we may assume to be convex (like all mirrors of the period), is, as it were, turned inside-out by Britomart's concave instrument.[8] Both women look into fair mirrors to see *themselves* (a point that Spenser stresses), yet the images with which they are presented are different. Britomart sees 'A comely knight, all arm'd in complete wize' (III. ii. 24. 2): the image, although she does not yet know it, of her appointed husband. In so far as Artegall presents an analogy for the Earl of Leicester, Elizabeth too has seen this vision, but if it ever existed it has entirely vanished. The Queen's fate, instead, is altogether closer to that which Britomart momentarily imagines for herself. Not knowing of her fated union, she complains to Glauce that her 'wicked fortune',

> Can haue no end, nor hope of my desire,
> But feed on shadowes, whiles I die for food,
> And like a shadow wexe, whiles with entire
> Affection, I doe languish and expire.
> I fonder, then *Cephisus* foolish child,
> Who hauing vewed in a fountaine shere
> His face, was with the loue thereof beguild;
> I fonder loue a shade, the bodie farre exild.   (III. ii. 44. 2–9)

Glauce at once responds with sound counsel:

> Nought like (quoth she) for that same wretched boy
> Was of himselfe the idle Paramoure;
> Both loue and louer, without hope of ioy,
> For which he faded to a watry flowre.
> But better fortune thine, and better howre,
> Which lou'st the shadow of a warlike knight;
> No shadow, but a bodie hath in powre:
> That bodie, wheresouer that it light,
> May learned be by cyphers, or by Magicke might.   (III. ii. 45)

Britomart is 'much cheard' (III. ii. 47. 1) by Glauce's words, but a mere two cantos earlier the poet has affirmed that Elizabeth *is* to see shadows by means of a mirror, and that same formulation is to be found in the previous Proem. Britomart in King Ryence's closet thus presents one of

---

[8] On the construction of mirrors of the period, see Grabes, *Mutable Glass*, 4. On mirrors and prophecy see esp. pp. 36–62; on Spenser specifically, see pp. 150–67 and 180. There is an extensive tradition of commentary on Britomart's mirror, especially from feminist and Lacanian perspectives. The episode is very important e.g. in Elizabeth Bellamy's *Translations of Power: Narcissism and the Unconscious in Epic History* (Ithaca, NY: Cornell University Press, 1992) and Linda Gregerson's *The Reformation of the Subject: Spenser, Milton, and the English Protestant Epic*, Cambridge Studies in Renaissance Literature and Culture, 6 (Cambridge: Cambridge University Press, 1995).

the most troubling 'mirrors' that the Queen may find in the first instalment. The image of '*Cephisus* foolish child' (Narcissus) entranced by his own reflection is only one of the mirrors with which Elizabeth is presented 'her selfe to see' (III. Proem. 5. 6), and it must be well veiled. Yet, as an image it expresses an undeniable logic: for the aged Queen there is nowhere to look but on the picture of herself as embodied in 'antique history': she must 'feed on shadowes' presented to her by the poet. To compass her future 'by cyphers, or by Magicke might' is an exceptionally dangerous enterprise.

Beside the 'antique Image' of the Queen's 'great auncestry', Merlin's history can also be compared to that found in less exalted spheres. The notion that a mirror should 'whilome' have afforded Britomart the first glimpse of her future neatly encapsulates a number of the paradoxes surrounding the Renaissance practice of political prophecy. From Medieval times, those who claimed to have found ancient prophecies routinely dated them earlier than the real time of composition and retold historical facts as part of the supposed prophecy.[9] As Sharon Jansen says, 'the greater part of most political prophecy was really history disguised as prophecy: historical events were treated as if they had not yet occurred'.[10] Spenser's Merlin is a particularly extreme example of this general trend.[11]

The events narrated in the second and third cantos of Book III need to be read in the context of contemporary political prophecy—especially as it operated at the height of the Alençon marriage crisis, in the years 1579–80. Elizabeth in 1579, and Britomart in Cantos ii and iii, have marriage in mind, and both are surrounded by a maelstrom of prophecy. In the light of this disturbing parallel, it is the hated Alençon who becomes the nightmarish mirror image of Artegall.

The kinds of reworking and reflection earlier observed between the first and second instalment of *The Faerie Queene* are also in evidence here.

---

[9] See Rupert Taylor, *The Political Prophecy in England* (New York: Columbia University Press, 1911), 7. The same feature was, incidentally, also to be found in Irish prophecies, with which it is probable Spenser would have had contact. For observations on Irish prophecies, see Eugene O'Curry, *Lectures on the Manuscript Materials of Ancient Irish History* (Dublin: James Duffy, 1861), 390–6.

[10] Sharon L. Jansen, *Political Protest and Prophecy under Henry VIII* (Woodbridge: Boydell Press, 1991), 15.

[11] The approach was to be taken still further by Thomas Heywood in a work entitled *The Life of Merlin, Sirnamed Ambrosius: His Prophesies, and Predictions Interpreted; and their Truth Made good by our English Annalls* (1641), which interchanged the standard British chronicle with a transparent (but nevertheless laboriously explicated) prophecy.

In 1580 Spenser had already begun work on his great poem;[12] and, although published a decade later, its treatment of prophecy bears the imprint of the crisis years 1579–80. The works which *were* published in those years—*The Shepheardes Calender* and the *Three Proper and Wittie Familiar Letters*—bear that imprint still more clearly. Both are concerned with and make use of political prophecy. An examination of these texts and those that surrounded them can cast some light on the dark recesses of Merlin's cave and King Ryence's closet.

The Tradition of Political Prophecy

At the time Spenser was writing, 'prophecy' could denote a wide range of texts and activities: from apocalyptic rantings on the streets of London by the likes of William Hacket, to the interpretation of biblical passages carried out by certain preachers with puritan leanings.[13] *Political* prophecy constitutes a subset of this broad field, and while it un-doubtedly interconnects with a great number of other subsets, it is not unreasonable to refer to it as a distinct form. It was defined by the first full academic study of the literary genre, that of Rupert Taylor, as 'any expression of thought, written or spoken, in which an attempt is made to foretell coming events of a political nature'.[14] It is an activity distinct from prediction: political prophecy (although often obscured by in-scrutable symbolism) reads very much like history written in the future tense. It had originated (in Taylor's view as a literary exercise) with the work of Geoffrey of Monmouth, but had soon developed into an instru-ment of analysis, persuasion, and sedition. Stylistically, Taylor notes ten forms of prophetic composition—most notably the Sibylline (which gives clues by means of initial letters) and Galfridian (which does the same by means of animal symbolism). As we can tell from the State Papers, and from numerous manuscript remains, in the sixteenth cen-tury such prophecies were both extremely popular and politically suspect; and at their centre stood the figure of Merlin.

As Glauce's conflation of 'cyphers' and 'Magicke might' suggests, it is doubtful if many readers distinguished astrological forecasts from other

---

[12] Spenser tells Harvey he intends to send him a part of the poem in the first of the *Three Proper and Wittie Familiar Letters* (1580). See Selincourt and Smith (eds.), *Works*, 612.

[13] On Hacket, see *DNB*. On 'The Prophesyings', see Patrick Collinson, *Elizabethan Puritan*, 51, 126, and 168–96.

[14] Taylor, *Political Prophecy*, 2.

predictions delivered oracularly by seers such as Merlin.[15] Certainly, the title-page of Henry Howard's *Defensative Against the Poyson of Supposed Prophesies* (1583) amalgamates 'olde paynted bookes, espositions of Dreames, Oracles, Revelations, Invocations of damned spirites, Judicialles of Astrologie, or any other kinde of pretended knowledge whatsoever', going on to condemn each with venom.[16] As Howard points out, all were proscribed by statute: already in 1402 Henry IV had directed a law against Welsh minstrels, and in 1542 Henry VIII had made it a felony 'to declare any false prophecy upon occasion of arms fields, letters, names, cognizances, or badges'.[17] The law had been repealed under Edward VI, but later reinstated, repealed again under Mary, and reinstated by Elizabeth.[18] As the statute of 1562 explained:

> Sithence the Expiration and Ending of the Statute made in the Time of King *Edward* the Sixth, intituled, *An Act against fond and fantastical Prophecies*, divers evil disposed Persons, inclined to the stirring and moving of Factions, Seditions and Rebellions within this Realm, have been the more bold to attempt the like Practices in feigning, imagining, inventing and publishing of such fond and fantastical Prophecies, as well concerning the Queen's Majesty, as divers honourable Personages, Gentlemen and others of this Realm, as was used and practised before the making of the said Statute, to the great Disquiet, Trouble and Peril of the Queen's Majesty, and of this her Realm.[19]

Those who 'advance, publish and set forth by Writing, Printing, Signing or any other open Speech or Deed' any such prophecy, face in the first instance a one-year term of imprisonment and a severe fine.

For the monarch who lacked an heir, prophecy constituted an especially serious threat. While, ultimately, the greatest outpouring of proph-

---

[15] On the absence of this distinction in the mind of the general populace, see Keith Thomas, *Religion and the Decline of Magic: Studies in Popular Beliefs in Sixteenth and Seventeenth Century England* (London: Weidenfeld & Nicolson, 1971), 409. Glauce's reference to 'cyphers' should also alert us to the fact that the numerological patterning described by Mills and others need not, of itself, be associated with an untroubled 'world picture'. Political prophets were as likely to seize upon a perceived numerical pattern as any other—the anonymous manuscript prophecy in British Library, Harley MS 559, fol. 39ᵃ, for example, attributes great significance to the numbers 6 and 1. In the same way, the fact that Merlin's words 'But yet the end is not' echo Matthew 24: 6 by no means eliminates the threat they carry.

[16] *Defensative*, sig. A1ᵃ.

[17] John Raithby (ed.), *Statutes at Large*, 10 vols. (London: George Eyre & Andrew Strahan, 1811), Anno 4° Hen. IV (1402), XXVII, vol. i. 545; Anno 33° Hen. VIII (1541–2), XIV, vol. ii. 187.

[18] Raithby, *Statutes*, Anno 1° Edw. VI (1547), XII. i, vol. ii. 256 [repeal]; Anno 3° & 4° Edw. VI (1549), XV, vol. ii. 295 ['An Act against fond and fantastical Prophecies']; Anno 1° Mariæ (1553), I, vol. ii. 323 [repeal]; Anno 5° Elizabethæ (1562), XV, vol. ii. 440.

[19] Anno 5° Elizabethæ (1562), XV, vol. ii. 440.

etic literature was to accompany the Civil War, the Stuarts initially seemed to find political prophecy a less threatening form.[20] Significantly, the accession of James I was to be marked by the publication, by the King's printer, of *The Whole Prophecy of Scotland*—a collection of political prophecies attributed to Merlin and others which would clearly have been illegal during Elizabeth's reign.[21] Prophecies such as Cranmer's in *Henry VIII* (5. 4. 14–55) or the apparition of a dynasty of succeeding kings in *Macbeth* had less subversive potential for a king ensured of a male heir.[22] The eighth of Banquo's ancestors, who, Macbeth observes, 'bears a glass | Which shows me many more' (4. 1. 118–19) may well have directed his mirror at the King himself, thereby reflecting an ongoing line of which the reigning Sovereign was a part.[23] Confronted by the failure of his own dynasty, the horrified Macbeth provides a perfect inversion of Britomart. The positions of Shakespeare's and Spenser's royal audiences are likewise reversed: King James sees Macbeth who (by means of the prophetic mirror) also sees him, just as Britomart (hearing Merlin's prophecy) sees *and is seen by* Elizabeth. Where James smiles at the mirror-gazer's distress in the assurance of an ongoing succession, Elizabeth, conversely, may look on a smiling Britomart and be reminded of the failure of the Tudor line. Unlike the Stuarts, Tudor monarchs from Henry VIII onwards could find little comfort in prophetic mirrors: Jansen's study of political prophecy under Henry shows how, in part as a result of the lack of a male heir, prophetic utterance became 'not simply a way of understanding the present' but a way of shaping it—a weapon with which the dispossessed attacked the state.[24]

Nor was an interest in political prophecy restricted to the margins: Harington made use of the famous HEMPE prophecy in his secret

---

[20] On the explosion of prophetic literature at the time of the Civil War, see Bernard Capp, *Astrology and the Popular Press: English Almanacs 1500–1800* (London: Faber & Faber, 1979).

[21] *The Whole Prophecy of Scotland* (1603). The prophecies were certainly circulated in manuscript before this date; one, copied around 1600 but composed earlier, exists in the British Library (see Sloane MS 1802).

[22] William Shakespeare, *King Henry VIII*, ed. John Margeson (Cambridge: Cambridge University Press, 1990), and *Macbeth*, ed. A. R. Braunmuller (Cambridge: Cambridge University Press, 1997). Marie Axton, in *The Queen's Two Bodies: Drama and the Elizabethan Succession* (London: Royal Historical Society, 1977), 116, contrasts Cranmer's prophecy with a more equivocal Elizabethan example.

[23] Braunmuller (ed.), notes that the eight kings reflect the eight Stuarts who had thus far ruled Scotland. However, he believes that the 'glass' is not a looking-glass but a magic crystal (196–7 nn.).

[24] Jansen, *Political Protest*, 18. See also L. Coote, 'A Language of Power: Prophecy and Public Affairs in Later Medieval England', in *Prophecy: The Power of Inspired Language in History*, 17–30.

'Tract on the Succession to the Crown' circulated a year before the Queen's death; and in search of a solution to the marriage crisis, Cecil himself arranged for the Queen's horoscope to be cast.[25] If we are to take at all seriously the near-hysterical pronouncements of Francis Coxe's tract, *The Wickednesse of Magicall Sciences* (1561), we must conclude that, at least in the early part of Elizabeth's reign, it was a business in which all strata of society engaged.[26] Before Elizabeth's much-praised punishment of the 'Astrologers, the starre gasers, and Prognosticatours' (sig. A1[a]), Coxe tells us, such people 'so blinded and bewytched the wittes of men, that scant durst thei credit God his self, if it semed that their blinded prophesies any time would make contradiction' (sig. A4[b]). If Coxe is exaggerating, he is certainly not alone in doing so: as Taylor observes, 'the Englishman of the late Middle Ages and early Renaissance seems to have been proverbial for his love of secular prophecies and his belief in them'.[27] In particular, prophecies proliferated at times of crisis. Keith Thomas's survey concludes that 'prophecies of one kind or another were employed in virtually every rebellion or popular rising which disturbed the Tudor state'.[28] When Glauce speaks of a prospective marriage which 'May learned be by cyphers, or by Magicke might' it is surely likely that Spenser's readers would have associated these words at least as much with political and astrological prophecy as with national providential history.

Certainly, even within Elizabethan court circles, prophecy could be

---

[25] *A Tract on the Succession to the Crown*, ed. Clements R. Markham (London: J. B. Nichols & Sons, 1880), 17. Harington, writing in 1602, refers to what he calls the 'blynde prophesye' that 'After Hempe is sowen and growen | Kings of England shall be none' (where 'Hempe' is read as referring to Henry, Edward, Mary, Philip, and Elizabeth). He finds a comforting interpretation for the prophecy (in line with his own political objectives) by suggesting that if James were to succeed to the throne all subsequent kings would be kings of Britain. John Heywood's *Life of Merlin* (1641) quotes a more gruesome version of the prophecy, again noting the 'great feare' surrounding the final years of Elizabeth's reign and the way in which James's accession 'proved this augury true, though not according to the former imagination' (p. 361). On William Cecil's use of astrology, see A. N. MacLaren, 'Prophecy and Providentialism in the Reign of Elizabeth I', in Bertrand Taithe and Tim Thornton (eds.), *Prophecy: The Power of Inspired Thought in History 1300–2000* (Stroud: Sutton Publishing, 1997), 31–50 (42).

[26] *The Wickednesse*, The English Experience, 501 (1561; repr. Amsterdam: Theatrum Orbis Terrarum, 1972).

[27] Taylor, *Political Prophecy*, 84–5.

[28] Thomas, *Religion and the Decline*, 398. Additionally significant is his observation that the Irish, in particular, were dependent on prophecies. See also C. W. Previté-Orton, 'An Elizabethan Prophecy', *History*, 2 (1917–18), 207–18; Jonathan K. Van Patten, 'Magic, Prophecy, and the Law of Treason in Reformation England', *The American Journal of Legal History*, 27 (1983), 1–32; and Richard L. Kagan, *Lucrecia's Dreams: Politics and Prophecy in Sixteenth-Century Spain* (Berkeley: University of California Press, 1990).

utilized as an instrument of praise: prophecies were addressed to Elizabeth and received by her. In large part, however, praise took the form of old prophecies whose wonderful outcomes were made to square with the conditions of the present age. Had Stanza 50 (beginning 'But yet the end is not') been excluded, Merlin's prophecy would have fitted comfortably into this uncontroversial mode. The hidden 'ghastly spectacle' that may be foreseen by Merlin, however, reminds us of the more questionable side of prophecy. Merlin, it is true, has spoken nobly of 'the streight course of heauenly destiny, | Led with eternall prouidence' (III. iii. 24. 3–4), but in Elizabethan England that course was widely known to be more crooked. Henry Howard, the Earl of Northumberland, for example, had, in the *Defensative Against the Poyson of Supposed Prophesies*, laid claim precisely to this 'streight course'. In the letter to Francis Walsingham that prefaced his work, he stated that, just as Joseph and Saint Philip, although 'not privie to the plotte which GOD had set in heaven', 'could not choose but passe' along a predestined 'beaten way',

So from the sixteenth yeere of mine age, untyll this present daye, (I knowe not whether by instinct of providence, or warning by mishaps of some that went before) my manner hath beene in the course of all my reading, to store up all such reasons and examples, as occurred eyther in Philosophie, the civill lawes, divinitie, or histories, to the ruine of pretended Prophetes, and their Prophecies: although in trueth I could no more foresee what accident might move mee afterward to dispose and marshall them in order for mine owne defence, then either *Joseph* or *Phillippe* knew what should betide them in their journey.

(sigs. ¶2ᵇ–¶3ᵃ)

Howard's words are as pious as Merlin's, but behind his high-minded pronouncements lay less altruistic reasoning. A letter recorded in the Calendar of State Papers tells us that, less than a year before, he had written to Walsingham protesting that 'the prophecy touching Her Majesty was utterly unknown to him', and that he had 'no knowledge of the book of babies in my Lord of Oxford's hands'.[29] The fact that another member of the Howard family—the unlucky Duke of Norfolk—had ended his life on the scaffold in part because of his involvement in political prophecy is likely to have been an additional motivating factor.[30]

---

[29] Robert Lemon (ed.), *Calendar of State Papers, Domestic Series* (London: Longman, Brown, Green, Longmans & Roberts, 1856), ii. 70.

[30] For extensive documentation concerning the Ridolfi plot, including a number of references to prophecy, see William Murdin (ed.), *A Collection of State Papers Relating to Affairs In the*

In part as a reaction to a significant change in the political climate surrounding prognostication, the dangerous meddling with prophecies that
had made Howard a subject of suspicion, was, in this preface, magically
transformed into the workings of providence. So too the dangerous
insights of Merlin may be transmuted into an explication of the workings
of God in the establishment of the Tudor dynasty—yet the magic can
never be entirely convincing.

Spenser and Political Prophecy (1569–1580)

Edmund Spenser's own 'beaten way' along the path of prophecy can be
traced as far back as the late 1560s. While still in his teens, the poet produced his first published work as a translator of Jan van der Noot's
unashamedly prophetic text: the *Theatre for Worldlings*. The *Theatre* is made
up of a set of epigrams and sonnets accompanied by woodcut illustrations and a prose commentary. As van der Noot's none too brief 'Brief
declaration' makes clear, the purpose of this accompanying material is to
direct the reader in his or her interpretation of the poems: specifically
to see them as visions of the overthrow of the church of Rome foreshadowed in the Book of Revelation. This biblically interpretative sense
of the word 'prophecy' was clearly an influence on Spenser's treatment
of the legend of holiness in Book I of *The Faerie Queen*: here too St
John the Divine's vision of the future was placed alongside a reading
of actual church history. But there is another way in which the *Theatre*
anticipates aspects of Spenser's later prophetic practice. For, ten years
later, the poet was himself to publish a work structured around woodcuts, and accompanied by prose commentary. Like the *Theatre*, Spenser's
Shepheardes Calender uses such apparatus to draw the reader into a particular mode of reading that again encourages a search for the prophetic.

Unlike van der Noot's confident Protestant diatribe, the 'generall
argument' that prefaces *The Shepheardes Calender* is quite explicit about the
provisional and partial nature of interpretation. In it, Spenser's mysteri-

---

Reign of Queen Elizabeth from the Year 1571 to 1596 (London: William Bowyes, 1759). In the record
of the examination of Norfolk's servant Robert Higford on 16 September 1571, Sir Thomas
Smith asks, 'Whither he hath not knowen, or hard that ther wer som in *England* who travailed
by Astronomye, or Art Magick, or such Arts, to understand what should become of the *Scottish
Quene*, or hir Mariage, or of the Persone that should succede the Quene's Majesty that now is'.
Higford denies any knowledge, but admits that the Duke showed him 'a folishe Prophecye'
(p. 71). The matter crops up occasionally in the ongoing investigation, although little further
evidence emerges. See also Thomas, *Religion and the Decline*, 405.

ous editor, E.K., coyly tells us that, while he can divide the Eclogues into a number of 'formes or ranckes', there are 'a few onely except, whose speciall purpose and meaning I am not privie to' (p. 419). The editor repeatedly backs away from outright assertion, yet, as Richard Rambuss has observed, in alluding so often to his role as both explicator and obfuscator of secrets, E.K. is calculatedly spurring his readers on in the effort of identifying more covert meanings.[31] The final paragraph of E.K.'.s opening 'Epistle' is a case in point. It opens promisingly: 'Now as touching the generall dryft and purpose of his Æglogues'.[32] The subsequent clauses of this first sentence, however, emphatically crush the reader's expectations: 'I mind not to say much, him selfe labouring to conceale it'. There follows an at first glance ramshackle series of sentences, from which it is necessary to quote at length. Having 'long wandred in the common Labyrinth of Love', E.K. tells us, the poet:

Compiled these xij. Æglogues, which for that they be proportioned to the state of the xij, monethes, he termeth the SHEPHEARDS CALENDAR, applying an olde name to a new worke. Hereunto have I added a certain Glosse or scholion for thexposition of old wordes and harder phrases: which maner of glosing and commenting, well I wote, wil seeme straunge and rare in our tongue: yet for somuch as I knew many excellent and proper devises both in wordes and matter would passe in the speedy course of reading, either as unknowen, or as not marked, and that in this kind, as in other we might be equal to the learned of other nations, I thought good to take the paines upon me, the rather for that by meanes of some familiar acquaintaunce I was made privie to his counsell and secret meaning in them, as also in sundry other works of his. (p. 418)

The first of the works that the editor says 'slepe in silence' is Spenser's 'Dreames', a title that, in itself, already highlights prophetic associations. On one level, of course, E.K. can claim to be facilitating only our aesthetic appreciation of the verse, but this does not go far in explaining 'the generall dryft and purpose' of the Eclogues. That purpose, which the poet is 'him selfe labouring to conceale', is associated with the 'olde name', the 'straunge and rare' gloss, and the 'counsell and secret meaning' of Spenser's text; all three of these apparently disparate elements highlight essential components of political prophecy.

---

[31] Richard Rambuss, *Spenser's Secret*, 53.
[32] *The Shepheardes Calender*, in *Complete Poetical Works*, ed. Smith and de Selincourt, 418. Subsequent page references appear in the text and are to this edition (folio references, however, are to the 1st edn.). With the *Calender mise en page* is particularly important: even the use of upper case for the work's title in the passage below is significant, as the only use of upper-case text in a dense body of prose it effectively draws the eye to this crucial passage.

In considering the old names that appear in the *Calender*, the reader is, in a number of ways, nudged into an exploration of prophecy. Both of Spenser's self-acknowledged models—Virgil and Chaucer—were widely believed to have been prophets.[33] Virgil was renowned for the vision in his Fourth Eclogue, and Chaucer's works as Spenser would have encountered them included a prophetic allegory known as 'The Ploughman's Tale'.[34] The work depicts the conflict between the monks and the true church, and is noticeably Galfridian in its symbolism. Spenser may well be alluding specifically to this prophetic tale from a pastoral teller when in the epilogue to the *Calender* he refers to 'the Pilgrim that the Ploughman playde awhyle' (p. 467) as one of those poets that the *Calender* 'dare not' match. The more conventional reading of that allusion—as a reference to Langland's *Piers Plowman*—in any case also points to a text that was widely credited as prophetic. Paul McLane, in addition, has noted the connections between Spenser's *Calender* and Skelton's *Colin Clout*. Skelton as well as Spenser, he argues, calls upon Colin Clout as a figure from medieval times associated with the prophetic voice of God, as well as of the common people.[35]

The persona of Colin Clout was very much related to popular, unofficial, and potentially seditious traditions of prognostication. That both Skelton and his character were recognized as political prophets is clear from their appearance in manuscripts of the period. One commonplace book of the earlier half of the sixteenth century, for example, contains an extract from Skelton's 'Colin Cloute' referring to Cardinal Wolsey. It begins: 'some men thynke that ye shall have penaltie' and ends 'and lett colen clowte alone', with the addition of a colophon reading 'the propfecy of Skelton/1529'.[36] Under the name of Colin Clout, of course,

---

[33] The poet, and especially the pastoral poet, was of course well established in the role of 'seer' (on vatic authority, see e.g. Patrick Cheney, *Spenser's Famous Flight*, esp. 77–148). The spiritual or careerist aspects of the vatic could, however, easily overlap with the strong political tradition of the genre (on which see e.g. Annabel Patterson, *Pastoral and Ideology: Virgil to Valéry* (Oxford: Clarendon Press, 1988)).

[34] For the text of the Ploughman's tale, see *Chaucerian and Other Pieces*, ed. Walter W. Skeat (Oxford: Clarendon Press, 1897), a supplement to Skeat's *Works of Geoffrey Chaucer*, 6 vols. (Oxford: Clarendon Press, 1894). John N. King's work has argued for Spenser's 'emulation of the archaic diction, style, and characterization' of this work—for details, see *Spenser's Poetry and the Reformation Tradition* (Princeton, NJ: Princeton University Press, 1990), 4.

[35] Paul E. McLane, 'Skelton's *Colyn Cloute* and Spenser's *Shepheardes Calender*', *SP* 70 (1973), 141–59 (143), see also Roland Greene, 'Calling Colin Clout', *Spenser Studies*, 10 (1992), 229–44, and Andrew Hadfield, '"Who knowes not Colin Clout?": The Permanent Exile of Edmund Spenser', *Literature, Politics and National Identity: Reformation to Renaissance* (Cambridge: Cambridge University Press, 1994), 170–201.   [36] British Library, Lansdowne MSS, 762, fol. 71ᵃ.

E.K. has told us 'the Author selfe is shadowed' under the 'basenesse' of which name 'it semeth, he chose rather to unfold great matter of argument covertly' (p. 418). 'Colin Cloute', the first gloss of *The Shepheardes Calender* tells us, 'is a name not greatly used, and yet have I sene a Poesie of M. Skeltons under that title'.

In 'applying an olde name to a new worke', *The Shepheardes Calender* is most explicitly advertising its connections with a work still more directly concerned with prophecy. On this matter E.K. is even less forthcoming. But for the Elizabethan reader his aside about this 'olde name' would surely be enough: the old *Kalender of Shepardes* was amongst the most popular and widely consulted works of the Tudor age.[37] A collection assembled by an anonymous French author that first appeared in English at the beginning of the sixteenth century, it was at its core a work of Astrology. Like Spenser's work, the old *Kalender* had an archaic quality and featured woodcuts and naïve yet learned debates between shepherds.[38] That the old *Kalender* was indeed associated with unwarranted prognostication is confirmed when we note that in his tract against prophecies John Harvey explicitly extended his attack on them to the materials taken not only from '*Pierce Plowmans* satchell', but also those 'newly collected out of the old shepherds *Kalender*'.[39] According to Harvey, it is precisely this drawing of the new from the old that makes prophecy so dangerous. 'Chronicles . . . other famous books, and many old smokie paperbookes', he notes, are 'upon every new occasion, strange accident, perilous exigence, or whatsoever other notable occurrence, againe and againe revived, by way of fresh, and currant matter to serve present turnes, and to feede the working humor of busie and tumultuous heads, continually affecting some innovation, or other' (sig. A4ᵃ). In the move from 'old smokie paperbooks' to 'innovation' Harvey astutely draws our attention to the kind of transformative rereading of history in which Renaissance prophecy in general—and *The Shepheardes Calender* in particular—is engaged.

[37] The work is first published in English in 1503 and continues to appear into Elizabeth's reign and beyond. I refer to STC 22410 (1518). For a fuller description of the *Kalender*, and for evidence of the tremendous popularity and utility of it and later almanacs, see Capp, *Astrology*, 20–60. For a detailed study of Spenser's borrowing from the *Kalender* and other astrological works, see J. Michael Richardson, *Astrological Symbolism in Spenser's 'The Shepheardes Calender': The Cultural Background of A Literary Text*, Studies in Renaissance Literature, 1 (Lewiston, NY: Edwin Mellen Press, 1989).

[38] The discussion between two shepherds on the number of stars (sig. A4ᵃ), for example, ends up dealing with the question of free will in relation to the influence of heavenly bodies.

[39] John Harvey, *A Discoursive Probleme Concerning Prophesies* (1588), 62.

Nor was the medieval French *Kalender* the only work of its kind. Every year saw the appearance of at least a handful of prognostications, almanacs, or astrological calendars. Looking at a typical early-Elizabethan almanac, the *Prognostication Made for the Yeere of our Lorde 1566*, we discover a text that bears an even more striking physical resemblance to *The Shepheardes Calender*.[40] This work, too, is structured around woodcuts depicting appropriate rural scenes for every month: June, for example, showing the work of sheep-shearing. Examining the two side by side, we can be in no doubt that the poet drew upon this pre-existing form.

The background to the *Prognostication*, incidentally, provides another illustrative instance of the opaque manœuvring that characterizes the world of popular prophecy. It is, in fact, the work of the same Francis Coxe who had, five years earlier, railed so passionately against all forms of astrology in *The Wickednesse of Magical Sciences*. That pamphlet was in fact a panicked response to its author's severe public punishment at the hands of the Privy Council on grounds of sorcery. In his hurried publication, Coxe was forced to abjure even mainstream astrology, which, as he himself could testify, was 'bayte or trayne to far greater mischeves' (sig. A6[b]). By 1566, it seems, Coxe felt strong enough to resist that temptation.

Both the *Kalender of Shepardes* and the *Prognostication*, it is true, are generally rather cautious and prosaic in their pronouncements. The horoscopes in the *Kalender of Shepardes* remained the same over decades of reprints. For generation after generation those with the star sign Gemini were destined to be bitten by dogs and (in the case of women) needed to be married at 15 if they were to remain chaste. Coxe's prognostication contains the same peculiar mix of the specific and the general. In January on 'the first quarter of the .xxvii. day at .iii. of the clock after noone', there will be 'raine with some frost' (fol. 7[b]), yet this remarkably exact meteorological prediction is immediately undermined when we note that it is preceded by the ludicrously vague warning that the winter will bring a variety of illnesses (fol. 6[a]). Such bland predictions pose little risk of exposure for the prognosticator.

As Coxe and the translator of the French *Kalender* were no doubt aware, the government was very much averse to the publication of

---

[40] Francis Coxe (1565/66). Coxe's *Prognostication* is typical of literally hundreds of Almanacs appearing in the *Short Title Catalogue: 1475–1640*, ed. A. W. Pollard and G. R. Redgrave, 3 vols. (London: Bibliographical Society, 1986). The model for the *Prognostication*'s illustrations can be traced at least as far back as the xylographically printed single-strip vellum perpetual almanacs, several of which survive from the early 16th cent.

prophecies with an overt political content, and after 1571 the almanacs' section on political prognostication 'was reduced to extremely vague and ambiguous generalizations, and this remained so until 1640'.[41] This crackdown on the explicitly political, however, did not mean that the almanacs were entirely frivolous. The *Kalender of Shepardes* supplements its horoscopes and astrological tables with sections from the Apocalypse of St John, and Coxe begins his work with a grim warning that the coming eclipse of the moon is a sign of God's intention 'utterly to destroye us' if there is not immediate repentance (fol. 2[b]). The crackdown after 1571 also marks these texts as part of an older and more suspect tradition; by advertising its connection with them, Spenser's *Calender* was sending out some subtle messages to its readership.

Alongside the 'olde name', E.K.'s paragraph addressing the 'generall dryft and purpose' of the eclogues also stressed the 'Glosse or scholion' which was to accompany them. The gloss functions not so much to explicate as to draw attention: without it 'many excellent and proper devises both in wordes and matter would passe in the speedy course of reading, either as unknowen, or as not marked'. Astute readers are likely to have picked up on associations beyond those about which E.K. is explicit: specifically, they may well have perceived parallels with the interpretative glosses that usually accompanied manuscript prophecies.

From the beginning political prophecies had been accompanied by notes and interpretations, and had served as the basis for elaborate commentaries. When no other commentary was provided, marginal or interlinear notes frequently supplied the information needed for an understanding of the prophecies.[42] One mid-sixteenth-century book of manuscript prophecies in the British Library has at least four different types of commentary.[43] These include an initial subject index, numerous marginal annotations, an interpretative summary in prose, and an extensive key at the end of the volume giving meanings for the Galfridian symbols.[44] Most of the prophecies in the manuscript derive from paradigms that appeared several hundreds of years earlier, yet the commentary clearly gave them present-day application. One set of marginalia applies specific parts of a prophecy to each of the years between 1576 and the reign of the last king before Antichrist in 1580 (fol. 78[a]).

[41] Capp, *Astrology*, 29.
[42] See Taylor, *Political Prophecy*, 109.
[43] British Library, Sloane MS 2578.
[44] British Library, Sloane MS 2578, fols. 1[b]–4[a]; 18[a] (and ibid.); 112[b]; and 112[b]–116[b] respectively.

The features of this manuscript are characteristic of a good number of other political prophecies—the annotations of another, for example, applying its concluding prognostication to the year 1590.[45] Crucially, these prophecies are brought to life only by means of what we might call their 'Glosse or scholion'. Readers would be able to interpret a prophecy such as that of the 'Lily' and the 'Son of May', for example, because the recto of this page of verse contains a key assigning these symbols to the French and English Kings.[46] The interpreter and prophet are (or must appear to be) separate persons: commentary and prophecy may well be written in the same hand, but ultimately the prophecy must be rooted in a more ancient and distant source. It was this fundamental distinction that allowed the same prophecies to survive for generation after generation—the repeated failure of such prognostication was the failure of the gloss, not the prophecy.

Like manuscript prophecies of the time, *The Shepheardes Calender* is made up of a text that is inextricably tied to a body of commentary. Like them it makes use of an interpreter who is made to stand apart from an archaic, difficult, and even venerable set of verses—an interpreter on whom its readers are (it is claimed) dependent in their interpretation. It is in those portions of *The Shepheardes Calender* that are directly concerned with prophecy, such as the July Eclogue, that we see most clearly the way in which the gloss exploits and comments upon its workings.

The July Eclogue consists of a dialogue between the shepherds Thomalin and Morrell concerning the relative merits of hill and dale, a fairly transparent allegory displaying the rival attractions of the corrupt and remote Roman church, and the lowly, accessible Protestant one. The Eclogue also plays more directly on the politics of the day. According to Thomalin, the good shepherds of the 'lowly leas' were formerly instructed by 'old Algrind' (l. 126). 'Algrind', in its first spelling, is a perfect anagram of Grindal—the reform-minded Archbishop of Canterbury whose positions on controversial issues such as clerical vestments are subtly worked into the discussion.[47] In the last three speeches, however, matters are still further complicated by unannounced shifts in

---

[45]   British Library, Harley MS 559, fols. 39–48.

[46]   The correspondences between symbols and persons are often specific to individual prophecies, the present example refers to a key in British Library, Harley MSS, 559, fol. 2ᵇ, which glosses a prophecy on the verso of that page.

[47]   For the best survey of these views, see Patrick Collinson, *Archbishop Grindal 1519–1583: The Struggle for a Reformed Church* (London: Jonathan Cape, 1979). For an up-to-date overview of the concerns of this passage, see *Shorter Poems*, ed. McCabe, 543–5.

the positions of both Algrind and Morrell. In the penultimate speech, Algrind, the exponent of the 'lowly leas', is newly described as a shepherd 'great in gree' who provides a lesson only by means of his own 'ill' example. Unwisely seating himself 'upon a hill', Algrind was—tragically—struck upon the head by a shellfish dropped by an eagle. Hearing this news, the Shepherd Morrell fleetingly changes his tone to one of confident prognostication:

> Ah good *Algrin*, his hap was ill,
>   but shall be better in time.
> Now farwell shepheard, sith thys hyll
>   thou hast such doubt to climbe.   (July, ll. 229–32)

Morrell's lines are the last in the Eclogue, and are the only ones that appear over the page directly above and beside the dense print of E K 's gloss (fol. 30ᵇ).[48] The gloss on the name 'Algrin' is also the last of the July section—this despite the name's four earlier appearances in the Eclogue. The note itself acknowledges this omission in a demonstratively casual manner: 'Algrin', we are told, is 'the name of a shepheard afforesayde, whose myshap he alludeth to the chaunce, that happened to the Poet Æschylus, that was brayned with a shellfishe' (fol. 30ᵇ). As so often, E.K.'s commentary at first glance fails to live up to its promise: instead of access to the text's 'secret meaning', readers are apparently fobbed off with a rather stale Classical allusion. Those elements of the Eclogue that require interpretation—most notably the very Galfridian 'Eagle' (with a capital 'E')—are left unglossed. It would be a mistake, however, to pass too quickly over any reference in Spenser to the fate of a poet; upon closer inspection the gloss on 'Algrin' constitutes the nexus for a number of lines that are concerned with the matter of prophecy.

Aeschylus, as canny readers of the work would surely have noticed, was famously the victim of a misunderstood oracle: the apocryphal story held that the poet was presented with the prophecy that something 'thrown from the sky' would kill him. Thinking to avoid his fate, Aeschylus is said to have climbed a high mountain, only to be struck on the head by an eagle that mistook the poet's bald head for a rock on which to smash the shell of its prey.[49] The parallel with Grindal is an

---

[48] This and subsequent folio references are to the 1st edn.: Edmund Spenser, *The Shepheardes Calender* (1579; repr. Menston: Scholar Press, 1968).

[49] The story can be traced back to an 11th-cent. Florentine manuscript which included *The Life of Aeschylus*. A version of the story, and an overview of its sources, can be found in Mary R. Lefkowitz, *The Lives of the Greek Poets* (London: Duckworth, 1981), 72–3.

intriguing one. The Archbishop was himself a believer in portents.[50] More significantly, however, he had been the victim of controversy surrounding the prophesyings—the exercises in communal biblical interpretation that had excited the wrath of Elizabeth. Grindal's forthright refusal, in 1576, to accept the Queen's authority over the matter had resulted in his suspension from office and virtual house arrest: the 'lingring payne' of Thomalin's description. On the one hand the Eclogue appears to bemoan this fall, but on the other, it could also be read as a criticism of Grindal's initial acceptance. The debate between hill and dale that stands at the centre of the July Eclogue is, then, also a representation of the conflicting attractions and dangers of high office. Grindal's case provides the crux for this discussion: the Archbishop accepted his appointment with the greatest reluctance, yielding, he claimed, only after pondering the example provided by God's treatment of Jonah (whose futile attempt to escape a divine summons to the calling of prophecy had resulted in his imprisonment within the whale).[51] E.K.'s commentary mimics this indecision by glossing the emblems concerning ambition that follow the Eclogue (themselves already a kind of gloss on what has come before) with unusual even-handedness. Gradually the gloss allows more light to fall on the text's 'secret meaning': references to Doctors in religion, and in particular the line 'sequestred from all ambition' (fol. 30ᵇ), guide the reader to interpret the Eclogue in the context of specific political and religious controversies.

By means of the commentary on Aeschylus, the *Calender* hints that both Grindal and the poet (in the figure of Colin Clout) have been left in 'lingring payne' by recent events connected with prophecy. The *Calender* was published at the end of 1579. It was this year that, in Anne MacLaren's view, saw a crisis in the 'particular kind of "political prophecy" that emerged in England with the accession of Elizabeth'.[52]

---

[50] In the light of the discussion below, it is significant that the Archbishop believed, in particular, in the warnings provided by earthquakes. Buell notes that in a 1575 exchange between Grindal and Parker, the former (in the face of Parker's scepticism) had stood out firmly for the significance of a recent earthquake. In 1580, he observes, Grindal was to sanction an order for public prayer in response to the earthquake at issue in the Spenser/Harvey *Letters*. For details, see Llewllyn M. Buell, 'Elizabethan Portents: Superstition or Doctrine?', in Louis B. Wright (ed.), *Essays, Critical and Historical, Dedicated to Lily B. Cambell* (Berkeley: University of California Press, 1950), 27–44 (33).

[51] See Collinson, *Archbishop Grindal*, 214 and 222. Jonah himself provides a double example of the dangers of prophecy: the prophet being greatly angered by the failure of his prognostication of the overthrow of Nineveh (Jonah: 1–4).

[52] MacLaren, 'Prophecy', 31 and 42–6.

This crisis most dramatically played itself out in the events surrounding the publication of John Stubbs's *Gaping Gulf,* a work in which Stubbs self-consciously adopted the stance of a prophet in order to oppose the prospective marriage between Elizabeth and Alençon, predicting dire consequences for the entire realm 'if the Lord forbid not the banes'.[53] On the Queen's orders, the Privy Council acted with extreme vigour to suppress the work. On 3 November, Stubbs and his publisher William Page had their hands publicly amputated—a fate still worse than Algrind's 'lingring payne'. Stubbs's printer, who was also Spenser's, only narrowly escaped the same fate. The spectacle of Stubbs's punishment, in MacLaren's words, 'signalled the point from which prophecy could be successfully labelled what Elizabeth called it in her proclamation: "fanatical divinations" calculated to appeal to "every most meanest person of judgement", in the interest of destabilizing the realm rather than reforming the commonweal'.[54]

The *Calender* was entered in the Stationers' Register almost exactly a month after the sentence on Stubbs was carried out.[55] At this point in Elizabeth's reign political prophecy was perhaps at its most dangerous and controversial; and Spenser's treatment of the eagle's unintentional assault provides an astute commentary on its precarious position. The eagle is usually read as an allusion to Elizabeth; but as a symbol it would also have had a wide range of prophetic associations. Eagles occur very frequently in political prophecy: the index to the aforementioned British Library manuscript contains no fewer than fifteen references to the bird.[56] The key too provides a great number of interpretations, including an eagle as Derby, another as Germany, an eagle with splayed wings as Kent, and a green eagle as Salisbury (fol. 115). The eagle was known as a bird of prophecy. The prophecy of Merlin Silvester was sometimes known as the Prophecy of the Eagle: Geoffrey refers to 'the Auguries of the Eagle' in the tragic conclusion of his *Historia,* and a number of later

[53] See *John Stubbs's 'Gaping Gulf' with Letters and Other Relevant Documents,* ed. Lloyd E. Berry (Charlottesville: University Press of Virginia, 1968), 1. Berry's introduction provides a clear overview of events, including connections with Spenser. See also Woudhuysen, 'Leicester's Literary Patronage', 87–9, for suggestions about connections with Sir Philip Sidney's use of prophetic shepherds. Stubbs, of course, was not charged for political prophecy, but rather under legislation constructed against slander of the Queen's husband—a title that the courts chose to extend to her suitor (see MacCaffrey, *Making of Policy,* 257).

[54] MacLaren, 'Prophecy', 46.

[55] It was entered in the Stationers' Register on 5 December of that year. See Arber (ed.), *Transcript of the Registers,* ii. 1576–95.

[56] BL, Sloane MS 2578 (fols. 1–4b).

manuscripts refer to it or claim to transcribe it.[57] The eagle (as both a symbol for, and destroyer of, the prophetic) constitutes a calculatedly equivocal presence in Spenser's text.

Algrind, moreover, has an earlier appearance in the work, again in an Eclogue concerned with religious controversy, and again in the context of a gloss that highlights the prophetic. The May Eclogue provides an even less informative commentary on Algrind ('the name of a shepheard'), yet the earlier gloss on 'Great Pan' (one of the longest in the poem) provides an extensive discussion on 'the ceasing of oracles' (p. 439). Still more provocative is a later gloss on 'signes of ill luck' (l. 332) which notes that the 'evill signe' provided by a stumbling goat corresponds to a number of such omens recorded in history. E.K. goes on in some detail to discuss a 'dangerous dreame' had by Richard III which turned out to be 'a shrewde prophecie' (p. 440).

Most striking of all is the *Calender*'s concluding December Eclogue. Its verse provides a crescendo of references to soothsaying and astrology, including 'a Comet or blasinge starre', 'the signes of heauen', the eclipse of the moon, the shifting of Venus, and 'The soothe of byrds', with the gloss providing extensive comment on cosmology, 'sooth saying used in elder tymes' and other 'enchauntments and sorceries' (pp. 465–6). There is not space here to set out in full the suggestiveness of this concluding Eclogue; suffice to say that it is doubtful whether the prophecy of Colin Clout's own death, the eclipse of the moon, and the 'sodain rysing of the raging seas', would be without covert messages for the monarch or her courtiers.

Spenser and Political Prophecy after 1580

The Shepheardes Calender plays quite brilliantly on the tensions surrounding prophecy in the year of its publication—its allusive presentation calls up a wide range of prophetic texts and draws upon their qualities. Using prophecy, it hints darkly at the kind of future that might ensue as a result of an unwise marriage. As well as their secretive and political nature, however, the *Calender* also illustrates the dangerous unpredictability of prophecies—texts that can recoil upon the prophet, just as they impact upon society. Spenser must at the very least have been a ringside observer of this strange dynamic. His friend and early mentor, Gabriel

---

[57] Geoffrey, *History*, 283. For references to, and transcriptions of, this prophecy, see e.g. British Library, Cotton MSS, Faustina A. viii and Tiberius A. ix.

Harvey, is known to have been a student of astrology and was the reputed author of a number of almanacs. Most dramatically, Harvey was tainted when his two brothers, Richard and John, became embroiled in a national scare surrounding the prophecy of Regiomontanus.[58] At the time the *Shepheardes Calender* was published Spenser was probably already aware of his friend's concerns. And in the *Three Proper, and wittie, familiar Letters*—the exchanges between 'two Universitie men' (Edmund Spenser and Gabriel Harvey) published a year later—we find evidence not only of Harvey's concern about the matter, but also of his desire to establish a public position on it.

Given Gabriel Harvey's personal involvement with judicial astrology, it becomes apparent that the scholar's rational analysis of the causes of earthquakes—advertised as one of the chief attractions in the *Letters*— was intended to apply more generally to the well-documented apocalyptic panic of the early 1580s.[59] In fact, Harvey acknowledges this concern when he concedes that earthquakes are indeed 'terrible signes, and, as it were certaine manacing forerunners, and forewarners of the great latter day'. He goes on in some detail to list the events that have followed them: 'they have seemed to Prognosticate, and threaten to this, and that Citie, utter ruyne and destruction: to such a Country, a generall plague and pestilence: to an other place, the death of some mightie Potentate or great Prince: to some other Realme or Kingdome, some cruell imminent warres: and sundry the like dreadfull and particular Incidentes'.[60] Harvey's formal conclusion is that, while God is certainly warning his people about their sinful ways, it would be foolish to draw out of this any specific knowledge of divine intentions:

To make shorte, I cannot see, and would gladly learne, howe a man on Earth, should be of so great authoritie, and so familiar acquaintance with God in

---

[58] The prophecy, which appears to have been assembled by Kaspar Brusch, was effectively launched into the European public arena in Cyprian Leowitz's *De Conjuntionibus Magnis Insignioribus Superiorum Planetarum* (1564). It was published in London in 1573, thereafter appearing in numerous tranlations including that in Richard Harvey's *An Astrological Discourse upon the great and notable Conjunction of the two superior Planets* (1583). For full details see Walter B. Stone's analysis of the background to the fateful year 1588, 'Shakespeare and the Sad Augurs', *Journal of English and German Philology*, 52 (1953), 457–79.

[59] Stone's analysis of the background to the fateful year 1588 includes the 1580 earthquake among a number of events adding to the apocalyptic fears about the date 1583 (p. 463). On the Elizabethan understanding of earthquakes, see S. K. Heninger, Jr., *A Handbook of Renaissance Meteorology* (Durham, NC: Duke University Press, 1960), 128–34.

[60] Gabriel Harvey, 'A Pleasant and pithy familiar discourse, of the Earthquake in Aprill last', in *Three Proper, and wittie, familiar Letters* (1580), in *Works*, ed. Smith and de Selincourt, 617.

Heaven, (unlesse haply for the nonce he hath lately intertained some few choice singular ones of his privie Counsell) as to be able in such specialties, without any justifyable certificate, or warrant to reveale hys incomprehensible mysteries, and definitively to give sentence of his Majesties secret and inscrutable purposes.

(p. 617)

The religious position is beyond dispute—and a clear, if unheeded, warning to Gabriel's brothers John and Richard—yet in his slippage into the language of politics ('choice singular ones of his privie Counsell', 'justifyable certificate, or warrant', 'his Majesties secret and inscrutable purposes') Harvey nevertheless flags up a different brand of political/ prophetic knowledge.

With their switches between verse and prose, their Latin colophons, secretive pen names, and references to the unsayable, the *Letters* have much in common with the *Calender*. Both publications are to some degree collaborations between Spenser and Harvey, and both function in order to advertise secrets and gain influence. The cross-over between prophecy and political intrigue is once more in evidence. In his first letter Spenser (or rather 'Immerito') writing to 'Master G.H'. at 'Justinians Courte' speaks of the latter's 'secreate Studies' (p. 611), and goes on to talk about his own unpublished works, mentioning in particular his *Dreames* (the mysterious verses about which E.K. too had spoken). These, he says, have 'growen by meanes of the Glosse (running continually in maner of a Paraphrase) full as great as my *Calendar*' (p. 612). The text of the *Dreames* remains hidden. Yet in the letter that follows Harvey again asserts the power attached to his knowledge: he is able not only to calm a group of hysterical high-born individuals, but also to plumb their psyches, asserting to the gentlewomen 'you shall both this night, within somwhat lesse than two howers and a halfe, after ye be layed, *Dreame* of terrible straunge Agues, and Agonyes as well in your owne prettie bodyes, as in the mightie great body of the Earth' (p. 615). In Harvey's account the ladies are as impressed as everyone else by his esoteric learning, finding him 'marvellous privie to our dreames'. The word '*Dreame*', which is the only verb in the letter that does not appear in black letter Gothic type, may be intended to remind us of Spenser's similarly secretive composition; certainly it is one of a number of words that are likely to have caused a frisson of prophetic intimacy in a certain kind of reader.

An intriguing interconnection suggests itself: this time with a work that appeared a decade later. Immediately following her discoveries in the mirror, Britomart (in Book III of *The Faerie Queene*) begins to 'pant and quake, | As it an Earth-quake were' (III. ii. 42. 8–9). Could there be an echo here of Harvey's exposition on earthquakes published in the *Letters* ten years earlier? We know that at the time the letters were written Spenser had composed enough of *The Faerie Queene* to feel able to show a draft of it to Harvey; indeed, Harvey acknowledges the receipt of this draft in the letter that immediately follows the discourse on the earthquake. Certainly both Glauce's and Harvey's comforting speeches are a response to womanly panic: Harvey's gentlewomen 'nothing acquaynted with any such Accidentes' being 'marvellously daunted' and falling down to terrified prayers (p. 613). Britomart is likewise in danger of collapsing into 'despaire' (III. ii. 35. 6), and in accordance with Gabriel's prediction in the *Letters*, that night 'her selfe opprest, | Streight way with dreames, and with fantasticke sight | Of dreadfull things' (III. ii. 29. 3–5).

Having read Harvey's account Spenser may conceivably have included the reference to 'an Earth-quake' before enclosing the Britomart episode in his letter of reply.[61] Both Harvey and Glauce see themselves as knowledgeable counsellors in supernatural matters—believers who are also determined to treat their insights with caution. Whether or not there is a connection, it is sure that Gabriel's subtle arguments about the limits of prophecy had as little effect upon his brothers as Glauce's 'idle charmes' have on her charge. In 1583 Richard Harvey published his *Astrological Discourse upon the Great and Notable Conjunction of the Two Superior Planets*, a work that included a conventional almanac, and that took the form of a letter addressed to his brother Gabriel. In it Richard predicts a truly vast litany of disasters, showing '*as it were in a glasse*' (italics mine): 'great rain', 'extreame povertie', 'hunger', 'shipwracks', 'burnings', 'treason', 'rebellion', 'plague', 'war', 'notorious calamities', for 'great rulers and mightie governours', and 'an extraordinarye death and destruction of fishes'.[62] Richard acknowledges Gabriel's doubts about his enterprise, but also writes to him as an initiate, arguing 'that Judiciall

[61] Some backing for this admittedly speculative theory is offered by Bennett's argument in *The Evolution*, 153, that Book III is made up of the oldest most Ariostan part of Spenser's epic. That material, she suggests, was then reworked for publication in 1590. Such an argument would strengthen the claim forwarded here that Britomart's prophetic experiences bear the marks of an earlier political moment.

[62] Richard's list of the consequences of the conjunction goes on for tens of pages. The above quotations are taken from pp. 16, 19, and 28. They constitute but a modest selection of the predicted disasters.

Astrologie is neither any vaine and idle studie, nor forbidden and un-lawful Arte, your self having long since, taken some reasonable paines therein, and being able to say so much in the defence thereof' (sig. A2ᵇ). Richard refers specifically to Gabriel's oration upon the earthquake, claiming that 'in the earnester part of that Discourse' his brother also admits it as a terrible sign (p. 46). Richard goes on to refer to a story about Alexander the Great, who deliberately played down the signifi-cance of an eclipse of the moon in order not to alarm his soldiers (p. 69). Noting that it was Gabriel himself who drew his attention to this anec-dote, Richard implies that his brother's argument in the *Letters* is designed merely for public consumption: a false interpretation that does not reflect Gabriel's true opinion.

That same year, the youngest of the Harvey brothers (John) brought out *An Astrologicall Addition*, a publication that was, as its title indicates, a continuation of his brother Richard's earlier work on the same subject.[63] In it John again acknowledges Gabriel's objections to their studies, but also hints at his tacit support (sig. A5ᵃ). John, like Richard, eschews Gabriel's caution in favour of a more brash approach. Convinced of the accuracy of his analysis, he insists he 'may freely utter, that which I Astrologically conceive' (sig. C5ᵃ). Heavenly signs, old prophecies, and the general sinfulness of the age all lead him to conclude 'that some pro-phane helhound, some fierce and cruell *Antichrist*, some outragious and irreligious Mahomet, some Turkish Martial Tyrant shall arise, who will play the second *Athila*, or *Totilas*, by scourging the zealous people of God' (sig. C5ᵃ).

John and Richard's predictions caused widespread panic, not least because of the daringly specific time-scale for these events. The first stage would be heralded by a great wind erupting at high noon on Sunday 28 April 1583 (p. 7), with the whole period of cataclysm ending in 1593 on 21 March at 12:30 p.m. (sig. D6ᵃ).[64] John tells us he will not 'recapitu-late the horrors of the marveilous yeere, *1588.* or ... unfold other auncient predictions, & prophecies' (sig. E5ᵇ), but it is clear that he sets great store by them. Only in the final pages of their works do the brothers introduce a caveat: John ending with a warning, based on biblical precedent, that 'punishments decreed from above, are in some part alterable, upon humble signification of a contrite and reformed heart' (sig. E6ᵃ).

---

[63] John Harvey, *An Astrologicall Addition or Supplement to be Annexed to the Late Discourse upon the Great Conjunction of Saturne and Jupiter* (1583).

[64] For the best account of the false alarm surrounding the year 1583, see Stone.

This qualification, however, was not enough to save the Harvey brothers from the cataclysmic uneventfulness of 1583. John and Richard, it appeared, had constructed a self-fulfilling prophecy only so far as their own fortunes were concerned. The two were widely mocked and berated, and the cloud above their heads inevitably cast a shadow on Gabriel. The most telling irony, however, was to come about five years later when John Harvey published *A Discoursive Probleme Concerning Prophesies*. Like Henry Howard's *Defensative*, Harvey's tract was a transparent attempt to curry favour with the authorities. Ironically, in 1583 Howard had been writing in response to the public anxiety caused by John and Richard Harvey's own efforts.[65] In 1588 John Harvey was clearly attempting to replicate the success of his predecessor. For a second time, however, Harvey's attempt backfired. For in dismissing the HEMPE prophecy and (of more immediate importance) the prophecy concerning 'this present famous yeere, 1588, supposed the Great-woonderfull, and Fatall yeere of our Age', he discounted what for generations to come would be the two most widely cited examples of successful prognostication.[66]

John Harvey provides an exemplary case for the dangers of prophecy and over the years that followed Gabriel was not to be allowed to forget it. Nashe mercilessly ridiculed the prophetic pretensions of his family. Refusing to accept any distinction between the brothers, he openly proclaimed that Harvey had published his own work under the name of one of his siblings.[67] Harvey's attempts to defend his reputation, an effort that included the publication of a commendatory sonnet by Spenser, proved increasingly ineffective—Nashe manœuvring his opponent into such a corner that Gabriel was forced into a direct defence of Richard's *Astrological Discourse*.[68]

In 1593 Gabriel appended to his *New Letter of Notable Contents* what he himself called 'a straunge Sonet, intituled Gorgon, Or the wonderfull

[65] Howard, sig. ¶1ᵃ.

[66] Even Bacon's essay on prophecy was to cite these two as examples of the genuine article. See 'Of Prophecies', in *Francis Bacon: A Critical Edition of the Major Works*, ed. Brian Vickers (Oxford: Oxford University Press, 1996), 413–14.

[67] *The Works of Thomas Nashe*, ed. Ronald B. McKerrow, 5 vols. (Oxford: Basil Blackwell, 1958), i. 196 and 298. Given Harvey's almost certain involvement in the supposedly unauthorized printing of the *Letters*, his complicity in the publication of texts that (like the *Letters*) consistently cast Gabriel in the flattering role of judicious sage is perhaps not as unlikely as it first seems.

[68] See *Foure Letters, and certaine Sonnets*, in *The Works of Gabriel Harvey*, ed. Alexander B. Grosart, 3 vols. (London: Hazell, Watson, & Viney, 1584–5), i. 153–254. For Nashe's response to this defence in his *Strange Newes*, see *Works*, i. 308.

yeare'.[69] The sonnet, which appeared complete with a 'glosse' in verse, has proved largely inscrutable for generations of scholars. It begins by dismissing (as John had done) the now widely acknowledged miraculousness of 1588: for Gabriel, determinedly out of step with popular opinion, 'The wonder was, no wonder fell that yeare'. For him, instead, 'The fatall yeare of yeares is Ninety Three', a date that seems intended to combine a number of significant political turn-arounds on the Continent with the deaths of Greene and Marlowe and the appearance of an apology from Nashe. By means of the interplay between a number of envoys, a postscript, the gloss, and the sonnet, Harvey attempts to construct a prophetic satire in the mould of those that appeared in the *Calender*. Nashe, however, seems to have been more baffled than offended by what he termed the 'goggle-eyed sonet of Gorgon': by 1593 Gabriel had lost all authority in prognostication. The Harveys had overplayed their hand.

The Faerie Queene *(1590–1596)*

Spenser's and Gabriel Harvey's use of political prophecy in the two texts published in the period 1579–80 had been both sophisticated and daring. But events on both a national and personal level in the years that followed are likely to have made such use of the prophetic considerably more problematic. In 1581, following both the suppression of the Prophesyings and the public punishment of Stubbs, Parliament greatly strengthened the 1562 measures against prophecy. The relevant statute states that anyone who

> shall by setting or erecting of any Figure or Figures, or by casting of Nativities, or by Calculation, or by any Prophecying, Witchcraft, Conjurations or other like unlawful Means whatsoever, seek to know, and shall set forth by express Words, Deeds or Writings, how long her Majesty shall live or continue, or who shall reign as King or Queen of this Realm of *England* after her Highnesses Decease . . . shall suffer such Pains of Death and Forfeiture, as in case of Felony is used, without any Benefit of Clergy or Sanctuary.[70]

Merlin's prognostication in *The Faerie Queene*, but also Spenser's publications in the years 1579–80, must be seen in the light of this statute.

By 1590 prophecy had been both suppressed and harnessed by the

[69] *Works*, i. 295–7.
[70] Raithby, *Statutes*, Anno 23° Elizabethæ (1581), II. vi. vol. ii. 516.

Elizabethan establishment. Most remarkably, the HEMPE and especially Regiomontanus prophecies were transformed from forebodings
of doom to messages of comfort.[71] The providential quality of Merlin's
prophecy published that year appears to reflect this change. There is
something comic in the transformation of Geoffrey's obscure prophecy
(including such gems as 'the feet of those that bark shall be cut off')[72]
into a neat chronological survey of England's monarchs. Merlin's reaction to Glauce's forewarning of Britomart's death (beginning 'Now
haue three Moones with borrow'd brothers light, | Thrice shined faire,
and thrice seem'd dim and wan' (III. iii. 16. 1–2)) likewise mocks the
obscurity of Galfridian speech.[73] Glauce's 'smooth speeches', 'dis-
sembled womanish guyle', and 'vaine' search for 'Magicke spell' at once
invite a smile from Merlin (III. iii. 17. 1–7), and her insistence that these
events can have no 'naturall cause' (a phrase that echoes Gabriel Harvey)
send the prophet into fits of laughter, saying 'what needs this colourable
word, | To cloke the cause, that hath it selfe bewrayd?' (III. iii. 19. 3–4).
The bulk of the prophecy that follows is clear-cut history, almost entirely
free of Galfridian symbolism and interpreted by its speaker as 'the
streight course of heauenly destiny' (III. iii. 24. 3).

As time passed and Spenser moved on to publish a second instalment
in 1596, this message was given further leverage by means of the distant
perspective afforded by the prophecy of the first instalment. Not only
did it supposedly originate from the distant past of Arthurian myth; if
Harper and Bennett are right, it also came from the more recent past of
the early 1580s (or, from the date of publication, 1590).[74] As we have
seen, Merlin's prophecy to Britomart had concluded (but for its final
stanza) in a foreshadowing of national achievement. The 'royall virgin'
would 'Stretch her white rod ouer the *Belgicke* shore, | And the great
Castle smite so sore with all, | That it shall make him shake, and shortly
learne to fall' (III. iii. 49. 6–9). In 1590 that 'Castle' had still been the stuff
of hopeful prophecy, being a pun on Philip II's title as king of 'Castile'.[75]

---

[71] On the new attitude to prophecy following the events of 1583 and 1588, see Stone,
'Shakespeare and the Sad Augurs', 472–9. Such reversals (for good or ill) are a consistent
feature of political prophecy—Macbeth being a notable victim of such amphibology; see
Steven Mullaney, 'Lying Like Truth: Riddle, Representation and Treason in Renaissance
England', *ELH* 47 (1980), 32–47.   [72] See Monmouth, *History*, 174.
[73] Arguably Glauce's speech anticipates the burlesque prophecies (like that of *Lear*'s fool),
the first of which, according to Capp, appeared in the year following the first instalment's
publication (see *Astrology*, 33).
[74] See Harper, *Sources*, 190, and Bennett, *Evolution*, 134 and 153.
[75] Hamilton, *Faerie Queene*, 334 n.

In 1594 it had taken on the more solid form of Brest Haven, and a few months after the publication of the second instalment it could have stood for Cadiz, without doubt the English action that most caused Spain to 'shake'. Merlin's prophecy had been transformed by time into a more firmly grounded declaration of England's potential. Its prophetic nature had been validated: Elizabeth's 'rod' had stretched over the '*Belgicke* shore' in a way that could only have been dreamed of at the time of its composition.

Yet the traces of a more dangerous branch of prognostication are not entirely erased. The prophecy of Book III held within it some disturbing collective memories, and Britomart's attempt to dissociate herself from it when questioned by Redcrosse remains reminiscent of the kind of selective amnesia employed by the Harvey brothers and other prognosticators. At the time of its composition the prospect of a second Queen Mary may still have been a very real one. Right up until the Queen of Scots' execution in 1587, times of royal illness, like the near-fatal attack of smallpox that the Queen suffered in October 1562, opened, MacCaffrey tells us, 'for a horrifying moment vistas of ultimate chaos'; chaos that it is tempting to compare to Merlin's 'suddein fit'.[76]

At the time of the second instalment's publication the prospects for a Protestant succession were considerably better. By that stage Spenser's verse chronicle may have been ten years old, itself a kind of 'antiquity'. Rather than allowing the dynamic interrelationships between history, current affairs, and prophecy to ossify, however, in the second instalment Spenser was to extend them into a new dimension. In fact, by providing a new historical incarnation for Duessa in the figure of Mary Queen of Scots, Spenser conjured up a more personal 'ghastly spectacle' following the Queen's death in the shape of the highly offended King James. For in Book V the events dimly foreshadowed in Merlin's prophecy were to be clearly represented in the action of the romance plot. In that book too, Spenser was to replay earlier events by once again subjecting Britomart to a prophetic encounter. In Isis Church, Britomart has a 'wondrous vision', which is fuller of Galfridian symbolism than anything that has occurred earlier in the poem. In it:

> All sodainely she saw transfigured
> Her linnen stole to robe of scarlet red,
> And Moone-like Mitre to a Crowne of gold.   (V. vii. 13. 4–6)

---

[76] MacCaffrey, *Shaping of the Elizabethan Regime*, 141.

This transformation, which has been interpreted as a vision of the coronation ceremony, occasions 'An hideous tempest' and 'outragious flames' from the altar's 'holy fire' (V. vii. 14. 2–7).[77] The fire awakens a crocodile which devours 'Both flames and tempest', threatening to do the same to Britomart (V. vii. 15. 6). Ultimately, it impregnates Britomart, so that she 'forth did bring a Lion of great might; | That shortly did all other beasts subdew' (V. vii. 16. 6–7). Still more so in this case, the closeness of this prophetic dream to the contents of manuscript political prophecy (and even the early visions of the *Theatre for Wordlings*) needs to be recognized. The vision terrifies the priest in whom Britomart confides, leaving him 'with long locks vp-standing . . . Like one adawed with some dreadfull spright' (V. vii. 20. 7–8) in a way strongly reminiscent of Merlin's 'halfe extatick stoure'. The priest proceeds to provide a comforting interpretation of the vision, glossing the crocodile as Artegall and the Lion as the son Britomart shall bear. This is of course a perfectly satisfactory reading; had the episode been passed over to E.K. for editorial assistance, however, it is doubtful whether he would have provided a similarly innocuous clarification.

Still more so than historical ones, prophetic mirrors have the capacity to change their aspect depending on the political context in which they are read. Possible readers, at the time of the Alençon crisis, at the moment of 1590 publication, or of the 1596 second edition would all have seen the implications of Britomart's prophetic visions differently. Those of 1590 may have had a new confidence in the benign outcomes of prophecy, but they would also have had the memory of times when its associations were a great deal less comforting. Even today it is easy to assume the age of Elizabeth was one of national fulfilment and to blanch over the darker aspects of Britomart's prophetic episode. What this episode and its reconstructed background shows, perhaps more radically than any other in this study, is the way in which the form of historical material may be recast to alter implications for the reader. By shaping national chronicle history into prophecy Spenser may seem to have changed little beside the tense of his narration. Whether we stress

---

[77] Fletcher, *Prophetic Moment*, 277. René Graziani presents a more politicized reading of the episode, interpreting the Church as Parliament, and Britomart's dream as an allegory of Elizabeth's differences with it over the case of Mary Queen of Scots. For details, see 'Elizabeth at Isis Chruch', *PMLA* 79 (1964), 376–89. For McCabe 'the episode in Isis Church vindicates the belief that the axis about which all such experiences revolve is that of divine justice. It represents the ultimate expression of the historical sense informing all of the poem's Briton chronicles' (*Pillars*, 117).

providence or politics, however, it is clear that the interpretation of this narrative changed significantly as a result of the shift. In a culture attuned to such alterations the forms of history became a rich source of expression. The second and third cantos of Book III—containing elements of chronicle, chorography, analogy, and prophecy—exemplify the complexity of Spenser's dialogue with those forms.

Conclusion

This book has attempted to place Edmund Spenser in the context of different and coexisting conceptions of the past—in particular, those influenced by religious, nationalistic, and scholarly perspectives on history. It has examined Early Modern England's absorption, use, and critical awareness of diverse modes of historical narrative, and has argued for the significance of these modes in determining the writer's or reader's outlook on distant events. Exploring Spenser's poetry and prose in the light of such 'forms of history' it has illustrated the ways in which the poet engaged with the languages of history surrounding him.

The poet, it concludes, had a profound, playful, and above all multi-form sense of the past. He was deeply knowledgeable about the historical writing of his day—using it extensively across the full range of his literary production. Each of the six forms of history examined here held an important position in Elizabethan culture. They reinforced and sometimes challenged each other, and were individually used to perform distinct kinds of work. In Spenser we find a considered awareness and deployment of these six forms. We discover chronicle clashing with chorography or euhemerism supporting analogy. Antiquarianism is used to formulate political aims, and prophecy to express providence or warning. While there is overlap and conflict there is also the artful conjunction of modes. A focus on forms of history thus offers access to an important dialogue between a poet and his time.

The Elizabethan age was a period of particular prominence for history. Chronicles were being printed in unprecedented numbers; chorography blossomed over the course of the Queen's reign; the Society of Antiquaries was at its height; euhemeristic commentary proliferated; historical parallels were used with unsurpassed ingenuity; and political prophecies circulated widely, especially at moments of crisis. Whether consciously or not, writers and readers alike proved capable of discriminating and alternating between these modes of discourse—frequently within the same volume or oration.

Inevitably, boundaries were far from solid. Chronicles could contain or be turned into prophecies; antiquarian discourse was frequently embedded in chorography; and historical analogy could intrude into these as well as other genres. The forms that have been the subject of this book were not immutable categories (nor do they constitute the full range of historical writing that was available). But as ways of writing, speaking, or performing, they would have been encountered by a great many of Spenser's contemporaries. The fact that these 'forms of history' were generically ill defined need not detract from their cultural interest or significance. Indeed, the points at which modes of writing cross over into one another are often of particular importance. It is at these moments (such as the report of Caesar's invasion in Holinshed, or of Elizabeth's accession in Foxe) that the interconnections between form and meaning come most strongly to the fore.

   This cultural context could not fail to make its impression on an exceptionally intellectual poet. Although the degree of sophistication, self-awareness, and poetic judgement that he brought to such processes was exceptional, Spenser (in hybridizing and juxtaposing historical forms) conforms very much to the customs of his age. Spenser was, in the words of one recent critic, 'an aggressively inter-textual writer'.[1] He absorbed, imitated, and transformed sources from the biblical to the Classical and from the popular to the abstruse. His work is by turns ostentatious and artfully evasive about its influences; but rarely, if ever, casual. Spenser was a poet deeply interested in the relationship between his own texts and their models—concerned not just with their style and structure, but also with their ideological affinities. His 'forms', on whatever scale he adopts them, almost invariably come with attached critical histories. It is his recurrent tendency to place such forms in productive tension—to play upon their respective capacities, effecting both harmonies and discords.

   Spenser's engagement with 'chronicles', 'chorographies', 'antiquarianism', 'analogy', 'euhemerism', 'and 'prophecy' appears to have followed almost automatically from his reading of literary and historiographic sources. The two categories are at times scarcely separable. It is notable, for example, that Spenser's *View* should cite the *Aeneid* to illustrate antiquarian detail, or that Harington's 1591 translation of *Orlando Furioso* appeared complete with detailed historical commentary. A work such as Camden's *Britannia*, likewise, mingled its groundbreaking analysis with

---

[1] *Shorter Poems*, ed. McCabe, p. xix.

generous literary quotation. Even the scholarly Selden was to garnish his annotations to *Poly-Olbion* with verses. In Early Modern England, Deborah Shuger has suggested, the boundaries between conceptual territories were still largely drawn with dotted rather than solid lines.[2] This is certainly true of the lines between literature and history. Spenser took his self-coined tag of 'Poet historical' seriously, drawing upon both elements of the phrase. Whilst (in verse) he generously granted himself what such commentators as Harington and Selden call 'poetical license', that prerogative is itself frequently taken up in order to tackle the substance of history.[3]

Historical analogy underlies the entire design of Spenser's epic, but the complexities of his understanding are often seen best in individual lines, stanzas, and cantos. As he worked directly from contemporary chronicle compilations to construct the British chronicle, for example, Spenser isolated the qualities of that mode. He highlighted on the one hand its insistence on instruction and providence, and, on the other, its severe doubts about historical integrity. Again, when he used Harrison's 'Description' to locate Merlin in 'Deheubarth' or Camden to provide material for the 'Marriage of Thames and Medway', he deftly exploited chorography's unique structural capacity for uniting geography, history, and myth. Likewise, when he looked to establish an antiquarian grounding for his plans for the subjection and reform of Ireland, the methodology and outlook that characterized his models proved to have a major impact on the workings of his argument.

Spenser was familiar, too, with numerous mythological compendia and universal histories. The overlap that he found in them between poetry and history evidently fascinated him: at numerous points in his fiction he was to play upon the paradoxical logic of euhemerism. He and his readers were well schooled in the language of historical praise and pageantry. That mode was all but ubiquitous in public speechifying, and when Spenser came to address his sovereign or her generals he used it with political awareness and subtlety. Finally, when it came to delivering history as prophecy through the figure of Merlin, rival traditions inevitably forced themselves onto a poet whose literary output had exploited the vatic mode from the beginning. Whilst here (as elsewhere)

---

[2] Deborah Kuller Shuger, *Habits of Thought in the English Renaissance: Religion, Politics, and the Dominant Culture* (Berkeley: University of California Press, 1990), 11. See also Helgerson, *Forms*, 1–18 (esp. 18).

[3] Harington, *Orlando Furioso*, 18; Selden, *Poly-Olbion*, 210.

strong encomiastic and providential precursors existed, they were complicated by other (less edified) associations upon which Spenser also drew.

An exploration of the forms of history once more shows Spenser to be a supremely sensitive reader and adapter. Repeatedly, one is struck by the sureness of touch with which the poet draws threads of narrative from the fabric of the past. Melding genres and narratives he is able to give voice to multiform and even contradictory perspectives: from the providential to the political, from national destiny to localized myth. These complexities originate not just in the design of Spenser's compositions, but also in the ceaseless questioning drive that seems to have characterized the poet at work. 'Yet', 'But', and 'And' are among Spenser's favourite stanza openings—they are the marks of a poet who is instinctively aware of objections and alternatives.

Spenser's poetry is notable for instances of geographical and historical particularity, but also for its extraordinary temporal scope. Revealingly, the two often fall together, so that we hear vast histories in a cave in Maridunum or survey the remnants of several centuries on a sunny day by the Thames. It was Samuel Taylor Coleridge who concluded that Spenser's great poem belonged to 'the domains neither of history or geography'—a work whose 'marvellous independence and true imaginative absence of a particular space and time' he commended.[4] This book has attempted to show both how wrong and how right Coleridge was. In spite of his judgement, encounters with history and geography are dispersed throughout *The Faerie Queene* and are of vital concern in much of the rest of Spenser's output. As Coleridge rightly observed, however, these are not treated as static entities. Instead, historically allusive episodes have the capacity to propel the reader through time and space, not simply to a single event in history, but to a matrix of suggestive parallels, from the apocryphal past to hypothetical future achievements.

---

[4] *Coleridge's Miscellaneous Criticism*, ed. T. M. Raysor (London: Constable, 1936), 36. On this passage see Galbraith, *Architectonics*, 12–13.

Works Cited

Note: For books published before or shortly after the death of Edmund Spenser the place of publication, unless otherwise stated, is London.

PRIMARY SOURCES

Manuscripts

ANON., 'political prophecies', British Library, Harley MS 559.
—— 'political prophecies', British Library, Landsdowne MS 762.
—— 'political prophecies', British Library, Sloane MS 1802.
—— 'political prophecies', British Library, Sloane MS 2578.
FORMAN, SIMON, Papers including 'Book of Giants and Monstrous Forms', Bodl. MS Ashmole 244.
—— Papers, MS Ashmole 802.
GREBNER, PAUL, *Grebneri Vaticinia* (Magdeburg, 1585), Trinity College Cambridge, MS R. 16. 22.299.
SPENSER, EDMUND, *A View of the Present State of Ireland*, Cambridge University Library, MS Dd.14.28.1.
—— *A View of the Present State of Ireland*, Gonville and Caius, Cambridge, MS 188.221.
—— *A View of the Present State of Ireland*, Bodleain MS Gough Ireland 2.

Collections

A Collection of Curious Discourses written by Eminent Antiquaries upon Several Heads in our English Antiquities, ed. Thomas Hearne, 2 vols. (London: W. & J. Richardson, 1771).
A Collection of State Papers Relating to Affairs in the Reign of Queen Elizabeth from the Year 1571 to 1596, ed. William Murdin (London: William Bowyes, 1759).
Calendar of State Papers, Domestic Series, of the Reigns of Edward VI, Mary, Elizabeth 1547–1580, ed. Robert Lemon (London: Longman, Brown, Green, Longmans & Roberts, 1856).
Chaucerian and Other Pieces, ed. Walter W. Skeat (Oxford: Clarendon Press, 1897), a supplement to the *Works of Geoffrey Chaucer*, 6 vols. (Oxford, Clarendon Press, 1894).

Statutes at Large, ed. John Raithby, 10 vols. (London: George Eyre & Andrew Strahan, 1811).

The Historie of Ireland, Collected by Three Learned Authors, ed. Sir James Ware (Dublin: Society of Stationers, 1633).

Mirror for Magistrates, ed. Lily B. Campbell (Cambridge: Cambridge University Press, 1938).

Works by Individual Authors

ANON., *The Kalender of Shepardes* (1518).

—— '"A Discourse of Ireland" (*circa* 1599): A Sidelight on English Colonial Policy', ed. David Beers Quinn, *Proceedings of the Royal Irish Academy*, 47 (1942), 151–66.

—— '"A Treatise for the Reformation of Ireland" (1554–5)', ed. Brendan Bradshaw, *The Irish Jurist*, 16 (1981), 299–315.

APOLLODURUS, *The Library*, trans. Sir James George Frazer, Loeb Classical Library, 2 vols. (London: Heinemann, 1921; repr. 1961).

ARIOSTO, LUDOVICO, *Orlando Furioso*, trans. Barbara Reynolds, 2 vols. (London: Penguin, 1973; repr. 1975).

BACON, FRANCIS, *Francis Bacon: A Critical Edition of the Major Works*, ed. Brian Vickers (Oxford: Oxford University Press, 1996).

BEACON, RICHARD, *Solon His Folie; or A Politique Discourse Touching the Reformation of Common-Weales Conquered, Declined or Corrupted*, ed. Clare Carroll and Vincent Carey (Binghamton, NY: Medieval & Renaissance Texts & Studies, 1996).

BLUNDEVILLE, THOMAS, *The True Order of Wryting and Reading Hystories*, The English Experience, 908 (London, 1574; repr. Amsterdam: Theatrum Orbis Terrarum, 1979).

BODIN, JOHN, *Method for the Easy Comprehension of History*, trans. Beatrice Reynolds (New York: Columbia University Press, 1945).

BRY, THEODORE DE, *De Ontdekking van de Nieuwe Wereld* (Amsterdam: van Hoeve, 1979).

—— *A brief and true Report of the new found Land of Virginia: A Study of the de Bry Engravings*, intro. and ed. W. John Faupel (East Grinstead: Antique Atlas Publications, 1989).

CAMBRENSIS, GIRALDUS, *The History and Topography of Ireland*, trans. and ed. John J. O'Meara, Dolmen Texts, 4 (Dundalk: Dundalgan Press, 1951; repr. Atlantic Highlands, NJ: Humanities Press, 1982).

CAMDEN, WILLIAM, *Britannia* (1586).

—— *Britain*, trans. Philemon Holland (1610).

CAXTON, WILLIAM, *Chronicles of England*, The English Experience, 508 (1480; repr. Amsterdam: Theatrum Obis Terrarum, 1973).

CHAUCER, GEOFFREY, *Workes*, ed. John Stow (1561).

—— *The Complete Works of Geoffrey Chaucer*, ed. Walter W. Skeat, 7 vols. (Oxford: Clarendon, 1894–7).

CHASSANION, JEAN DE, *De Gigantibus* (Basle, 1580).

CHURCHYARD, THOMAS, *The Worthines of Wales* (1587; repr. London: Thomas Evans, 1776).

CONTI, NATALE, *Mythologies*, trans. Anthony Dimatteo (London: Garland, 1994).

COOPER, THOMAS, *Epitome of Chronicles* (1559).

COVELL, WILLIAM, *Polimanteia; or, The Meanes Lawfull and Unlawfull to Judge the Fall of a Common-Wealth* (1595).

COXE, FRANCIS, *The Wickednesse of Magical Sciences* (1561).

—— *A Prognostication made for the Yeere of our Lorde 1566* (1566).

CRESPIN, JEAN, *Actiones et Monumentes* (Geneva, 1560).

DANIEL, SAMUEL, *Poetical Works* (1602).

—— *The Civile Wures* (1609).

—— *The Collection of the History of England* (1634).

—— *The Complete works in Verse and Prose of Samuel Daniel*, ed. A. B. Grosart, 5 vols. (London: privately printed, 1885–99; repr. New York: Russell & Russell, 1963).

DERRICKE, JOHN, *The Image of Ireland* (1581).

DRAYTON, MICHAEL, *The Works of Michael Drayton*, ed. J. William Hebel, 5 vols. (Oxford: Shakespeare Head Press, 1931; repr. Oxford: Basil Blackwell, 1961).

DU BELLAY, JOACHIM, *Les Regrets et Autres Œuvres Poëtiques*, ed. J. Jolliffe and M. A. Screech (Geneva: Librairie Droz, 1966).

FOXE, JOHN, *Actes and Monuments* (1563).

—— *Actes and Monuments* (1570).

—— *Actes and Monuments* (1583).

GEOFFREY OF MONMOUTH, *The History of the Kings of Britain*, trans. Lewis Thorpe (London: Penguin, 1966).

GRAFTON, RICHARD, *Abridgement of Chronicles of England* (1563; 1564; 1570; 1572).

—— *A Manuell of the Chronicles of England* (1565).

—— *A Chronicle at Large* (1569).

—— *A Brief Treatise Conteyning many proper Tables and Easy Rules* (1582).

HAKLUYT, RICHARD, *The Principall Navigations, Voyages, Traffiques and Discoveries of the English Nation* (1589).

HALLE, EDWARD, *The Union of the Two Noble Families of Lancaster and York* (1550; repr. Menston: Scholar Press, 1970).

HARDYNG, JOHN, *The Chronicle*, ed. Richard Grafton, The English Experience, 805 (1543; repr. Amsterdam: Theatrum Orbis Terrarum, 1976).

HARINGTON, SIR JOHN, *Orlando Furioso in English Heroical Verse* (1591).

—— *A Tract on the Succession to the Crown* (1602), ed. Clements R. Markham (London: J. B. Nichols & Sons, 1880).

HARINGTON, SIR JOHN, *A Short View of the State of Ireland* (1605), ed. W. Dunn Macray (Oxford: James Parker & Co., 1879).

HARVEY, GABRIEL, *The Works of Gabriel Harvey*, ed. Alexander B. Grosart, 3 vols. (London: Hazell, Watson, & Viney, 1884–5).

HARVEY, JOHN, *An Astrologicall Addition* (1583).

——*A Discoursive Probleme Concerning Prophecies* (1588).

HARVEY, RICHARD, *An Astrological Discourse* (1583).

HESIOD, *The Homeric Hymns and Homerica*, trans. Hugh G. Evelyn-White, Loeb Classical Library (Cambridge, Mass.: Harvard University Press, 1914; repr. 1982).

HEYWOOD, THOMAS, *The Life of Merlin* (1641).

HIGDEN, RANULF, 'The English Polychronicon: A Text of John Trevisa's Translation of Higden's *Polychronicon* based on Huntingdon MS. 28561', ed. Richard Arthur Seeger (Unpublished doctoral dissertation, University of Washington, 1974).

HOLINSHED, RAPHAEL, *Chronicles* (1577).

——*Chronicles*, 3 vols. (1587).

——*Holinshed's Chronicles*, ed. Henry Ellis, 2nd edn., intro. Vernon Snow (London: J. Johnson, 1807; repr. New York: Ams Press, 1979).

HOWARD, HENRY (Earl of Northampton), *A Defensative Against the Poyson of Supposed Prophesies* (1583).

LAMBARDE, WILLIAM, *A Perambulation of Kent* (1576).

LANQUET, THOMAS, *An Epitome of Chronciles* (1549).

LELAND, JOHN, *The Itinerary of John Leland the Antiquary*, ed. Thomas Hearne, 3rd edition, 9 vols. (Oxford: James Fletcher & Joseph Pote, 1770).

LHUYD, HUMPHREY, *The Breviary of Britayne*, trans. Thomas Twyne (1579).

LUCRETIUS, *On the Nature of the Universe*, trans. R. E. Latham, 2nd edn., rev. John Godwin (London: Penguin, 1994).

MILTON, JOHN, *Paradise Lost*, ed. Scott Elledge, Norton Critical Edition (New York: Norton, 1975).

MOLYNEUX, THOMAS, 'Some Notes upon the Foregoing Account of the Giants Causway', *Philosophical Transactions*, 18 (1694), 175–82.

——'An Essay concerning Giants', *Philosophical Transactions*, 22 (1700), 487–508.

MONTAIGNE, MICHEL DE, *The Complete Essays*, trans. and ed. M. A. Screech (London: Penguin, 1987; repr. 1991).

MORE, ST THOMAS, *Richard III*, ed. Richard S. Sylvester, in *The Complete Works of St. Thomas More*, 12 vols., ed. Thomas M. C. Lawler, Germain Marc'Hadour, and Richard C. Marius (New Haven: Yale University Press, 1963–81), vol. ii.

NASHE, THOMAS, *The Works of Thomas Nashe*, ed. Ronald B. McKerrow, 2nd edn., rev. F. Wilson, 5 vols. (Oxford: Basil Blackwell, 1958).

OVID, *Metamorphoses*, ed. and trans. Frank Justus Miller, 3rd edn., rev. G. Goold, in *Ovid*, 6 vols., Loeb Classical Library (Cambridge, Mass.: Harvard University Press, 1977; repr. 1999), iii–iv.

PAYNE, ROBERT, *A Brief Description of Ireland*, English Experience, 548 (1589; repr. Amsterdam: Theatrum Orbis Terrarum, 1973).

PUTTENHAM, G., *The Arte of English Poesie* (1589).

RALEGH, SIR WALTER, *The Discoverie of the Large, Rich and Bewtiful Empire of Guiana* (1596).

—— *The History of the World* (1614).

—— *The History of the World*, ed. C. A. Patrides (Philadelphia: Temple University Press, 1971).

SACKVILLE, THOMAS, and THOMAS NORTON, *Gorboduc; or Ferrex and Porrex*, ed. B. Cauthern, Jr. (London: Edward Arnold, 1970).

SHAKESPEARE, WILLIAM, *King Henry VIII*, ed. John Margeson (Cambridge: Cambridge University Press, 1990).

—— *Macbeth*, ed. A. R. Braunmuller (Cambridge: Cambridge University Press, 1997).

SIDNEY, SIR PHILIP, *The Complete Works of Sir Philip Sidney*, ed. Albert Feuillerat, 4 vols. (Cambridge: Cambridge University Press, 1912–16).

—— *The Correspondence of Philip Sidney and Hubert Languet*, ed. William Aspenwall Bradley, Humanist's Library, 5 (Boston: Merrymount Press, 1912).

—— *Sir Philip Sidney*, ed. Katherine Duncan-Jones (Oxford: Oxford University Press, 1989; repr. 1991).

SPENSER, EDMUND, *The Shepheardes Calender* (1579; repr. Menston: Scholar Press, 1968).

—— *Three Proper, and Wittie, Familiar Letters* (1580).

—— *The Faerie Queene* (1590).

—— *The Faerie Queene* (1596).

—— *Spenser: Poetical Works*, ed. J. C. Smith and E. de Selincourt (Oxford: Oxford University Press, 1912; repr. 1970).

—— *The Works of Edmund Spenser: A Variorum Edition*, ed. Edwin Greenlaw *et al.*, 8 vols. (Baltimore: Johns Hopkins University Press, 1949).

—— *The Faerie Queene*, ed. A. C. Hamilton (London: Longman, 1977).

—— *The Yale Edition of the Shorter Poems of Edmund Spenser*, ed. William A. ORAM *et al.* (New Haven: Yale University Press, 1989).

—— *A View of the State of Ireland*, ed. Andrew Hadfield and Willy Maley (Oxford: Blackwell, 1997).

—— *Edmund Spenser: The Shorter Poems*, ed. R. A. McCabe (London: Penguin, 1999).

—— *The Faerie Queene*, ed. A. C. Hamilton (London: Longman, 2001).

STOW, JOHN, *The Chronicles of England* (1580).

—— *Annales of England* (1592).

—— *A Summarie of the Chronicles of England* (1598).

STOW, JOHN, *Survay of London* (1598).

STUBBS, JOHN, *John Stubbs's 'Gaping Gulf' with Letters and Other Relevant Documents*, ed. Lloyd E. Berry (Charlottesville: Folger Shakespeare Library, 1968).

TASSO, TORQUATO, *Jerusalem Delivered*, trans. and ed. Ralph Nash (Detroit: Wayne State University Press, 1987).

THOMAS OF ERCELDOUNE, *The Romance and Prophecies of Thomas of Erceldoune*, ed. James A. H. Murray (London: Early Modern Text Society, 1875).

VAN DER NOOT, JAN, *A Theatre for Worldlings* (1569; repr. New York: Scholars Facsimiles and Reprints, 1937).

VERGIL, POLYDORE, *De Inventibus Rerum*, ed. Beno Weiss and Louis C. Pérez, Bibliotheca Humanistica & Reformatorica, 56 (Nieuwkoop: De Graaf, 1997).

VIRGIL, *Works*, trans. H. Rusdton Fairclough, 2 vols. (London: William Heinemann, 1918).

WARNER, WILLIAM, *Albions England* (1592).

——*Albions England* (1602).

WHITE, ROLAND, 'Roland White's "A Discourse Touching Ireland" (*c.* 1569)', ed. Nicholas Canny, *Irish Historical Studies*, 20 (1977), 439–63.

——'Roland White's "The Disorders of the Irishry" (1571)', ed. Nicholas Canny, *Studia Hibernica*, 19 (1979), 147–60.

SECONDARY SOURCES

ABBOTT, EDWIN A., *Bacon and Essex: A Sketch of Bacon's Earlier Life* (London: Seeley, Jackson, & Halliday, 1877).

ADLER, WILLIAM, *Time Immemorial: Archaic History and Its Sources in Christian Chronography from Julius Africanus to George Syncellus* (Washington: Dumbarton Oaks Research Library, 1989).

ALBANO, ROBERT A., *Middle English Historiography* (New York: Peter Lang, 1993).

ALLEN, DON CAMERON, *Image and Meaning: Metaphoric Traditions in Renaissance Poetry* (Baltimore: Johns Hopkins University Press, 1968).

ALSTON, R. C., *Books with Manuscript: A Short Title Catalogue of Books with Manuscript Notes in the British Library* (London: British Library, 1994).

ALPERS, PAUL J., *The Poetry of 'The Faerie Queene'* (Princeton: Princeton University Press, 1967)

ALTER, ROBERT B., 'Sacred History and the Beginnings of Prose Fiction', *Poetics Today*, 1 (1980), 143–62.

ANDERSON, JUDITH H., 'The Antiquities of Fairyland and Ireland', *Journal of English and Germanic Philology*, 86 (1987), 199–214.

——'"Mine Actour": Spenser's Enabling Fiction and Eumnestes' "Immortall Scrine"', in George M. Logan and Gordon Teskey (eds.), *Unfolded Tales: Essays on Renaissance Romance* (Ithaca, NY: Cornell University Press, 1989), 16–31.

——Donald Cheney, and David A. Richardson (eds.), *Spenser's Life and the Subject of Biography* (Amherst, Mass.: University of Massachusetts Press, 1997).

Anderson, Ruth Leila, *Elizabethan Psychology and Shakespeare's Plays*, University of Iowa Humanistic Studies, 3 (Iowa City: Iowa University Press, 1927).

Anon., 'MS Notes to Spenser's "Faerie Queene"' *N&Q* 202 (1957), 509–15.

Aptekar, Jane, *Icons of Justice: Iconography and Thematic Imagery in Book V of 'The Faerie Queene'* (New York: Columbia University Press, 1969).

Arber, Edward (ed.), *A Transcript of the Registers of the Company of Stationers of London*, 5 vols. (London: privately published, 1876).

Auerbach, Erich, *Scenes from the Drama of European Literature* (New York: Meridean, 1959).

Axton, Marie, *The Queen's Two Bodies: Drama and the Elizabethan Succession* (London: Royal Historical Society, 1977).

Babb, Lawrence, *The Elizabethan Malady: A Study of Melancholia in English Literature from 1580 to 1642* (East Lansing. Michigan State College Press, 1951).

Baker, David J., '"Some Quirk, Some Subtle Evasion": Legal Subversion in Spenser's *A View of the Present State of Ireland*', *Spenser Studies*, 6 (1986), 147–65.

——*Between Nations: Shakespeare, Spenser, Marvell, and the Question of Britain* (Stanford, Calif.: Stanford University Press, 1997).

——'Spenser and the Uses of British History', in Patrick Cheney and Lauren Silberman (eds.), *Worldmaking Spenser: Explorations in the Early Modern Age* (Lexington, Ky.: University of Kentucky Press, 2000), 193–203.

Bal, Mieke, *Narratology: Introduction to the Theory of Narrative*, trans. Christine van Boheemen (Toronto: University of Toronto Press, 1985).

Bates, Catherine, *The Rhetoric of Courtship in Elizabethan Language and Literature* (Cambridge: Cambridge University Press, 1992).

Baybak, Michael, Paul Delany, and A. Kent Hieatt, 'Placement "In the Middest" in *The Faerie Queene*', *Papers on Language and Literature*, 5 (1969), 227–34.

Beal, Peter, *Index of English Literary Manuscripts*, 2 vols. (London: Mansell, 1980).

Bellamy, Elizabeth, *Translations of Power: Narcissism and the Unconscious in Epic History* (Ithaca, NY: Cornell University Press, 1992).

Bennett, Josephine Waters, *The Evolution of 'The Faerie Queene'* (Chicago: University of Chicago Press, 1942).

Berger, Harry, Jr., *The Allegorical Temper: Vision and Reality in Book 2 of Spenser's 'Faerie Queene'*, Yale Studies in English, 137 (New Haven: Yale University Press, 1957).

——'Archaism, Immortality, and the Muse in Spenser's Poetry', *The Yale Review*, 58 (1968), 214–31.

——'Two Spenserian Retrospects: The Antique Temple of Venus and the Primitive Marriage of Rivers', *Texas Studies in Literature and Language*, 10 (1969),

5–25 (repr. in *Revisionary Play: Studies in the Spenserian Dynamics* (Berkeley: University of California Press, 1988), 195–214).

BERGER, HARRY, JR., 'The Structure of Merlin's Chronicle in *The Faerie Queene* III (iii)', *Studies in English Literature*, 9 (1969), 39–51.

——*Revisionary Play: Studies in the Spenserian Dynamics* (Berkeley: University of California Press, 1988).

BERNHEIMER, RICHARD, *Wild Men in the Middle Ages: A Study in Art, Sentiment, and Demonology* (Cambridge, Mass.: Harvard University Press, 1952).

BEST, NICHOLAS, *The Knights Templar* (London: Weidenfeld & Nicolson, 1997).

BLACKBURN, WILLIAM, 'Spenser's Merlin', *Renaissance and Reform*, 4 (1980), 179–98.

BLITCH, ALICE FOX, 'The Mutabilitie Cantos: "In Meet Order Ranged"', *English Language Notes*, 7 (1969–70), 179–86.

BONDANELLA, PETER E., *Machiavelli and the Art of Renaissance History* (Detroit: Wayne State University Press, 1973).

BOOTH, STEVEN, *The Book Called Holinshed's Chronicles: An Account of its Inception, Purpose, Contributors, Contents, Publication, Revision, and Influence on William Shakespeare* (San Francisco: Book Club of California, 1968).

BORRIS, KENNETH, *Spenser's Poetics of Prophecy in 'The Faerie Queene' V*, English Literary Studies Monograph Series, 52 (Victoria, BC: University of Victoria Press, 1990).

——*Allegory and Epic in English Renaissance Literature: Heroic Form in Sidney, Spenser, and Milton* (Cambridge: Cambridge University Press, 2001).

BRADEN, GORDON, 'Riverrun: An Epic Catalogue in *The Faerie Queene*', *ELR* 5 (1975), 25–48.

BRADSHAW, BRENDAN, ANDREW HADFIELD, and WILLY MALEY (eds.), *Representing Ireland: Literature and the Origins of Conflict, 1534–1660* (Cambridge: Cambridge University Press, 1993).

BRADY, CIARÁN, 'Spenser's Irish Crisis: Humanism and Experience in the 1590s', *Past & Present*, 111 (1986), 17–49.

——'Court, Castle, and Country: The Framework of Government in Tudor Ireland', in Ciarán Brady and Raymond Gillespie (eds.), *Natives and Newcomers: Essays on the Making of Irish Colonial Society 1534–1641* (Dublin: Irish Academic Press, 1986), 22–49.

——'The Road to the *View*: On the Decline of Reform Thought in Tudor England', in Patricia Coughlan (ed.), *Spenser and Ireland: An Interdisciplinary Perspective* (Cork: Cork University Press, 1989).

BREEN, JOHN M., 'Imagining Voices in *A View of the Present State of Ireland*: A Discussion of Recent Studies Concerning Edmund Spenser's Dialogue', *Connotations*, 4 (1994–5), 203–28.

——'Spenser's "Imaginatiue Groundplot": *A View of the Present State of Ireland*', *Spenser Studies*, 12 (1998), 151–68.

BRINK, JEAN R., 'Constructing the *View of the Present State of Ireland*', *Spenser Studies*, 11 (1990), 203–28.

—— *Michael Drayton Revisited*, Twayne's English Authors Series, 476 (Boston: Twayne Publishing, 1990).

—— 'Who Fashioned Edmund Spenser?: The Textual History of Complaints', *SP* 88 (1991), 153–68.

BROOKS, N., *History and Myth, Forgery and Truth: An Inaugural Lecture Delivered in the University of Birmingham on 26th January 1986* (Birmingham: University of Birmingham, 1986).

BROWN, RICHARD DANSON, *'The New Poet': Novelty and Tradition in Spenser's 'Complaints'*, Liverpool Texts and Studies, 32 (Liverpool: Liverpool University Press, 1999).

BUELL, LLEWLLYN M., 'Elizabethan Portents: Superstition or Doctrine?', in *Essays, Critical and Historical, Dedicated to Lily B. Campbell*, ed. Louis B. Wright (Berkeley: University of California Press, 1950), 27–44

BULGER, THOMAS F., *The Historical Changes and Exchanges as Depicted by Spenser in 'The Faerie Queene'* (Lewiston, NY: Edwin Mellen Press, 1993).

BURKE, PETER, *The Renaissance Sense of the Past* (London: Edward Arnold, 1969).

BURROW, COLIN, *Edmund Spenser* (Plymouth: Northcote House, 1996).

—— *Epic Romance: Homer to Milton* (Oxford: Clarendon Press, 1993).

CALDWELL, JAMES RALSTON, 'Dating a Spenser Harvey Letter', *PMLA* 41 (1926), 568–74.

CAMBINO, MERCEDES MAROTO, '"Methinks I see an evil unespied": Visualizing Conquest in Spenser's *A View of the Present State of Ireland*', *Spenser Studies*, 14 (1998), 169–94.

CANINO, CATHERINE G., 'Reconstructing Lord Grey's Reputation: A New View of the *View*', *Sixteenth Century Journal*, 29 (1998), 3–18.

CANNY, NICHOLAS, 'Reviewing *A View of the Present State of Ireland*', *Irish University Review*, 26 (1996), 252–67.

—— *Making Ireland British, 1580–1650* (Oxford: Oxford University Press, 2001).

CAPP, BERNARD, *Astrology and the Popular Press: English Almanacs 1500–1800* (London: Faber & Faber, 1979).

—— 'The Political Dimension of Apocalyptic Thought', in C. A. Patrides and Joseph Wittreich (eds.), *The Apocalypse in English Thought and Literature: Patterns, Antecedents and Repercussions* (Manchester: Manchester University Press, 1984), 93–125.

CARROLL, CLARE, 'Spenser and the Irish Language: The Sons of Milesio in *A View of the Present State of Ireland, The Faerie Queene*, Book V and the *Leabhar Gabhála*', *Irish University Review*, 26 (1996), 281–90.

CAVANAGH, SHEILA T., '"Licentious Barbarism": Spenser's View of the Irish and *The Faerie Queene*', *Irish University Review*, 26 (1996), 268–80.

CÉARD, JEAN, 'La Querelle des géants et la jeunesse du monde', *The Journal of*

Medieval and Renaissance Studies, 8 (1978), 37–76.

CHAUDHURI, SUKANTA, 'The Rebirth of Time: Tradition, History and the Renaissance Mind', in Sukanta Chaudhuri (ed.), *Renaissance Essays for Kitty Scoular Datta* (Calcutta: Oxford University Press, 1995), 26–51.

CHENEY, PATRICK GERARD, '"Secret Powre Unseene": Good Magic in Spenser's Legend of Britomart', *Studies in Philology*, 85 (1988), 1–28.

——*Spenser's Famous Flight: A Renaissance Idea of a Literary Career* (Toronto: University of Toronto Press, 1993).

CHUILLEANÁIN, EILÉAN NÍ, 'Forged and Fabulous Chronicles: Reading Spenser as an Irish Writer', *Irish University Review*, 26 (1996), 237–51.

COLERIDGE, SAMUEL TAYLOR, *Coleridge's Miscellaneous Criticism*, ed. T. M. Raysor (London: Constable, 1936).

COLIE, ROSALIE, *The Resources of Kind: Genre-Theory in the Renaissance*, ed. Barbara K. Lewalski (Berkeley: University of California Press, 1973).

COLLINS, CYNTHIA, 'The Golden Age and the Iron Age of Gold: The Inversion of Paradise in the Cave of Mammon', *Comitatus*, 20 (1989), 43–58.

COLLINSON, PATRICK, *The Elizabethan Puritan Movement* (London: Jonathan Cape, 1967).

——*Archbishop Grindal 1519–1583: The Struggle for a Reformed Church* (London: Jonathan Cape, 1979).

—— 'Truth and Legend: The Veracity of John Foxe's Book of Martyrs', in A. C. Duke and C. A. Tamse (eds.), *Clio's Mirror: Historiography in Britain and the Netherlands*, Britain and the Netherlands, 8 (Zutphen: Walburg Pers, 1985), 31–54.

——*Elizabethan Essays* (London: The Hambledon Press, 1994).

COOK, PATRICK J., *Milton, Spenser, and the Epic Tradition* (Aldershot: Scholar, 1996).

COOKE, JESSICA, 'The Beginning of the Year in Spenser's *Mutabilitie Cantos*', *N&Q*, NS 42 (1995), 285–6.

COOTE, L., 'A Language of Power: Prophecy and Public Affairs in Later Medieval England', in Bertrand Taithe and Tim Thornton (eds.), *Prophecy: The Power of Inspired Language in History, 1300–2000* (Stroud: Sutton Publishing, 1997), 17–30.

COUGHLAN, PATRICIA (ed.), *Spenser and Ireland: An Interdisciplinary Perspective* (Cork: Cork University Press, 1989).

—— '"Some Secret Scourge Which Shall by her Come unto England": Ireland and Incivility in Spenser', in Patricia Coughlan (ed.), *Spenser and Ireland: An Interdisciplinary Perspective* (Cork: Cork University Press, 1989), 46–75.

—— 'The Local Context of Mutabilitie's Plea', *Irish University Review*, 26 (1996), 320–41.

COVINGTON, F. F., 'Spenser's Use of History in the *View of the Present State of Ireland*', *University of Texas Bulletin*, Studies in English, 4 (1924), 5–38.

COX, VIRGINIA, *The Renaissance Dialogue: Literary Dialogue in its Social and Political Contexts, Castiglione to Galileo* (Cambridge: Cambridge University Press, 1992).

CUMMINGS, R. M. (ed.), *Spenser: The Critical Heritage* (New York: Barnes & Noble, 1971).

CURRAN, JOHN EDWARD, JR., 'Poets Historical and the Historical Revolution: Roman Britain in Renaissance Poetry' (unpublished doctoral dissertation, University of Virginia, 1996).

——'Spenser and the Historical Revolution: Briton Moniments and the Problem of Roman Britain', *Clio: A Journal of Literature, History, and the Philosophy of History*, 25 (1996), 273–92.

CURRY, PATRICK, *Prophecy and Power: Astrology in Early Modern England* (Cambridge: Polity Press, 1989).

DAVIS, ELLEN F., *Swallowing the Scroll: Textuality and the Dynamics of Discourse in Ezekiel's Prophecy*, Journal for the Study of the Old Testament Supplement Series, 78 (Sheffield: Almond Press, 1989).

DAWSON, JANE E. A., 'The Apocalyptic Thinking of the Marian Exiles', in *Prophecy and Eschatology*, ed. Michael Wilks, Studies in Church History, 10 (Oxford: Blackwell, 1994), 75–92.

DeNEEF, A. LEIGH, '"The Ruins of Time": Spenser's Apology for Poetry', *SP* 76 (1979), 262–71.

DOBIN, HOWARD, *Merlin's Disciples: Prophecy, Poetry, and Power in Renaissance England* (Stanford, Calif.: Stanford University Press, 1990).

DONNO, ELIZABETH STORY, 'Some Aspects of Shakespeare's Holinshed', *Huntington Library Quarterly*, 50 (1987), 229–48.

DUBROW, HEATHER, 'The Arraignment of Paridell: Tudor Historiography in *The Faerie Queene*, III.ix', *SP* 87 (1990), 312–27.

DUFF, DAVID (ed.), *Modern Genre Theory* (London: Longman, 2000).

DUMVILLE, DAVID N., *Histories and Pseudo-histories of the Middle Ages* (Aldershot: Variorum, 1990).

DUNSEATH, T. K., *Spenser's Allegory of Justice in the 'Faerie Queene' V* (Princeton: Princeton University Press, 1968).

DuROCHER, RICHARD J., 'Guiding the Glance: Spenser, Milton, and "Venus Looking Glas"', *Journal of English and Germanic Philology*, 92 (1993), 325–41.

ECKHARDT, CAROLINE D., 'Prophecy and Nostalgia: Arthurian Symbolism at the Close of the English Middle Ages', in Mary Flowers Braswell and John Bugge (eds.), *The Arthurian Tradition: Essays in Convergence* (Tuscaloosa: University of Alabama Press, 1988), 109–27.

ELDEVIK, RANDI, '*The Faerie Queene* II.x.18–19', *Spenser Studies*, 12 (1998), 207–14.

ELSKY, MARTIN, *Authorizing Words: Speech, Writing and Print in the English Renaissance* (Ithaca, NY: Cornell University Press, 1989).

ERICKSON, WAYNE, 'Spenser's Letter to Ralegh and the Literary Politics of *The Faerie Queene*'s 1590 Publication', *Spenser Studies*, 10 (1992), 139–74.

——*Mapping 'The Faerie Queene': Quest Structures and the World of the Poem*, Garland Studies in the Renaissance, 3 (New York: Garland Publishing, 1996).

EVANS, JOAN, *A History of the Society of Antiquaries* (Oxford: Society of Antiquaries, 1956).

FAIRHOLT, F. W., *Gog and Magog, The Giants in Guildhall; Their Real and Legendary History. With an Account of other Civic Giants, at Home and Abroad* (London: John Camden Hotten, 1859).

FERGUSON, ARTHUR B., *Clio Unbound: Perception of the Social and Cultural Past in Renaissance England*, Duke Monographs in Medieval and Renaissance Studies, 2 (Durham, NC: Duke University Press, 1979).

—— *Utter Antiquity: Perceptions of Prehistory in Renaissance England* (Durham, NC: Duke University Press, 1993).

FERGUSON, MARGARET W., '"The Afflatus of Ruin": Meditations on Rome by Du Bellay, Spenser, and Stevens', in Annabel Patterson (ed.), *Roman Images*, Selected Papers from the English Institute, NS 8 (Baltimore: Johns Hopkins University Press, 1984), 23–50.

FERRIS, INA, 'The Historical Novel and the Problem of Beginning: The Model of Scott', *The Journal of Narrative Technique*, 1 (1988), 73–82.

FICHTER, ANDREW, '"And nought of *Rome* in *Rome* perceiu'st at all": Spenser's *Ruines of Rome*', *Spenser Studies*, 2 (1981), 183–92.

—— *Poets Historical: Dynastic Epic in the Renaissance* (Yale: Yale University Press, 1982).

FINKE, LAURIE A., 'Spenser for Hire: Arthurian History as Cultural Capital in *The Faerie Queene*', in Martin B. Schichtman and James Carley (ed.), *Culture and the King: The Social Implications of the Arthurian Legend: Essays in Honor of Valerie M. Lagorio* (New York: State University of New York Press, 1994), 211–33.

FLETCHER, ANGUS, *The Prophetic Moment: An Essay on Spenser* (Chicago: University of Chicago Press, 1971).

FLETCHER, ANTHONY, and PETER ROBERTS (eds.), *Religion, Culture and Society in Early Modern Britain: Essays in Honour of Patrick Collinson* (Cambridge: Cambridge University Press, 1994).

FOUCAULT, MICHEL, *The Archaeology of Knowledge*, trans. A. M. Sheridan Smith (London: Tavistock, 1972; repr. London: Routledge, 1995).

FOWLER, ALASTAIR, 'Oxford and London Marginalia to *The Faerie Queene*', *N&Q* 206 (1961), 416–19.

FOX, ALISTAIR, 'Prophecies and Politics in the Reign of Henry VIII', in Alistair Fox and John Guy (eds.), *Reassessing the Henrican Age: Humanism, Politics and Reform 1500–1550* (Oxford: Basil Blackwell, 1986), 77–94.

FREEMAN, THOMAS, 'Notes on a Source for John Foxe's Account of the Marian Persecution in Kent and Sussex', *Historical Research*, 67 (1994), 203–11.

FRENCH, PETER J., *John Dee: The World of an Elizabethan Magus* (London: Routledge & Kegan Paul, 1972).

FRYE, SUSAN, *Elizabeth I: The Competition for Representation* (Oxford: Oxford University Press, 1993).

FUSSNER, F. SMITH, *Tudor History and the Historians* (New York: Basic Books, 1970).

GAFFNEY, CARMEL, 'Colin Clouts Come Home Againe' (unpublished doctoral dissertation, University of Edinburgh, 1982).

GALBRAITH, DAVID IAN, *Architectonics of Imitation in Spenser, Daniel, and Drayton* (Toronto: University of Toronto Press, 2000).

GALINSKY, G. KARL, *The Herakles Theme: The Adaptations of the Hero in Literature from Homer to the Twentieth Century* (Oxford: Basil Blackwell, 1972).

GANS, NATHAN A. 'Archaism and Neologism in Spenser's Diction', *Modern Philology*, 76 (1978–9), 377–9.

GLEASON, JOHN B., 'Opening Spenser's Wedding Present: The "Marriage Number" of Plato in the "Epithalamion"', *ELR* 24 (1994), 620–37.

GLESS, DARYLL J., *Interpretation and Theology in Spenser* (Cambridge: Cambridge University Press, 1994).

GOLDBERG, JONATHAN, *Endlesse Worke: Spenser and the Structures of Discourse* (Baltimore: Johns Hopkins University Press, 1981).

GOTTFRIED, RUDOLF B., 'Spenser Recovered: The Poet and Historical Scholarship', in Richard C. Frushell and Bernard J. Vondersmith (eds.), *Contemporary Thought on Edmund Spenser* (London: Feffer & Simons, 1975), 61–79.

—— 'The Date of Spenser's *View*', *Modern Language Notes*, 52 (1937), 176–80.

GRABES, HERBERT, *The Mutable Glass: Mirror-Imagery in Titles and Texts of the Middle Ages and English Renaissance*, trans. Gordon Collier (Cambridge: Cambridge University Press, 1982).

GRAFTON, ANTHONY, *Joseph Scaliger: A Study in the History of Classical Scholarship*, 2 vols. (Oxford: Clarendon Press, 1983–93).

—— *The Footnote: A Curious History* (London: Faber & Faber, 1997).

—— *Bring Out Your Dead: The Past as Revelation* (Cambridge, Mass.: Harvard University Press, 2001).

GRANSDEN, ANTONIA, *Historical Writing in England: c.550–c.1307* (London: Routledge & Kegan Paul, 1974–82; repr. London: Routledge, 1996).

—— *Historical Writing in England, II: c. 1307 to the Early Sixteenth Century* (London: Routledge, 1996).

GRAZIANI, RENÉ, 'Elizabeth at Isis Chruch', *PMLA* 79 (1964), 376–89.

GREENBLATT, STEPHEN, *Renaissance Self-Fashioning: From More to Shakespeare* (Chicago: University of Chicago Press, 1980).

GREENE, ROLAND, 'Calling Colin Clout', *Spenser Studies* 10 (1992), 229–44.

—— 'A Primer of Spenser's Worldmaking: Alterity in the Bower of Bliss', in Patrick Cheney and Lauren Silberman (eds.), *Worldmaking Spenser: Explorations in the Early Modern Age* (Lexington, Ky.: University of Kentucky Press, 2000), 9–31.

GREENE, THOMAS M., *The Light in Troy: Imitation and Discovery in Renaissance Poetry*, The Elizabethan Club Series, 7 (New Haven: Yale University Press, 1982).

GREGERSON, LINDA, *The Reformation of the Subject: Spenser, Milton, and the English Protestant Epic*, Cambridge Studies in Renaissance Literature and Culture, 6 (Cambridge: Cambridge University Press, 1995).

GROSS, KENNETH, *Spenserian Poetics: Idolatry, Iconoclasm, and Magic* (Ithaca, NY: Cornell University Press, 1985).

GRUNDY, JOAN, *The Spenserian Poets: A Study in Elizabethan and Jacobean Poetry* (London: Edward Arnold, 1969).

GUIBBORY, ACHSAH, *The Map of Time: Seventeenth-Century English Ideas of Pattern in History* (Urbana, Ill.: University of Illinois Press, 1986).

HADFIELD, ANDREW, 'Briton and Scythian: Tudor Representations of Irish Origins', *Irish Historical Studies*, 28 (1993), 390–408.

—— *Literature, Politics and National Identity: Reformation to Renaissance* (Cambridge: Cambridge University Press, 1994).

—— 'The "sacred hunger of ambitious minds": Spenser's Savage Religion', in Anthony Fletcher (ed.), *Religion, Culture and Society in Early Modern Britain: Essays in Honour of Patrick Collinson* (Cambridge: Cambridge University Press, 1994), 27–42.

—— 'Was Spenser's *A View of the Present State of Ireland* Censored? A Review of the Evidence', *N&Q* 239 (1994), 459–63.

—— 'Who is Speaking in Spenser's *A View of the Present State of Ireland*? A Response to John Breen', *Connotations*, 4 (1994–5), 233–41.

—— (ed.), *Edmund Spenser* (London: Longman, 1996).

—— *Edmund Spenser's Irish Experience: Wilde Fruit and Salvage Soyl* (Oxford: Clarendon Press, 1997).

—— 'Spenser, Drayton, and the Question of Britain', *Review of English Studies*, 51 (2000), 582–99.

—— BRENDAN BRADSHAW, and WILLY MALEY (eds.), *Representing Ireland: Literature and the Origins of Conflict, 1634–1660* (Cambridge: Cambridge University Press, 1993).

HAIGH, CHRISTOPHER (ed.), *The Reign of Elizabeth I* (London: Macmillan, 1984).

HALE, J. R. (ed.), *The Evolution of British Historiography: From Bacon to Namier* (London: Macmillan, 1967).

—— *Renaissance Europe 1480–1520* (London: Fontana Press, 1971; repr. 1985).

HALL, WILLIAM KEITH, 'From Chronicle to Chorography: Truth, Narrative, and the Antiquarian Enterprise in Renaissance England' (unpublished doctoral dissertation, University of North Carolina, 1995).

—— 'A Topography of Time: Historical Narration in John Stow's *Survey of London*', *SP* 88 (1991), 1–15.

HALLOWELL, ROBERT E., 'Ronsard and the Gallic Hercules Myth', *Studies in the Renaissance*, 9 (1962), 242–55.

HAMILTON, A. C., 'On Annotating Spenser's *The Faerie Queene*: A New Approach to the Poem', in Richard C. Frushell and Bernard J. Vondersmith (eds.),

Contemporary Thought on Edmund Spenser (London: Feffer & Simons, 1975), 41–60.

—— ed., *The Spenser Encyclopedia* (Toronto: University of Toronto Press, 1990).

HAMILTON, DONNA B., and RICHARD STRIER (eds.), *Religion, Literature and Politics in Post-Reformation England, 1540–1688* (Cambridge: Cambridge University Press, 1996).

HARPER, CARRIE ANNA, *The Sources of the British Chronicle History in Spenser's 'Faerie Queene'* (Philadelphia: John C. Winston, 1910).

HARRIS, RONALD WILLIAM, 'Telling Stories, Inventing Histories: The Reception and Revision of the British History in Early Modern England' (unpublished doctoral dissertation, University of Wisconsin, 1996).

HAZELTINE, HAROLD DEXTER, *Selden as Legal Historian: A Comment in Criticism and Appreciation* (Weimar: Hermann Böhlaus, 1910).

HEFFNER, RAY, 'Spenser's *View of Ireland*: Some Observations', *Modern Language Quarterly*, 3 (1942), 507–16.

HELGERSON, RICHARD, *Self-Crowned Laureates: Spenser, Jonson, Milton and the Literary System* (Berkeley: University of California Press, 1983).

—— '"Barbarous Tongues": The Ideology of Poetic Form in Renaissance England', in H. Dubrow and Richard Strier (eds.), *The Historical Renaissance: New Essays on Tudor and Stuart Literature and Culture* (Chicago: University of Chicago Press, 1988).

—— *Forms of Nationhood: The Elizabethan Writing of England* (Chicago: University of Chicago Press, 1992).

HENINGER, S. K., JR., 'The Orgoglio Episode in *The Faerie Queene*', *ELH* 26 (1959), 171–87.

—— *A Handbook of Renaissance Meteorology: With Particular Reference to Elizabethan and Jacobean Literature* (Durham, NC: Duke University Press, 1960).

—— 'The Tudor Myth of Troy-novant', *South Atlantic Quarterly*, 61 (1962), 378–87.

—— 'Opening Remarks to "The Interface Between Poetry and History: Gascoigne, Spenser, Drayton"', *SP* 87 (1990), 109–10.

—— 'Spenser and Sidney at Leicester House', *Spenser Studies*, 8 (1990), 239–50.

HERENDEEN, WYMAN H., 'The Rhetoric of Rivers: The River and the Pursuit of Knowledge', *SP* 78 (1981), 107–27.

—— *From Landscape to Literature: The River and the Myth of Geography* (Pittsburgh: Duquesne University Press, 1986).

—— 'Wanton Discourse and the Engines of Time: William Camden—Historian among Poets-Historical', in Maryanne Cline Horowitz *et al.* (eds.), *Renaissance Rereadings: Intertext and Context* (Urbana, Ill.: University of Illinois Press, 1988), 142–58.

HIGHLEY, CHRISTOPHER, 'Spenser and the Bards', *Spenser Studies*, 12 (1998), 77–104.

HIGHLEY, CHRISTOPHER, *Shakespeare, Spenser, and the Crisis in Ireland*, Cambridge Studies in Renaissance Literature and Culture, 23 (Cambridge: Cambridge University Press, 1997).

HODGSON, SIDNEY, *The Worshipfull Company of Stationers and Newspaper Makers: Notes on its Origin and History* (London: Stationers Hall, 1953).

HOFFMAN, KATHERINE A., 'Reading History in the *Orlando Furioso* and *The Faerie Queene*' (unpublished doctoral dissertation, Northwestern University, 1991).

HOUGH, GRAHAM, 'First Commentary on *The Faerie Queene*: Annotations in Lord Bessborough's Copy of the First Edition of *The Faerie Queene*', *Times Literary Supplement*, Thursday 9 April 1964, 294.

——(ed.), *The First Commentary on 'The Faerie Queene': Being an Analysis of the Annotations in Lord Bessborough's Copy of the First Edition of 'The Faerie Queene'* (n.p.: privately published, 1964).

HULSE, CLARK, 'Samuel Daniel: The Poet as Literary Historian', *Studies in English Literature*, 19 (1979), 55–70.

——'Spenser, Bacon and the Myth of Power', in H. Dubrow and Richard Strier (eds.), *The Historical Renaissance: New Essays on Tudor and Stuart Literature and Culture* (Chicago: University of Chicago Press, 1988).

HUME, ANTHEA, *Edmund Spenser: Protestant Poet* (Cambridge: Cambridge University Press, 1984).

HUNTER, W. B. (ed.), *The English Spenserians: The Poetry of Giles Fletcher, George Wither, Michael Drayton, Phineas Fletcher and Henry More* (Salt Lake City: University of Utah Press, 1977).

IREDALE, ROGER O., 'Giants and Tyrants in Book Five of *The Faerie Queene*', *Review of English Studies*, NS 17 (1966), 373–81.

JAMES, MERVYN, *Society, Politics and Culture: Studies in Early Modern England* (Cambridge: Cambridge University Press, 1986).

JANSEN, SHARON L., *Political Protest and Prophecy under Henry VIII* (Woodbridge: Boydell Press, 1991).

JARDINE, LISA, 'Encountering Ireland: Gabriel Harvey, Edmund Spenser, and English Colonial Ventures', in Brendan Bradshaw, Andrew Hadfield, and Willy Maley (eds.), *Representing Ireland: Literature and the Origins of Conflict, 1534–1660* (Cambridge: Cambridge University Press, 1993), 60–75.

JOHNSON, FRANCIS R., *A Critical Bibliography of the Works of Edmund Spenser Printed Before 1700* (Baltimore: Johns Hopkins University Press, 1933).

JUDSON, ALEXANDER C., *The Life of Edmund Spenser* (Baltimore: Johns Hopkins University Press, 1945).

KAGAN, RICHARD L., *Lucrecia's Dreams: Politics and Prophecy in Sixteenth-Century Spain* (Berkeley: University of California Press, 1990).

KELLY, HENRY A., *Divine Providence in the England of Shakespeare's Histories* (Cambridge, Mass.: Harvard University Press, 1970).

KENDRICK, T. D., 'The Elfin Chronicle', *Times Literary Supplement*, Saturday, 7 February 1948, 79.

—— *British Antiquity* (London: Methuen, 1950; repr. 1970).

KERMODE, FRANK, *Shakespeare, Spenser, Donne: Renaissance Essays* (London: Routledge & Kegan Paul, 1971).

KIDD, COLIN, *British Identities before Nationalism: Ethnicity and Nationhood in the Atlantic World, 1600–1800* (Cambridge: Cambridge University Press, 1999).

KING, ANDREW, *'The Faerie Queene' and Middle English Romance: The Matter of Just Memory* (Oxford: Oxford University Press, 2000).

KING, JOHN N., *English Reformation Literature: The Tudor Origins of the Protestant Tradition* (Princeton: Princeton University Press, 1982).

—— *Spenser's Poetry and the Reformation Tradition* (Princeton: Princeton University Press, 1990).

KINNEY, ARTHUR F., *Humanist Poetics: Thought, Rhetoric, and Fiction in Sixteenth-Century England* (Amherst, Mass.: University of Massachusetts Press, 1986).

KLEIN, BERNHARD, 'The Lie of the Land: English Surveyors, Irish Rebels and *The Faerie Queene*', *Irish University Review*, 26 (1996), 207–25.

KOLLER, KATHRINE, 'The Travayled Pilgrime by Stephen Batman and Book Two of *The Faerie Queene*', *Modern Language Quarterly*, 3 (1942), 535–41.

KRIER, THERESA M., *Gazing on Secret Sights: Spenser, Classical Imitation, and the Decorums of Vision* (Ithaca, NY: Cornell University Press, 1990).

LANE, MICHAEL (ed.), *Introduction to Structuralism* (New York: Basic Books, 1970).

LAX, ADRE, and G. W. MOST, *Studies in the Derveni Papyrus* (Oxford: Oxford University Press, 1997).

LEFKOWITZ, MARY R., *The Lives of the Greek Poets* (London: Duckworth, 1981).

LENNON, COLM, *Richard Stanihurst the Dubliner 1547–1618: A Biography with Stanihurst's Text 'On Ireland's Past'* (Blackrock: Irish Academic Press, 1981).

LEVIN, HARRY, *The Myth of Golden Age in the Renaissance* (Bloomington, Ind.: Indiana University Press, 1969).

LEVINE, JOSEPH M., *Humanism and History: Origins of Modern English Historiography* (Ithaca, NY: Cornell University Press, 1987).

LEVY, F. J., *Tudor Historical Thought* (San Marino: The Huntington Library, 1967).

LEWALSKI, BARBARA KIEFER (ed.), *Renaissance Genres: Essays on Theory, History, and Interpretation* (Cambridge, Mass.: Harvard University Press, 1986).

LEWIS, C. S., *The Allegory of Love: A Study in Medieval Tradition* (Oxford: Oxford University Press, 1936).

—— *Spenser's Images of Life*, ed. Alastair Fowler (Cambridge: Cambridge University Press, 1977).

LINDENBAUM, PETER, 'Sidney's *Arcadia* as Cultural Monument and Proto Novel', in Cedric C. Brown and Arthur F. Marotti (eds.), *Texts and Cultural Change in Early Modern England* (Basingstoke: Macmillan, 1997), 80–94.

LIVINGSTONE, CAROLE ROSE, *British Broadside Ballads of the Sixteenth Century: A*

Catalogue of the Extant Sheets and an Essay (New York: Garland Publishing, 1991).

LOADES, DAVID M., *The Tudor Court*, New Appreciations in History, 18 (London: The Historical Association, 1989).

LOEWENSTEIN, DAVID A., '*Areopagita* and the Dynamics of History', *Studies in English Literature*, 28 (1988), 77–93.

LOGAN GEORGE M., and GORDON TESKEY (eds.), *Unfolded Tales: Essays on Renaissance Romance* (Ithaca, NY: Cornell University Press, 1989).

LOTHERINGTON, JOHN (ed.), *The Tudor Years* (London: Hodder & Stoughton, 1994).

LOTSPEICH, HENRY GIBBONS, *Classical Mythology in the Poetry of Edmund Spenser*, Princeton Studies in English, 9 (Princeton: Princeton University Press, 1932).

LUBORSKY, RUTH SAMSON, 'The Allusive Presentation of *The Shepheardes Calender*', *Spenser Studies*, 1 (1980), 29–57.

—— 'The Illustrations to *The Shepheardes Calender*', *Spenser Studies*, 2 (1981), 3–53.

LUPTON, JULIA REINHARD, 'Mapping Mutability: or Spenser's Irish Plot', in Andrew Hadfield (ed.), *Edmund Spenser* (London: Longman, 1996), 211–31 (first publ. in Brendan Bradshaw, Andrew Hadfield, and Willy Maley (eds.), *Representing Ireland: Literature and the Origins of Conflict, 1534–1660* (Cambridge: Cambridge University Press, 1993), 93–115).

MCCABE, RICHARD A., 'The Masks of Duessa: Spenser, Mary Queen of Scots, and James VI', *ELR* 17 (1987), 224–42.

—— *The Pillars of Eternity: Time and Providence in 'The Faerie Queene'* (Dublin: Irish Academic Press, 1989).

—— 'Self-Consuming Discourse: Spenserian Poetics and the 'New' New Criticism', *Review*, 13 (1991), 185–99.

—— 'Edmund Spenser, Poet of Exile', *Proceedings of the British Academy*, 80 (1991), 73–103.

MACCAFFREY, ISABELL G., *Spenser's Allegory: The Anatomy of Imagination* (Princeton: Princeton University Press, 1976).

MACCAFFREY, WALLACE T., *The Shaping of the Elizabethan Regime: Elizabethan Politics 1558–1572* (Princeton: Princeton University Press, 1968).

—— *Queen Elizabeth and the Making of Policy, 1572–1588* (Princeton: Princeton University Press, 1981).

—— *Elizabeth I: War and Politics 1588–1603* (Princeton: Princeton University Press, 1992).

—— *Elizabeth I* (London: Edward Arnold, 1993).

MCCANLES, MICHAEL, '*The Shepheardes Calender* as Document and Monument', *Studies in English Literature*, 22 (1982), 5–19.

MACCARTHY-MORROGH, MICHAEL, *The Munster Plantation: English Migration to Southern Ireland 1583–1641* (Oxford: Clarendon Press, 1986).

MCCOY, RICHARD C., *The Rites of Knighthood: The Literature and Politics of*

Elizabethan Chivalry, The New Historicism, 7 (Berkeley: University of California Press, 1989).

McEACHERN, CLAIRE, *The Poetics of Nationhood, 1590–1612*, Cambridge Studies in Renaissance Literature and Culture, 13 (Cambridge: Cambridge University Press, 1996).

McELDERRY, BRUCE ROBERT, JR., 'Archaism and Innovation in Spenser's Poetic Diction', *PMLA* 47 (1932), 144–70.

McKISACK, MAY, *Medieval History in the Tudor Age* (Oxford: Clarendon Press, 1971).

McLANE, PAUL E., 'Skelton's *Colyn Cloute* and Spenser's *Shepheardes Calender*', *SP* 70 (1973), 141–59.

MacLAREN, A. N., 'Prophecy and Providentialism in the Reign of Elizabeth I', in Bertrand Taithe and Tim Thornton (eds.), *Prophecy: The Power of Inspired Language in History: 1300–2000* (Stroud: Sutton Publishing, 1997), 31–50.

MacLEAN, GERALD M., *Time's Witness. Historical Representation in English Poetry, 1603– 1660* (Madison, Wis.: University of Wisconsin Press, 1990).

MacLURE, MILLAR, 'Spenser and the Ruins of Time', in Judith M. Kennedy and James A. Reither (eds.), *A Theatre for Spenserians* (Manchester: Manchester University Press, 1973), 3–18.

MALEY, WILLY, *A Spenser Chronology* (Basingstoke: Macmillan Press, 1994).

—— 'Spenser's *View* and Stanyhurst's *Description*', *N&Q* 241 (1996), 140–2.

—— 'Dialogue-wise: Some Notes on the Irish Context of Spenser's *View*', *Connotations*, 6 (1996–7), 67–77.

—— *Salvaging Spenser: Colonialism, Culture and Identity* (Basingstoke: Macmillan, 1997).

—— 'Sir Philip Sidney and Ireland', *Spenser Studies*, 12 (1998), 223–7.

MANLEY, LAWRENCE, 'The Emergence of a Tudor Capital: Spenser's Epic Vision', in *Literature and Culture in Early Modern London* (Cambridge: Cambridge University Press, 1995), 168–211.

MANNING, JOHN, 'Notes and Marginalia in Bishop Percy's Copy of Spenser's *Works* (1611)', *N&Q* 229 (1984), 225–7.

MASLEN, KEITH I., 'Three Eighteenth-Century Reprints of the Castrated Sheets in Holinshed's Chronicles', *The Library*, 13 (1958), 120–4.

MASSINGHAM, H. J., *Fee, Fi, Fo, Fum; or The Giants in England*, Psyche Miniatures, 5 (London: Kegan Paul, Trench, Trubner & Co., 1926).

MENDYK, STAN A. E., *'Speculum Britanniae': Regional Study, Antiquarianism and Science in Britain to 1700* (Toronto: University of Toronto Press, 1989).

METZGER, BRUCE M., and MICHAEL D. COOGAN (eds.), *The Oxford Companion to the Bible* (Oxford: Oxford University Press, 1993).

MILLER, DAVID LEE, *The Poem's Two Bodies: The Poetics of the 1590 Faerie Queene* (Princeton: Princeton University Press, 1988).

—— 'The Earl of Cork's Lute', in Judith H. Anderson, Donald Cheney, and

David A. Richardson (eds.), *Spenser's Life and the Subject of Biography* (Amherst, Mass.: University of Massachusetts Press, 1996), 146–71.

MILLICAN, CHARLES BOWIE, *Spenser and 'The Table Round': A Study in the Contemporaneous Background for Spenser's Use of the Arthurian Legend*, Harvard Studies in Comparative Literature, 8 (Cambridge, Mass.: Harvard University Press, 1932).

MILLS, JERRY LEATH, 'Spenser and the Numbers of History', *Philological Quarterly*, 55 (1976), 281–7.

——— 'Spenser's Letter to Raleigh and the Averroistic *Poetics*', *English Language Notes*, 14 (1977), 246–9.

MOMIGLIANO, A. D., 'Ancient History and the Antiquarian', in *Studies in Historiography* (London: Weidenfeld & Nicolson, 1966; repr. 1969), 1–39 (first publ. in *Journal of the Warburg and Courtauld Institutes*, 13 (1950), 285–315).

MONTROSE, LOUIS ADRIAN, 'Of Gentlemen and Shepherds: The Politics of Elizabethan Pastoral Form', *ELH* 50 (1983), 415–59.

——— 'Renaissance Literary Studies and the Subject of History', *ELR* 16 (1986), 5–12.

——— 'The Elizabethan Subject and the Spenserian Text', in Patricia Parker and David Quint (eds.), *Literary Theory/Renaissance Texts* (Baltimore: Johns Hopkins University Press, 1986), 303–40.

——— 'Spenser's Domestic Domain: Poetry, Property, and the Early Modern Subject', in Margreta De Grazia, Maureen Quilligan, and Peter Stallybrass (eds.), *Subject and Object in Renaissance Culture*, Cambridge Studies in Renaissance Literature and Culture, 8 (Cambridge: Cambridge University Press, 1996), 83–130.

MOODY, T. W. (ed.), *A New History of Ireland*, 10 vols. (Oxford: Clarendon Press, 1976–).

MORONEY, MARYCLAIRE, 'Spenser's Dissolution: Monasticism and Ruins in *The Faerie Queene* and *The Vewe of the Present State of Ireland*', *Spenser Studies*, 12 (1998), 105–32.

MULLANEY, STEVEN, 'Lying Like Truth: Riddle, Representation and Treason in Renaissance England', *ELH* 47 (1980), 32–47.

NICHOLS, JOHN (ed.), *The Progresses and Public Processions of Queen Elizabeth* (Edinburgh: privately published, 1788).

NICHOLSON, HELEN, *The Knights Templar: A New History* (Stroud: Sutton, 2001).

NISBET, ROBERT, *History of the Idea of Progress* (London: Heinemann, 1980).

NOHRNBERG, JAMES, *The Analogy of The Faerie Queene* (Princeton: Princeton University Press, 1976).

NORBROOK, DAVID, *Poetry and Politics in the English Renaissance* (London: Routledge, 1984).

O'CALLAGHAN, MICHELLE, *The 'Shepheards Nation': Jacobean Spenserians and Early Stuart Political Culture, 1612–1625* (Oxford: Oxford University Press, 2000).

O'CONNELL, MICHAEL, *Mirror and Veil: The Historical Dimension of Spenser's 'The Faerie Queene'* (Chapel Hill, NC: University of Carolina Press, 1977).

O'CONNOR, JOHN J., 'Terwin, Trevisan, and Spenser's Historical Allegory', *SP* 87 (1990), 328–40.

O'CURRY, EUGENE, *Lectures on the Manuscript Materials of Ancient Irish History* (Dublin: James Duffy, 1861).

OAKESHOTT, WALTER, 'Carew Ralegh's Copy of Spenser', *The Library*, NS 26 (1971).

ONEGA, SUSANA, and JOSÉ ANGEL GARCÍA LANDA (eds.), *Narratology: An Introduction* (London: Longman, 1996).

ONG, WALTER J., 'Spenser's *View* and the Tradition of the "Wild" Irish', *Modern Language Quarterly*, 3 (1942), 561–71.

ORUCH, JACK B., 'Spenser, Camden, and the Poetic Marriages of Rivers', *SP* 64 (1967), 606–24.

OSGOOD, CHARLES G., 'Spenser's English Rivers', *Transactions of the Connecticut Academy of Arts and Sciences*, 23 (1920), 65–108.

—— *A Concordance to the Poems of Edmund Spenser* (Washington: Carnegie Institution of Washington, 1915; repr. Gloucester, Mass.: Peter Smith, 1963).

OWEN, W. J. B., 'The Structure of *The Faerie Queene*', *PMLA* 68 (1953), 1079–100.

PARKER, ROBERT, 'Early Orphism', in A. Powell (ed.), *The Greek World* (London: Routledge, 1995), 488.

PARRY, GRAHAM, *The Trophies of Time: English Antiquarians in the Seventeenth Century* (Oxford: Oxford University Press, 1995).

PATRIDES, C. A. (ed.), *Aspects of Time* (Manchester: Manchester University Press, 1976).

—— and JOSEPH WITTREICH (eds.), *The Apocalypse in English Renaissance Thought and Literature* (Manchester: Manchester University Press, 1984).

PATTERSON, ANNABEL, *Reading between the Lines* (London: University of Wisconsin Press, 1993).

—— *Reading Holinshed's Chronicles* (Chicago: University of Chicago Press, 1994).

—— 'Sir John Oldcastle as a Symbol of Reformation Historiography', in Donna B. Hamilton and Richard Strier (eds.), *Religion, Literature, and Politics in Post Reformation England: 1540–1688* (Cambridge: Cambridge University Press, 1996), 6–21.

PIGGOTT, STUART, *Ancient Britons and the Antiquarian Imagination: Ideas from the Renaissance to the Regency* (London: Thames & Hudson, 1989).

POCOCK, J. G. A., 'British History: A Plea for a New Subject', *Journal of Modern History*, 47 (1974), 601–28.

—— *The Ancient Constitution and the Feudal Law: A Study of English Historical Thought in the Seventeenth Century: A Reissue with Retrospect* (Cambridge: Cambridge University Press, 1987).

POLLARD, A. W., G. R. REDGRAVE, *et. al.*, *A Short Title Catalogue of Books Printed in*

England, Scotland and Ireland, 2nd edn., 3 vols. (London: Bibliographical Society, 1976–91).

POPE, NANCY, *National History in the Heroic Poem: A Comparision of the Aeneid and The Faerie Queene* (New York: Garland Publishing, 1990).

PRESCOTT, ANNE LAKE, 'Drayton's Muse and Selden's "Story": The Interfacing of Poetry and History in *Poly-Olbion*', *SP* 87 (1990), 128–35.

—— *French Poets and the English Renaissance: Studies in Fame and Transformation* (New Haven: Yale University Press, 1978).

—— 'Spenser (Re)Reading Du Bellay: Chronology and Literary Response', in Judith H. Anderson, Donald Cheney, and David A. Richardson (eds.), *Spenser's Life and the Subject of Biography* (Amherst, Mass.: University of Massachusetts Press, 1996), 131–45.

—— 'Foreign Policy in Fairyland: Henri IV and Spenser's Burbon', *Spenser Studies*, 14 (2000), 189–214.

PREVITÉ-ORTON, C. W., 'An Elizabethan Prophecy', *History*, 2 (1917–18), 207–18.

QUINT, DAVID, *Origin and Originality in Renaissance Literature: Versions of the Source* (Yale: Yale University Press, 1983).

RADCLIFFE, DAVID HILL, *Edmund Spenser: A Reception History* (Columbia: Camden House, 1996).

RAMBUSS, RICHARD, *Spenser's Secret Career*, Cambridge Studies in Renaissance Literature and Culture, 3 (Cambridge: Cambridge University Press, 1993).

RASMUSSEN, CARL J., '"How Weak Be the Passions of Woefulness": Spenser's *Ruins of Time*', *Spenser Studies*, 2 (1981), 159–82.

RATHBORNE, ISABEL E., *The Meaning of Spenser's Fairyland*, Columbia University Studies in English and Comparative Literature, 131 (New York: Columbia University Press, 1937).

—— 'The Elfin Chronicle', *The Times Literary Supplement*, 24 April 1948, 233.

READ, DAVID, *Temperate Conquests: Spenser and the Spanish New World* (Detroit: Wayne State University Press, 2000).

REED, REGINA BALLA, 'Rebellion, Prophecy and Power in Four Works of the English Renaissance' (unpublished doctoral thesis, State University of New York at Buffalo, 1970).

RHU, LAWRENCE F., 'After the Middle Ages: Prophetic Authority and Human Fallibility in Renaissance Epic', in James L. Kugel (ed.), *Poetry and Prophecy: The Beginnings of a Literary Tradition* (Ithaca, NY: Cornell University Press, 1990), 163–84.

RICHARDSON, J. MICHAEL, *Astrological Symbolism in Spenser's 'The Shepheardes Calender': The Cultural Background of A Literary Text*, Studies in Renaissance Literature, 1 (Lewiston, NY: Edwin Mellen Press, 1989).

RICŒUR, PAUL, *Time and Narrative*, trans. Kathleen McLaughlin and David Pellauer, 3 vols. (Chicago: University of Chicago Press, 1983–5).

ROCHE, THOMAS, JR., *The Kindly Flame: A Study of the Third and Fourth Books of Spenser's 'Faerie Queene'* (Princeton: Princeton University Press, 1964).

RODGERS, CATHERINE, *Time in the Narrative of 'The Faerie Queene'* (Salzburg: Institut für Englische Sprache und Literatur, 1973).

ROSSI, JOAN WARCHOL, *'Britons Moniments*: Spenser's Definition of Temperance in History', *ELR* 15 (1985), 42–58.

RØSTVIG, MAREN SOFIE, 'Canto Structure in Tasso and Spenser', *Spenser Studies*, 1 (1980), 177–200.

—— *Topomorphical Approach to Renaissance Poetry* (Oslo: Scandinavian University Press, 1994), 347–54.

SAID, EDWARD W., *Beginnings: Intention and Method* (Baltimore: Johns Hopkins University Press, 1975).

SANDLER, FLORENCE, '*The Faerie Queene*: an Elizabethan Apocalypse', in C. A. Patrides and Joseph Wittreich (eds.), *The Apocalypse in English Thought and Literature: Patterns, Antecedents and Repercussions* (Manchester: Manchester University Press, 1984), 148–74.

SATTERTHWAITE, ALFRED W., *Spenser, Ronsard, and Du Bellay: A Renaissance Comparison* (Port Washington, NY: Kennikat Press, 1960).

SAYLE, C. E. (ed.), *Early Printed Books in the University Library Cambridge*, 5 vols. (Cambridge: Cambridge University Press, 1900).

SCANLAN, THOMAS, *Colonial Writing and the New World, 1583–1671: Allegories of Desire* (Cambridge: Cambridge University Press, 1999).

SCHNAPPER, ANTOINE, 'Persistance des Géants', *Annales ESC* 41 (1986), 177–200.

SCHOENFELDT, MICHAEL C., *Bodies and Selves in Renaissance England: Physiology and Inwardness in Spenser, Shakespeare, Herbert, and Milton,* Cambridge Studies in Renaissance Literature and Culture, 34 (Cambridge: Cambridge University Press, 1999).

SEZNEC, JEAN, *The Survival of the Pagan Gods: The Mythological Tradition and Its Place in Renaissance Humanism and Art,* trans. Barbara F. Sessions, Bollingen Series, 38 (New York: Pantheon Books, 1953).

SHAPIN, STEVEN, *A Social History of Truth: Civility and Science in Seventeenth-Century England* (Chicago: University of Chicago Press, 1994).

SHERMAN, WILLIAM H., *John Dee: The Politics of Reading and Writing in the English Renaissance* (Amherst, Mass.: University of Massachusetts Press, 1995).

SHROEDER, JOHN W., 'Spenser's Erotic Drama: The Orgoglio Episode', *English Literary History*, 29 (1962), 140–59.

SHUGER, DEBORAH KULLER, *Habits of Thought in the English Renaissance: Religion, Politics, and the Dominant Culture* (Berkeley: University of California Press, 1990).

—— 'Irishmen, Aristocrats, and Other Barbarians', *Renaissance Quarterly*, 50 (1997), 494–525.

SILBERMAN, LAUREN, *Transforming Desire: Erotic Knowledge in Books III and IV of 'The Faerie Queene'* (Berkeley: University of California Press, 1995).

SMITH, ROLAND M., 'Spenser, Holinshed, and the *Laebhar Gabhála*', *Journal of English and Germanic Philology*, 43 (1944), 390–401.

—— 'The Irish Background of Spenser's *View*', *Journal of English and Germanic Philology*, 42 (1942), 499–515.

SOUTHERN, R. W., 'Aspects of the European Tradition of Historical Writing: 3. History as Prophecy', *Transactions of the Royal Historical Society*, NS 22 (1972), 159–81.

SPURGEON, PATRICK O'DYER, 'The Poet Historical, A Study of Renaissance Methods and Uses of History' (unpublished doctoral thesis: University of Tennessee, 1963).

STEPHENS, WALTER, *Giants in Those Days: Folklore, Ancient History, and Nationalism* (Lincoln, Nebr.: University of Nebraska Press, 1989).

STERNBERG, MEIR, *Expositional Modes and Temporal Ordering in Fiction* (Baltimore: Johns Hopkins University Press, 1978).

STEWART, SUZAN, *On Longing: Narratives of the Miniature, the Gigantic, the Souvenir, the Collection* (Baltimore: Johns Hopkins University Press, 1984).

STONE, WALTER B., 'Shakespeare and the Sad Augurs', *Journal of English and German Philology*, 52 (1953), 457–79.

STRONG, SIR ROY, *The Tudor and Stuart Monarchy: Pageantry, Painting, Iconography*, 3 vols. (Woodbridge: Boydell Press, 1995–8).

SULLIVAN, GARRETT A., JR., *The Drama of Landscape: Land, Property, and Social Relations on the Early Modern Stage* (Stanford, Calif.: Stanford University Press, 1998).

TATLOCK, J. S., *The Legendary History of Britain: Geoffrey of Monmouth's 'Historia Regum Britainniae' and its Early Vernacular Versions* (Berkeley: University of California Press, 1950).

TAYLOR, JOHN, *The Universal Chronicle of Ranulf Higden* (Oxford: Clarendon Press, 1966).

TAYLOR, RUPERT, *The Political Prophecy in England* (New York: The Columbia Press, 1911).

TESKEY, GORDON, 'Mutability, Genealogy, and the Authority of Forms', *Representations*, 41 (1993), 104–22.

——*Allegory and Violence* (Ithaca, NY: Cornell University Press, 1996).

THOMAS, KEITH, *Religion and the Decline of Magic: Studies in Popular Beliefs in Sixteenth and Seventeenth Century England* (London: Weidenfeld & Nicolson, 1971).

THOMPSON, J. A. F., 'John Foxe and some Sources for Lollard History: Notes for a Critical Appraisal', in *Studies in Church History, II*, ed. G. J. Cuming (London: Thomas Nelson & Sons, 1965), 251–7.

TILLYARD, E. M. W., *The Elizabethan World Picture* (London: Chatto & Windus, 1943).

——*Shakespeare's History Plays* (London: Chatto & Windus, 1944; repr. Penguin, 1986).

TODD, MARGO (ed.), *Reformation to Revolution: Politics and Religion in Early Modern England* (London: Routledge, 1995).

TROMPF, G. W., *The Idea of Historical Recurrence in Western Thought: From Antiquity to the Reformation* (Berkeley: University of California Press, 1979).

UHLIG, CLAUS, *Klio und Natio: Studien zu Spenser und der Englischen Renaissance* (Heidelberg: Universitätsverlag, 1995).

ULREICH, JOHN C., JR., 'Making Dreams Truths, and Fables Histories: Spenser and Milton on the Nature of Fiction', *SP* 87 (1990), 363–77.

VAN ES, BART, 'The Life of John Dixon, *The Faerie Queene*'s First Annotator', *N&Q* 246 [NS 48] (2001), 259–61.

VAN NORDEN, LINDA, 'The Elizabethan College of Antiquaries' (unpublished doctoral dissertation, University of California at Los Angeles, 1946).

——'Celtic Antiquarianism in the "Curious Discourses"', in Louis B. Wright (ed.), *Essays, Critical and Historical, Dedicated to Lily B. Cambell* (Berkeley: University of California Press, 1950), 65–70.

VAN PATTEN, JONATHAN K., 'Magic, Prophecy, and the Law of Treason in Reformation England', *The American Journal of Legal History*, 27 (1983), 1–32.

VINK, JAMES, 'Spenser's "Easterland" as the Columban Church of Ancient Ireland', *Éire- Ireland*, 25 (1990), 96–106.

WALL, JOHN N., JR., 'The English Reformation and the Recovery of Christian Community in Spenser's *The Faerie Queene*', *SP* 80 (1983), 142–62.

——*Transformations of the Word* (Athens, Ga.: University of Georgia Press, 1988).

WALTERS, H. B., *The English Antiquaries of the Sixteenth, Seventeenth, and Eighteenth Centuries* (London: Edward Walters, 1934).

WARD, H. L. D. (ed.), *Catalogue of Romances in the Department of Manuscripts in the British Museum*, 3 vols. (London: Longmans, 1883).

WATERHOUSE, WILLIAM C., 'Spenser's Irenius and the Nature of Dialogue', *N&Q* 237 (1992), 355–7.

WELLS, ROBIN HEADLAM, *Spenser's 'Faerie Queene' and the Cult of Elizabeth* (London: Croom Helm, 1983).

WHIGHAM, FRANK, *Ambition and Privilege: The Social Tropes of Elizabethan Courtesy Theory* (Berkeley: University of California Press, 1984).

WHITE, HAYDEN, *Metahistory: The Historical Imagination in Nineteenth-Century Europe* (Baltimore: Johns Hopkins University Press, 1973).

WILKIN, GREGORY, 'Spenser's Rehabilitation of the Templars', *Spenser Studies*, 11 (1990), 89–100.

WILKS, MICHAEL (ed.), *Prophecy and Eschatology*, Studies in Church History, 10 (Oxford: Blackwell, 1994).

WILLIAMS, GLANMOR, 'Prophecy, Poetry, and Politics in Medieval Tudor Wales', in H. Hearder and H. R. Loyn (eds.), *British Government and Administra-*

tion: Studies Presented to S. B. Chrimes (Cardiff: University of Wales Press, 1974), 104–16.

WILLIAMS, KATHLEEN, *Spenser's 'The Faerie Queene': The World of Glass* (London: Routledge & Kegan Paul, 1966).

WILSON, ELKIN CALHOUN, *England's Eliza*, Harvard Studies in English, 20 (Cambridge, Mass.: Harvard University Press, 1939; repr. New York: Octagon Books, 1966).

WILSON, JEAN, *Entertainments for Elizabeth I*, Studies in Elizabethan Culture, 2 (Woodbridge: Brewer, 1980).

WILSON, RAWDON, 'Images and "Allegoremes" of Time in the Poetry of Spenser', *ELR* 4 (1974), 56–82.

WITTREICH, JOSEPH ANTONY, JR., *Visionary Poetics: Milton's Tradition and his Legacy* (San Marino: Huntington Library, 1979).

—— *'Image of that Horror': History, Prophecy, and Apocalypse in 'King Lear'* (San Marino: Huntington Library, 1984).

WOJCIK, JAN, and RAYMOND-JEAN FROTAIN (eds.), *Poetic Prophecy in Western Literature* (London: Associated University Press, 1984).

WOOLF, D. R, 'Genre into Artifact: the Decline of the English Chronicle in the Sixteenth Century', *The Sixteenth Century Journal*, 19 (1988), 321–54.

—— 'Community, Law, and State: Samuel Daniel's Historical Thought Revisited', *Journal of the History of Ideas*, 49 (1988), 61–84.

—— *The Idea of History in Early Stuart England: Erudition, Ideology and 'The Light of Truth' from the Accession of James I to the Civil War* (Toronto: University of Toronto Press, 1990).

—— 'Of Danes and Giants: Popular Beliefs about the Past in Early Modern England', *Dalhousie Review*, 71 (1991), 166–209.

—— *Reading History in Early Modern England* (Cambridge: Cambridge University Press, 2000).

WOUDHUYSEN, H. R., 'Leicester's Literary Patronage: A Study of the English Court 1578–1582' (unpublished doctoral thesis, University of Oxford, 1980).

YATES, FRANCES A., 'The Elfin Chronicle', *Times Literary Supplement*, July 3 1948, 373.

—— *Astraea: The Imperial Theme in the Sixteenth Century* (London: Routledge & Kegan Paul, 1975).

Index